HER WORDS, MY VOICE

HEIDI RAMER

Find your voice,
tell your story!
Blessings,
Heidi

LifeRich Publishing is a registered trademark of The Reader's Digest Association, Inc.

LifeRich Publishing books may be ordered through booksellers or by contacting:

LifeRich Publishing
1663 Liberty Drive
Bloomington, IN 47403
www.liferichpublishing.com
844-686-9607

Scripture quotations are taken from the Holy Bible, New International
Version®. NIV®. Copyright © 1973, 1978, 1984 by International Bible
Society. Used by permission of Zondervan. All rights reserved.

ISBN: 978-1-4897-4530-9 (sc)
ISBN: 978-1-4897-4532-3 (hc)
ISBN: 978-1-4897-4531-6 (e)

Library of Congress Control Number: 2022921618

Printed in the United States of America

LifeRich Publishing rev. date: 12/21/2022

To my mother.

You knew that someday, in my own time, I
would take this journey with you.
I have always heard your voice, and now the world will too.
Thank you for trusting me to be your vessel.
I pray this is the story you would have wanted me to tell.

CONTENTS

FOREWORD

For thirty-six years, I was the spouse of Karen, the mother in this book, until her untimely death in 2001. My wife was a victim of rape, and I became a secondary victim.

I'm also a retired teacher with thirty-three years of experience. In my second career, I was a chaplain in a retirement home and then a hospital and hospice chaplain for a total of fifteen years. I've been a spiritual director for eighteen years. I coauthored a children's picture book, *Maria's Kit of Comfort*, that shows how to use play experiences to help children express their fears and anxiety following disasters or traumatic experiences. I have spent a lifetime dealing with people's feelings.

I am the father of the author, Heidi, as well.

I lived in the same home as Heidi and her mother, Karen, but I didn't understand the depth of their anguish. I knew about Karen's pain and sleepless nights, but through Heidi's writing, I became aware of the deep suffering that Karen experienced. I knew Karen was absent for extended periods of time in our lives, but now I have a new understanding about the effects of such absences on Heidi.

Our family ate meals together, attended church regularly, and appeared to be a normal middle-class family. Heidi and I did dishes together and jogged together. I supported her by attending her cross-country meets, gymnastic competitions, and swim meets.

I taught elementary school while Karen worked as a consultant for the state and taught classes in early childhood education at the local college. Therefore, I was home during summers and school breaks to care for our children. I wanted to be a loving, caring parent who allowed my children to be independent, learning from their mistakes. I was not the parent who would ask questions to pry into my children's relationships. I observed and listened to their comments concerning various friends. I approved of many of their friends, and never openly disapproved of their decisions unless I was concerned about their safety.

When Karen told me she had been raped she said, "Don't ask any names or details." She could not tell me then, but she journaled the details years later. The abuse was too painful to deal with, so her body simply chose to bury it. But the pain lurked there, waiting to be expressed. The children and I walked on pins and needles every day. We were captured by the fear that we would say the wrong thing, causing Karen to explode and fall apart. She never explained to us at the time what she was feeling. Instead, she wrote her deepest feelings in her journals. Karen was gifted with expressive words of feeling.

Heidi, our daughter, has the same gift of using words to weave thoughts together with feelings. She uses this gift to bring you *Her Words, My Voice*.

The book begins with the sexual abuse as recorded in Karen's journals. At the same time, Heidi reflects how her mother's abuse also affected her life. Karen engaged in years of counseling and contemplative spiritual prayer and reflection to regain health and sanity. Heidi writes eloquently and honestly about how she struggled with her anger and anxiety into marriage and motherhood. Heidi shares her vulnerability of being a secondary victim and how she has become a caring, compassionate secondary survivor.

The whole range of Heidi's feelings—from anger and anxiety to love and compassion—comes through over years of counseling and reflecting in her own journaling. Heidi's vulnerability witnesses that, while we can be close to giving up, with the help of ministers, counselors, and supportive friends, we can find peace and wholeness in this life through God's grace.

If you have experienced trauma as a victim or as a secondary victim, you may discover part of your story in this book. To know that you are not alone and to hear how other victims learned to heal from the trauma may offer you hope.

With utmost respect, I offer my heartfelt thanks to Heidi for hearing the call to write her mother's story woven with her own. Wounded souls reach out when they have healed enough to care for others.

With compassion,
David

PROLOGUE

My mother was raped for the first time in 1979. She was sexually assaulted at least twelve more times by the same man over the next three years—a man had she known and trusted long before the abuse. She was emotionally tormented by him for the next twenty. Upon her untimely death in 2001, my father handed me a canvas bag full of handwritten journals. He had not read them; nor did he want to. He had lived her story by her side and did not care to rehash it from her perspective. Somehow, he knew they were intended for me.

Trauma has a ripple effect. The body's natural coping mechanism is to bury something that is too painful to deal with, but nothing is completely buried. It manifests in other ways, such as withdrawing from the people you love, the ones you cannot bear to witness your devastation. As the child who watched from the sidelines and lived in fear of losing her mother to this unimaginable pain, I earned the title of "secondary victim" and eventually "secondary survivor." I have a story as well—one that is entangled with hers from beginning to end. It is painful, heart-wrenching, reconciling, and hopeful.

In 1979, rapes were seldom reported. Maybe if they were random acts of violence connected to another crime, but never when they happened behind closed doors, perpetrated by a coworker, supervisor, or family friend. In these cases, the act was strictly an abuse of power.

Women were groomed to be vulnerable to men, to seek their approval and need their praise. Male predators wanted their victims to view the relationship as a mutually agreed upon affair and rationalized the woman's mute response as consent to do whatever he desired. Sometimes jobs were held in the balance, negotiated by being a quiet and seemingly willing participant. Almost always, these abuses of power were accompanied by a threat of physical harm, loss of employment, family ruin, or destruction of reputation.

During this era women endured repeated abuse, buried their trauma in the depths of their souls and put on a suitable face in order to carry on with their lives. In most cases, these women told no one—until a day, years later, when something triggered a memory, and there was safety in admitting they had been violated in the worst, most inhumane way.

Research tells us that significant trauma can have real health consequences and negatively affect longevity. It has been proved that physical and emotional trauma experienced over an extended period has the potential to shorten one's life by decades. In my personal experience, repeated abuse robbed my mother of thirty to forty years, but sadly that does not even take into account the years she was alive but not really living.

My mother's cathartic effort to free herself began in 1986 with pen and paper, recounting each individual incident as a way of fully recognizing what had been done to her. It was the commencement of her healing process. She wrote faithfully for fifteen years until mere days before her death. I have been the only witness to her words until now, but she was emphatic that her story be told. Her firsthand account of navigating living and dying at the same time is a gift she left, not only for me but also for you.

In 1987, my mom wrote in her journal, "If I should die, I want my story to be shared—the reason for my suffering and pain. I want people to know that rape destroys and kills—takes away the goodness of life."

In this book, as I interject her entries, I leave my mother's words in their organic state, completely untouched (other than removing some names). She wrote impeccably in a conversational tone. As I read, I could hear her unmistakable voice, as clear as my own. At times, I knew she was speaking directly to me, often to God, and sometimes entirely to herself as a means of hearing herself think. My hope is that, even if you don't know her, her tender and confident voice breaks through these pages. I pray that she speaks to you.

No one knows my mother in the intimate, ugly, and beautiful ways that I do. This is our story.

CHAPTER ONE

May 3, 1986

The day it began—when life as we knew it changed forever.

We weren't perfect, but we were a typical wholesome household—dad, mom, son, daughter, dog, cat, and so forth. My parents were both educators, Dad an elementary teacher and coach, Mom a professor at the local college. I was an athlete, and my brother was in musical theater. Our family lived on a modest income, in a modest home, and we were happy. Our home was centrally located in a small town of about five thousand people. We knew everyone in town, and everyone knew us—or at least thought they did. Rain, snow, or sunshine, we walked the three easy blocks to elementary school and three in the other direction to church. You could easily get anywhere else on a bicycle. Church was never optional; we went together as a family, sat together in the second row on the right side, and participated fully from an early age. We ate all meals together around the same table, we said grace, and the conversation flowed easily. Conversation in our home was always inclusive, fairly intelligent, frequently spirited, and rarely argumentative. My parents seldom drank and did not swear or raise their voices at us or at each other. My brother and I, at fifteen and seventeen, never fought. Often after dinner, Dad would do the dishes while the three of us would move over to the piano. Mom would play, and we would all sing. Our repertoire varied from *The Sound of Music* to John Denver to anything in the *Great American Songbook*! As I look back now, this all sounds a bit cheesy, but these are some of my favorite memories.

My mother was a smart, little woman. I say little because she was small in stature, about five foot three and 110 pounds, and smart because she was. She was well educated with a doctorate in early childhood education, which was pretty impressive for a female in the mid-1980s. She carried herself well and was always sharply dressed, with her short hair curled. I never knew her to wear makeup other than light foundation and blush. Her voice was soft but confident, and her words were intentional. She talked much more than my father and never left you wondering where she stood. It has occurred to me that she never used terms of endearment. None of us had pet names, not even my father. We were always called by our first names except when we were in trouble; then she used our first and middle names. She never minced words.

❧

Saturday afternoon, May 3, 1986

Yelling! Screaming! Swearing! Hateful words I had never heard within the walls that had protected us nearly all my life. This was so foreign in our home. What in the world had happened to cause this explosion? Seemingly, out of nowhere, in a matter of a few minutes, my family appeared to have fallen apart. From my ground floor bedroom, next to the kitchen, I heard their voices getting louder. My heart began to pound in my chest; I was frozen, unable to move but forced to listen. My mom and brother were arguing.

He verbally lashed out at her. "You're not much of a mother!"

"You son of a bitch, I hate you!" Mom screamed. "Get out. Get out of this house."

"I'm going to pack my shit and get the hell out of here!" he fired back.

"Good," was her only response.

Terrified and in shock over what I had just witnessed, I didn't bother to ask questions. I just needed to leave. I hopped on my bicycle and left.

Sara. I needed to tell someone. With numb legs and shaking hands, I rode the seven blocks to her house. It was a dangerous trip with my feet pedaling as fast as they could go and my hands frequently leaving the handlebars to wipe the tears from my face. Disheveled and visibly shaken, I knocked on the front door.

Oh, God, she isn't home, I thought, worried.

But her parents were not about to turn me away. They welcomed me to wait upstairs in her bedroom. Sara was my safe place, and so I curled up in a ball with my arms wrapped around my knees and waited.

Tears and more tears as I told Sara what I knew, which was truly little.

When my dad came to pick me up a few hours later, I had nothing left. I was emotionally void at that point. But the day was not over. Matt had returned home, and Mom had some explaining to do.

At the kitchen table, she began to speak. My brother was not at the root of her anger, only the trigger. Another man was the culprit, the source of her rage. My mother had been a victim of rape!

Her attacker had told her repeatedly, "You're not much of a lover."

In a fit of buried anger, Matt's words had resonated; they'd cut her to the core and taken her back to an experience she had not been able to touch for years. Once again, she had been reduced to nothing. She had been verbally assaulted and berated for what she was not. Her words were not meant for Matt; he was the unfair recipient of years of suppressed anger. But they had been uttered. Mom was remorseful and apologetic, but she could not take them back—the damage had been done.

Later that night, I wrote in my own journal, "What she told us totally devastated me and explained her anger but doesn't make up for what she said to Matt. She can't just tell him she didn't mean what she said and expect him to forget that it ever happened. My mind is now preoccupied with this thing, and I don't know if it will ever go away."

Weeks later, in stages (to my father first and then to Matt and me) more of the details unfolded. We would find out that this monster was someone we all knew. He had lived four blocks away from us for many years. He had gone to church with us. He and his wife had even shared meals with our family at our dining room table. Her rape had not been a random act of violence but a calculated, three-year bludgeoning of her body and soul. It had started seven years ago when he'd reached out to her with a professional opportunity that required them to travel the country together. She'd accepted eagerly but had walked away three years later, in April 1982, barely clinging to her life. She'd told no one.

Mom's first journal entry was dated February 27, 1986, just a couple of months prior to the big blowup with Matt. In her writings, she had barely begun to scratch the surface of the horror of the last seven years, but the experience was raw and present in her mind. She could hear his voice and feel the pressure of his weight. Her deeply buried anger was attempting to show its teeth, and she was afraid. She feared what she didn't yet know and what she would find as she began to dig. There had been a death, and she needed to work toward a resurrection. In the process, there would be ghosts to uncover—unearthed by the intensity of her anger and the depth of her fear.

Her first entry began with a verse from the book of Matthew in which Jesus is talking to his disciples. He says, "Take courage! It is I. Do not be afraid." If you look at the context surrounding this short verse, the disciples had just seen Jesus walking on the lake, and they thought he was a ghost.

After he spoke to them, Peter replied by saying, "Lord, if it's you, tell me to come to you on the water."

Jesus simply said, "Come."

In my mom's mind, Jesus was telling her it was time. He was asking her to come, to walk on the water, to come to the table where all are welcome. Healing meant putting her greatest fears aside and touching the truth. She could not go straight to the depths of the tomb but, rather, began by recalling the physical aftermath following three years of abuse. Once removed from the tension, her body began to absorb the trauma. It was killing her, and some days she was ready to let it:

> By May 1982, I was really sick. My skin and the whites of my eyes were gray. I looked absolutely horrible. It had been two months with no sleep. I went to the doctor and asked for a physical. Blood tests indicated liver malfunction and low blood counts. Rest was ordered, but I did not stop.

Four months after leaving the position (August 1982), she went to our pastor for counseling:

> I knew something was wrong, but I didn't know what. I went through several sessions before I even began to see the relationship between three years of devastating experiences and my present state of being. I didn't talk much. The story was so well hidden that I couldn't find it. Only bits and pieces came out. School started. I was

teaching—barely. I couldn't concentrate. Teaching and living were unbearable, but I continued to exist.

In September, I went back to the doctor. I needed medical help for sleep. We would try all sorts of sleeping pills—none worked. My body defied them all. I felt that, if I didn't get sleep, I would die. I did not see any value in continuing this type of existence. I still could not cry.

In October, I told my doctor about the counseling and being a victim of sexual abuse.

I am not aware of the details of what she told him, but my guess is that she barely described the depth of her trauma at that point, other than to say she had been raped. Honestly, I don't know that she had an absolute awareness of much more than that. For three years, she had trampled her ghosts and buried them in order to dismiss the shock of her reality and cope with day-to-day life. She had deprived herself of the opportunity to comprehend what had been done to her in order to simply survive. It was never a story that would be rattled off. It did not exist in the outer layer of her consciousness. Nevertheless, this small bit of sharing led to a degree of relief.

He reacted with extreme care and comfort. We talked about stress and its effects on the body. Our last hope was for me to run. He wrote a prescription for a beginning walking/running program. He was very methodical about my gradual progression. I was so sick—how could I ever run? But I was desperate. I followed his prescription to the exact word, and it worked. After four days I began to sleep—small amounts at first and then more. I felt promise. I continued counseling during the summer and winter of 1983. By January 1984, I stopped counseling. I was not opening up yet felt some peace with the progress I had made. The fear and anger remained buried. The actual touching of the entire experience never occurred; I wasn't ready.

CHAPTER TWO

Journal #1

The journal begins:

March 6, 1986. I fear admitting that I was responsible. In all my naivety, which I called trust, I fed the man's desires with my very presence. I mistook his compliments for flattery—I gave him exactly what he wanted. I don't recall my outward behavior to be any different with him than any other man—yet he read me in a way to satisfy himself.

I hate him for the injustice of the act. I hate him for taking advantage of my stupidity and naivety. I hate him for the pain he has caused me to endure—the mental anguish and the physical pain. I hate him for his low-lived act, his betrayal of my womanhood, my personhood, and my intimate self. I hate myself for falling prey to his manipulation. If only I'd been wiser to his flattery long before—I could have saved myself this mess. "If onlys" bring me no peace—just recognition that I didn't act responsibly or cautiously where I could.

I'm angry at me, my own responsibility. I'm angry that I gradually allowed myself to be trapped. Why couldn't I see what I was doing? "Whys" are like "If onlys." They get used when I try to escape the pain of my own responsibility.

I fear being punished by a just God who may judge me to have acted irresponsibly. I'm afraid to do so many things for fear of being "punished" for my naive acts. In addition, I fear what God thinks of me because of my death wishes for the man. I'm afraid to hate to the depth that I'd like because of my own punishment. I don't feel secure in expressing what I really feel. I don't want God or others to know—it doesn't seem good or right or acceptable to God to hate, to wish one dead. "Love your enemies … those who persecute you." If I loved, how could I ever justify wanting them dead? Maybe there's a hope—that I can express my feelings and be reconciled with God.

She was experiencing grief. Grief that results from trauma cannot be much different from that of a tragic loss. There had not been a physical death but, instead, a loss of life that would never exist in its intended form. This man had destroyed her in so many ways, and she had just begun to grieve the loss of her "self." For seven years, she had been in the first stage of denial. Denial is the space that gives us the grace to simply survive. For this eternity, all she *could* do was survive. Shock is the initial feeling. But as the shock wears off, it bleeds into emotional numbness, allowing your conscience to absorb only what it thinks it can handle. But neither the mind nor the body are meant to remain in denial long term. As her physical health continued to deteriorate, she began to acknowledge her reality and recognize her loss. As denial faded, the questions began to swirl as to how she, an intelligent thirty-five-year-old woman, had allowed this man to break her. She had unfairly turned to victim blaming. Perhaps it was easier to justify her own naivety. And then, finally, came anger and hatred. As I researched the stages of grief, reading that anger gives structure to nothingness made sense. It is the bridge, the connection to the source. She wrote:

> *March 13, 1986.* God, I want to be with you right now. I have the urge to "let go" with you. A door has been opened and I have the courage to be honest with you regarding the intensity of my feelings. For four years, I've known I was angry, but I've been afraid to admit the intensity and depth of that anger for fear of punishment from you. Psalm 58 has enabled me to search for the justness of my

personal anger. I am becoming convinced that my feelings toward this man are legitimate and that I can still be a worthy person and feel the thoughts I do toward someone who committed an unjust act. I find hope and comfort in the affirmation at the end of the Psalm about the reality of God's unseen justice. "Surely the righteous still are rewarded; surely there is a God who judges the earth."

It never occurred to me that you would want me to be angry and to show that anger. I now see the necessity of the expression. I am more convinced that you *do* hear my innermost cry of pain and hope for wholeness. The door is open; I believe in your healing power. I finally feel the importance of healing taking place during what seems to be a barren time. It is fruitless to pull up the roots of pain and claim that all is lost. Rather, in the midst of apparent barrenness, I am persuaded to continue to work with the expectation of a rich harvest to come. I am willing to wait, with faith in the outcome, for the appearance of the fruit of my pain and tears. I want to be whole—to no longer feel the fracturedness of life, to no longer have to live in two separate worlds. Someday I will feel whole again. Keep pushing me, Lord. Don't let me resign from the depth of this pain. Push me through to new heights, new understanding, new life.

Bargaining is the next stage of grief, although as we journey through the healing process, we undoubtedly float in and out of all stages. In the book, *On Grief and Grieving*, the authors state, "We do not enter and leave each individual stage in a linear fashion. We may feel one, and then another and back again." The "if onlys" from the beginning of this chapter are part of bargaining. And I assure you, she circled around to anger more times than I can count! Her bargaining at this point is for work and patience in exchange for healing. I love that she begs God to push her toward wholeness. Fortunately, in this moment, she had no understanding of the depth and gravity of what she was asking. If she had known her bargaining was leading her down a ten-year road, I firmly believe she would have hung up her sandals right then and there.

The next stage in the journey through grief? Depression. I don't think I need to expand. Depression is the natural, appropriate response to a great loss; however, this stage can feel as though it will last forever.

> *March 17, 1986.* I'm crying. I'm so distraught. When my life ceases to be busy, I become afraid—afraid of getting in touch with the real situation. I'm so split—a part of my life goes on as if nothing is wrong or upsetting in my life. The other part of me anguishes—oh so much. I feel today like I can't stand it.
>
> I'm so full of tears, of pain, of hurt, of anger, of fear. Oh God, sometimes I don't even know who I am, what I want, who I'm trying to hide from—myself, David, friends? Do I have any friends? Should I tell the whole story? Should David know?

∽

> *April 3, 1986.* My body is cold. I want to curl up, to retreat, to not feel—yet I know that's the path to death. Courage is what I need—to face pain and to endure pain. I need to see hope or a promise of hope.

∽

> *April 4, 1986.* Tears, a flood of them. Alone, more than I can bear. I need the courage to call someone. They said I could call; did they really mean it? I called. I went. I cried. There I was—a forty-two-year-old woman curled up to another woman—and I was able to cry.

For the first time, after seven years of secrecy, she told her story in its entirety to our pastor and his wife. There was so much power in admitting the truth—that she had been violated, repeatedly, and had hidden it for all these years. But the floodgates were now open. She had given birth to her story, and it was alive. It was going to rear its ugly head, and she could silence it no longer.

> *April 5, 1986.* The tears have flown freely in the last few days. So many years have passed since I've been able to cry. I'm beginning to sense and feel the width and breadth of my pain. Yes, I need to grieve. Grief is an expression of loss. Have I really thought about what I've lost, or have I not grieved because the pain of what's been lost is too difficult to bear? I believe the latter—to not grieve is to avoid pain.
>
> I'm grieving over the loss of a sense of wholeness. With each repeated rape, I felt more diminished—all of me—my sense of self, my spirit, my oneness with David. I was stripped of all the valuable possessions that were mine—my sense of self, my sense of goodness, my sense of cleanliness, my courage, trust, and faith in the human race that all things work together for good. Each time I was diminished into an object—something that could be used and abused for another's pleasure. Objects exist. They don't feel or give. They respond to forces in the environment—external not internal.
>
> Somewhere deep in the core of my being, a whimper is heard. I want to feel, to give, to break forth from my prison. And so, I grieve—an effort to break through the wall that has imprisoned me for seven years.

The whimper—the tiny voice from within that says, *I am not ready to die!* In a matter of thirty days, she had moved through all five stages of grief and reached acceptance, a place where she realized her past and understood that her future must change to accommodate its brokenness. Undoubtedly, over the next ten years, she would move in and out of these stages multiple times, especially anger and depression.

This entire chapter takes place chronologically prior to chapter 1, so at this point, I don't know what I didn't know. Understanding the space in which she was currently existing makes the trigger understandable. I cannot imagine I didn't notice her struggle, but I was a mere child, and my eyes were not fully opened to her emotional state until the blowup with my brother. After seven years, she had become an expert at disguising her attempt at living and appearing normal.

> *April 26, 1986.* It's been sixteen days since I've written— sixteen days of hell, confusion, extreme sense of brokenness, wandering, and failing at so many things I've attempted to do. I've even considered ending my life. At moments, I absolutely did not care about me or anyone else. My pain and anguish seemed so great that the only imminent release seemed to be death. But taking my life would only create more problems and questions. Why should my suffering be spread among others at a time when I chose to act irresponsibly? I feel consumed by physical pain—let alone the emotional. I hate this. I hate life—so empty and devoid of meaning.
>
> I'm ready to attempt to move within myself to the recesses of my mind and spirit I've yet to touch for seven years. Like a seed planted in the unfertilized, barren ground of my soul and spirit, it pushes for birth in spite of my continued trampling of its possibilities. I've denied its presence, its knowledge. I didn't know consciously it existed. I still don't know what exists within, but it pushes on with tremendous thrust—the inner self wants to be identified. Is this the source of new life? Allowing recognition to that which is buried?
>
> I am ready to try. I can't talk about it, but I am going to try to write it. My body says, "Write!" I am convinced there is reason to do this.

I share this inner dialogue not to expose the intimate crevices of her soul but to shed light on the constant turmoil within the mind of a rape victim. I hate that she even questioned her responsibility in his actions— that her incessant suffering was somehow the consequence of her naivety. And I hate that she legitimately felt guilty for hating him. But she was ready. She had come to terms with unearthing her pain and had justified her anger. She had the desire to heal. But healing meant facing the truth, and the truth was ugly. In our minds there are dungeons where we house the things we don't want to acknowledge. Becoming whole requires giving life to these dry bones, not to relive the horrors but to recognize their existence.

CHAPTER THREE

Disaster in Waiting

Somewhere between April 26 and May 7, 1986, she reflected back and wrote the following:

> In summer 1979, I resigned my job with the State Department of Public Welfare to begin teaching part-time at the college in the fall. I was restless—ready to create, to do, to produce—but no direction. The phone call came. He was frustrated with no services for young children following natural disaster. His request: "You ought to do something in this area." My mind immediately clicked. I saw possibilities—a chance to integrate my knowledge of emotional development of children and play and how to organize programs for children, an opportunity to create! Just what I wanted, and my schedule allowed me to pursue it. Four hours later, I called him back and relayed my ideas. He told me to begin reading, planning, putting ideas on paper. I was committed; this felt right. It was a new venture—no other person or agency was doing this—and I was in the driver's seat. I read studied, wrote and thought; good ideas need incubation. But I had never experienced disaster. He put me "in waiting" for the next natural disaster, and his office would provide the means for me to go and observe and talk to children and parents.

In mid-September 1979, Hurricane Fredrick hit Mobile, Alabama.

We met at the airport. I sat in on meetings with disaster personnel. He drove me to the damaged areas. We spent time at the Red Cross emergency shelters. I observed children, sat and talked to parents, talked to Red Cross personnel—all the time integrating what I heard and saw with the plan circulating in my head. In the midst of this disaster, I was elated because I saw possibilities.

The first night in Mobile, I stayed with a doctor and his family and eight other people. The second night, he drove me to Pensacola, Florida, for the night; it seemed far out of the way to me. As we looked for a motel, he asked if I wanted a double or a single bed. My innocent reply was, "I could sleep in either." At his request, I remained in the car while he went in to make the arrangements. We drove to a first-floor room on the other side of the motel, and he carried in my suitcase. He slid his off his shoulder and shut the door. I remember asking, "Where's your room?" and he said, "I'm with you, kid"

I froze. I went into the bathroom, locked the door, and stared into the mirror. No voice. No tears. No thoughts. Absolutely frozen. *No* is the only word that comes to mind as I recall this. Is the *no* what I was thinking? Or is the *no* what my body feels now—don't go on? But I will. I must. I must touch this experience.

When I emerged from the bathroom, he had lain his suitcase open on one of the beds and placed mine there too. That said to me that only one bed was left. I don't remember any conversation that evening. I watched some TV while he did some paperwork and made phone calls—one to his wife! He finally suggested *we* go to bed. I remember his next words: "My birthday was two days ago. I decided the greatest present I could receive would be to sleep with and make love to a slender, good-looking woman. I've been waiting for this for the last two days."

He went to the toilet and brushed his teeth—all with the bathroom door open! Was he afraid I would escape?

I was paralyzed. I sat in a chair. He pulled the covers back on the bed and patted the place where he wanted me. I sat on the bed motionless. He walked over to his briefcase, and as he returned to the bed, he laid a small square envelope on the nightstand. Its contents, a condom. His comment, "I believe like the Boy Scouts—be prepared." The lights went out. I lay down and turned my back to him. I clung to the edge of the bed, curled up tight. His hands, his kisses, he forcefully uncurled my legs ... I only remember the thrust of being raped. He criticized me because I was uptight—couldn't relax—belonged to the older belief that women don't let go. I died. He left me and went to sleep. I returned to my curled-up position but never slept. I remember thinking, *No! No! No! Oh God, No!*

I have no recollection of anything until the airport in Mobile. I waited for my plane. He stood beside me—and thanked me!!! I flew to Atlanta by myself. I recall no one else being on the plane. I had a three-hour layover, and I remember roaming the whole time. I never sat down. I flew to Fort Wayne and worked at trying to pull myself together. At home, I told David I was tired and went to bed. Over the next few days, I constantly repeated myself and forgot things. David finally asked me what was wrong. Coincidentally, the phone rang, and it was my partner, my perpetrator. David told him about my absentmindedness, and he said, "People often respond like that after they've seen the destruction of a disaster." David bought the simple explanation. That became the explanation of my behavior for the next three years.

After recounting the first incident, she was still awake at 2:00 in the morning. She could not sleep, so she decided to continue writing. Her body was trying to speak, to tell her things. The memories had come forward, coupled with physical pain, and she was begging to be freed. She wrote often about severe pain in her abdomen, localized on the left side in one general area. I am intrigued by this pain because it was colon cancer that eventually took her life. Had the seeds of her demise been planted at such an early point? Had cancer found the weakness in her body and just waited to take root and grow?

> Do I have to pay such a heavy price? Lord, keep me free from illness, please. If spitting out my story will serve that purpose, then I'm ready. I want to be free and well. I do not want to be controlled by this experience any longer. I want to control my life—*with* God as my ultimate source of control, not *away* from God while trying to hide the ugliness.

In early October 1979, a few weeks after my initiation to *real* disaster, there was a training seminar for new disaster workers in Mont Eagle, Tennessee. We were together again. Certainly not this time—no, he wouldn't. But he did. We arrived late at night amid a downpour. It was a Holiday Inn, and two rooms had been reserved—the kind connected by a door, for easy access. When we went to our rooms, they *weren't* connected. He was angry and took me with him down to the front desk. A real scene, I was so embarrassed. He conjured up this story to the manager about us having "much work to do and it was important that we have two adjoining rooms." After all, he placed his reservation that way, and his request was not met. I wanted to die. I knew from the force of his confrontation with the manager that his intentions were not work. We were given two new rooms—adjoining. He never set foot in the second one—*never*.

The terror I remember from this time was, after he finished "his important work with me," he walked out of the bathroom and said, "Kid, I have some bad news.

The condom tore. It's possible that ..." and I never heard the rest. I never slept again that night. All I could think about was pregnancy. What if ... Oh God, what would happen? What about David? We went on to the seminar where I worried myself sick. He compensated by telling the participants about the important "new program" for children that *I* was designing. I think he felt obligated to construct something good out of a three-day experience that could have some serious consequences.

At the airport, we stood on the observation deck in the late afternoon sun. I was numb—void of all feeling from the events of this trip. I remember his arm around me and saying, "Oh, kid. I'm sorry. I'm sorry." He asked me about abortion. Could I do it? He would pay for it. My anger arose. How could he so easily make life decisions for me—for my body? I cried and asked him to leave me alone. I wanted to be alone. How could I go on? But I did. I returned home. In an effort to appear normal, I denied the whole experience ... but I counted the days until my next cycle was to begin. I was seven days late, but finally, I was relieved. He called almost daily to see if I had started and was insistent that I never say a word to David. David must not know our secret.

At this point, my father was still buying the excuse of the "disaster aftermath hangover" and had not drawn any connection between her withdrawal from life and her traveling companion. The day the relief from pregnancy was awarded, our family eagerly welcomed this same man into our home for college homecoming weekend. He had come to visit his son and had conveniently asked to stay at our house. He stayed through Monday morning, and after the rest of us had left for school, he took advantage of having her alone. Since she was not pregnant, they had nothing to worry about in his eyes. It was a safe time, and he wanted to "make love" to her again.

He pulled her into *my bedroom* and satisfied himself. Again, her paralysis set in, and he belittled her for not responding physically to him.

He rationalized her behavior by saying it must be difficult to "let go" in her own home. He told her she was a conservative, traditional young woman who had not been sexually liberated. He was no longer convinced that marriage was meant to be monogamous, believing, rather, that other experiences could enrich and electrify a marriage relationship. His coaxing and coaching never paid off. She was never going to be able to "let go." But her mind was becoming twisted enough that she began to believe something was wrong with her because she couldn't.

It's devastating for me to think that I unknowingly slept in that bedroom, in the same bed, for twelve years following that horrific event. Ironically, my father was usually the one to put me to bed. How painfully difficult it had to have been for her to even step foot through the door of my room during the remaining years we lived in that house! Maybe this was part of the disconnect between my mother and me as well.

A child's bedtime is such an intimate experience. Prior to this time, the winding down process had been our favorite time of the day. She would scratch my back with the best fingernails on earth, read, and sing. I can still hear her voice, soothing me into slumber. "There Was Once a Puffin" and "Wynken, Blynken, and Nod" were our most beloved. How do you sing to your daughter, tuck her in, let her know she is safe, and encourage her to dream sweet things in a bed where your body had been violated and your soul destroyed beyond recognition?

I have no memory of bedtime with her in my later years. When I was just eight years old, this man, this monster had already begun to rob me—specifically, of my mother.

There Was Once a Puffin

Florence Page Jaques

Oh, there once was a puffin
Just the shape of a muffin,
And he lived on an island
In the bright blue sea!

He ate little fishes,
That were most delicious,
And he had them for supper
And he had them for tea!

But this poor little puffin,
He couldn't play nothin',
For he hadn't anybody
To play with at all!

CHAPTER FOUR

Write On

Her recollection continued:

I did not see him again until February 1980 and was accepted into graduate school during that time. Upon learning this, he became concerned that my studies would cut into "our work" and began planning opportunities for us to be together. On his phone calls, he indicated how he was missing me—how dull his life was without me. I guess I came to believe I was special. In retrospect, he was adept at building my ego professionally; he called me the expert. He could inflate me by day and destroy me by night. I was his puppet, and he pulled the strings. In my paralysis, I allowed myself to be destroyed.

In February 1980, on Valentine's Day, he met me in Buffalo, New York. He arranged two days of meetings for us with families who were Love Canal victims. But he arranged it on the fourteenth, a day of love so he could have me again. It was also three days after my birthday, and he wanted to give me "his gift." We stayed in a cheap motel, something with "love" in the name. After dinner, he drove me to Niagara Falls, because that's a lover's haven. I remember standing there freezing with his hands all over me. I wanted to go see my brother, just eight miles away. My request was denied because he might suspect something. Besides, we had "work to do."

I was his object again that I night. I remember it—a night of pain, of no sleep, of risk and fear. I lay motionless while he satisfied himself. *Oh God*, I prayed. *I hate this. I don't want this. I don't like this.* Amid his sighs of satisfaction he said, "You still haven't loosened up. I really have a lot of work to do with you." He began to talk about feeling cheated, everything I did not do. And for the first time he said, "You are a *cold* person." That entered my being with the force of a knife. I can hear it today. I was lowered lower.

I flew from Buffalo to Pittsburgh to change flights. Storms and delays—then take off into blinding snow. I feared death. I began to fear God's punishment. That fear persisted for seven years. In my weaker moments, I still fear God's punishment. At home, I entered back into my wife and mother duties and prepared for graduate school.

As she remembered and wrote, she relayed the experience of having no feeling of any kind other than matter-of-fact reporting. The only feeling she could recall was paralysis—psychological paralysis. There was no other feeling, and it still existed seven years later. She experienced a sense of disbelief—that this was not really happening. She wondered, *Did it really happen?* Yet, she was able to pull the experiences out of the depths of her soul, name them, and describe them in detail.

Moving further into the process (which only took a few days) her body urged her to write on, to continue the journey of allowing herself to touch the reality of each experience. There was a sense of urgency to get it *all* written down and soon. She wanted to remove it all from her being. She described it like peeling an onion, removing one layer at a time and bringing momentary pain and discomfort. But there was also a small degree of relief, a sneak preview of peace, perhaps. Sleep was coming in differing amounts, but enough to keep her stable. Sleep, in her eyes, was always the catalyst to maintaining her health and, consequently, her life.

She was learning to cry. Tears were present just under the surface of herself. She was longing for someone to reach out and touch her injured soul. Her hurting spirit ventured out cautiously, as she was aware trust was not there. When those who knew her pain did not initiate the act of compassion, she interpreted that to mean she was not loved. She longed for a friend, was hungry for an extended hand. But what did she have to offer? Her cup had dripped its last drop a long time ago. Was she demanding, frightening, unworthy, dependent, selfish? How could she fill her cup just a little, so she had something to give?

In March 1980, I flew to New Windsor, Maryland, to colead the first training seminar for the disaster childcare program. I met some exciting women and spent my free moments talking with many of them about the program. I stayed in a room by *myself*. It was a relief to be around him and not be threatened. I was mistaken. This was his hometown and the day the seminar ended. He drove me to see his new home. To my dismay, his wife was not there. As soon as I discovered this, I knew I was caught. I barely remember this time. I was frozen with fear that his wife would come home. In the brief time we were there, she did call. He told her we were looking for some books. Liar! I was ashamed, again, to be a part of the scene. The excitement of the first seminar was soon dashed to ruins. Again, I had been manipulated. I was dazed—wanting to escape.

Following this trip, he began extending himself to me in other ways. Frequent phone calls to my office and cards with verses for a "special friend" were mailed to my college box so David would not intercept. I opened each one, read it, shredded it into bits, and deposited the myriad pieces into a covered waste can on campus. Within a week I began graduate school—a season whose five and a half years was dominated by memories of destructive experiences. As I engaged myself in intense studies, I found an escape. I lost myself for hours in the graduate library. Classes, papers, and projects became my area of concentration. I buried my experiences—did not give them room to surface so they could be dealt with in a healthy manner. He soon tracked me down with phone calls and cards sent to the university. I responded with

22

haste; I did not have time for him. I was intently working on a reorganization of my life—trying to be a full-time graduate student and yet maintain my role as wife and mother without threat to my family. He sensed he was being left out and stepped up his campaign with me.

At this moment, the tears and sobs reappear—my body and soul remember his invasion of my private world and professional world, as well as my personal world. I hurt so much right now—I want to be held, just to be present with someone who knows my pain. No one. Loneliness.

Alone became her way of life during the entire graduate program. She felt out of place on a large campus and turned down all invitations to join the other students for meals and nightly gatherings. She ate alone, studied alone, and drove the distance between home and school alone. During the week she lived alone in a cold, dark dormitory room. And on the weekends, she went numbly home to her family. She was indeed different, yet desperately in need of a friend.

But no one was someone I wanted to trust.

May 1980 was the second training seminar—this time at our local church camp. He flew here and picked me up. I remember the drive to camp—his hand on my leg, his comments about missing me and his growing dissatisfaction with his wife, his stories constructed to cover up what he was really doing, and his reminders never to share "our secret." At camp, we met with eighteen people who stayed in the staff house; however, two other rooms had been previously arranged separate from the seminar participants. I argued the benefit of spending time with the others. "I think seminar leaders need time alone to process, to think, to prepare so they're more efficient, therefore the need for us to be separate!" Oh, shit! Damn him and his so-called logic. "Come on, kid. I miss you."

Shortly into the night, he came into my room—no locks or even doors at camp! I froze. He moved my body over to make room for his. I said, "No, not here." The walls are thin, but he was insistent on me being quiet—I wanted to scream. There were people in the next room who respected me. There was no stopping him. I lost—as usual. I lay motionless, pulling the shades of the experience over my awareness. I lost touch. I lost the recognition of myself. I was rapidly becoming a nothing.

In mid-May 1980, two weeks later, a tornado hit Kalamazoo, Michigan. This was the piloting of the childcare disaster program. People were trained, and we were ready to initiate. I had just finished my last test of the semester and was ready for a break with my family. Instead, I was off to another disaster. A local pastor offered his home, but "we" insisted on staying at the church in sleeping bags. I set up camp in the nursery, and he, in the sanctuary. It looked good to those who stopped by ... I can't remember anything other than being a victim—again. I guess by now his actions were becoming routine. Did I expect them?

A few days in, we had an argument. I went to bed early—bored yet frightened of an angry man. Again, in the night (no locks on the doors), he came in, still full of anger at me. I was fearing for my life at that moment. He carries his anger, doesn't talk about it. It just becomes a physical expression, and I was the recipient. Place did not matter to him—this was a church. It was more than I could admit, and so I didn't. How could I do what I had done and *ever* be worthwhile, good, or forgiven. I lost any last thread of goodness I had.

The next day, the center opened, the pilot program began, and other people came to stay at the church. She was left alone for the rest of the week. She spent most of her time in the childcare center and was the one to respond to inquiries from the Red Cross and federal government personnel.

Her recognition for the program was growing, and she was getting all the attention. She was the creator, but *he* was the director. She would not unseat him in his moment of glory, and he let her know. She had become a threat, and his efforts at restraining her from becoming any greater than himself became more apparent.

A week later, after she'd returned home and attempted a family vacation, he called to tell her about another tornado in Nebraska. Would she abandon her family and fly to Nebraska? She was due back at graduate school the following week. She could not do it for him—he would have to go alone. She cried. For the first time, she had said no to him, but she had clearly disappointed him, and he let her know. Underneath it all, she knew that, emotionally, she could not handle another week with him so soon. Fear had also set in. Her two worlds had nearly collided in the presence of my father. This man was on the phone begging her to go; and my father, beside her, was reminding her of the necessity of a few more days with him before leaving again for graduate school. She was caught between her two worlds, being wanted by two men and pulled in two different directions. The need to live two separate lives became more apparent. In reality, she looked forward to moving back to school. The pressure at home was mounting. Her guilt was extremely high. And all her energy was spent on not saying anything that would make my father suspicious. It was all taking its toll.

She concluded this entry with the awareness of her numbness and physical pain. Her arms were tingling, her stomach and back were in pain, her vision was blurred, and she could not feel the pen in her fingers. Something significant was happening. She questioned being caught up in the numbness of her memory versus her body releasing emotion that had not been allowed to surface. She could no longer attach feeling to the experience she had just written. Release overload? She chose to stop and let the emotion continue without the pressure of putting it on paper.

CHAPTER FIVE

Resistance

Soon she picked her narrative back up:

In June 1980, I moved back into the graduate dorm for
ten weeks. It was a relief. I again pursued my studies with
intensity. I worked hard because it brought relief from the
emotional pain. I could be a student in high gear.

Two training seminars over the summer were
uneventful. His relations with me were "cool," but
approaching me in other ways seemed too risky. In
September 1980, we had a training seminar in McPherson,
Kansas. I looked forward to staying with some of my best
friends who had moved there a few years ago. I arranged to
stay with them—and so did he! We were housed together
for two nights—separate bedrooms. The first night, no
problem, but the second, I had stayed up until 3:00 a.m.
talking with my friend. Being very tired, I went to my
room, only to have him follow me—he had been waiting.
He accused me up staying up so late, talking so much. He
took hold of my arm and pulled me to the room he was
sleeping in, which was my friends' bedroom. The thought
of betraying my friends was almost as intense as betraying
God in the church in Kalamazoo. He was a monster, lying
in waiting for me, and he grabbed me again. I lost again.
When I protested, he threatened me with my friends
finding out. I swallowed my screams. I swallowed and
buried another experience. Oh, but I hurt. I could barely

face them the next morning. I had fallen victim again, in my best friends' home. How could he do that?

She struggled even more returning home this time. She had betrayed God, her husband, and now her best friend. How could any of them love or trust her if they knew? She was not worthy of anyone. She returned to graduate school very alone and dropped her fellowship, along with the money attached, because she couldn't stand the pressure. Pressure from all angles—to remain quiet, to return home every weekend, to be a satisfaction to others—was mounting. Her life of hell was slowly scratching the surface of her spirit. She escaped even more, withdrew; and became very tired, yet studious. She pulled away from everyone and everything except school. It was a likely excuse. Many people knew she was in graduate school and accepted her resignation from committees, parties, and friends. She chose to be alone, as doing so reduced the risk of anyone finding out anything. It was easier, less threatening.

In October 1980, I had been invited to go to Grand Island, Nebraska, to train a group of teachers on children and disaster. The arrangements had been made through his office, so he was aware and found a reason to go as well. The flight was a memorable (or painful) one. I had finally extracted the courage to ask about "our" relationship. His response was, "Why do you ask?" And before I could respond, he retorted with, "Damn you. Don't bother me with being analytical. Just enjoy it."

I bit my tongue and froze.

He added, "It's fun having someone special, someone slender, someone to fly around the country with. Enjoy it. Relax. Liberate yourself." And on that note, he pulled a *Playboy* magazine out of his briefcase. "This is what you need!"

I couldn't bear to look as he mocked me for my inability to liberate myself. Is this what he thought he was doing to me? No, the exact opposite was happening to me—I was the oppressed. Also in his briefcase, he carried a supply of condoms. He enjoyed pointing them out to me with childish remarks about being prepared. It was a constant threat to me everywhere we went. To me, it said, "Tonight I'll get you again!" I lived in fear, and it was becoming greater. He was becoming more impatient with me. After all this time, I was not succumbing to his wishes in an easy manner. I resisted, and he knew it. I hated him but didn't know it. I was trapped and didn't know the direction to get out. I was transformed to a nonbeing but wasn't aware at the time. I remember him entering my room that night with a flashlight but nothing more. I can only assume I fell prey once again.

In November 1980, we led a weekend seminar in New Windsor, Maryland. This time, he arranged for me to stay in his home. His wife was a participant in the seminar, and his behavior was strikingly different—very professional— no pats on my behind or any other suggestive behavior. I was enjoying this temperament and relief from threat. Or so I thought.

The last night, he came upstairs to my bedroom in the middle of the night. I was awakened by his touch and verbal threat of, "Don't make a sound." Can you imagine? His wife was downstairs, and he had the *gall* to invade my room while she slept. I made it clear he needed to get lost, and he did. The next morning, he was ice-cold as he drove me to the airport. As we got near, we drove past a Holiday Inn. His words, sharply, were, "If I had time, I'd take you in that motel and rape you!"

I panicked. For a moment, I thought he would, but then he drove on. *Rape?* That was the first time he'd used the word. It's obvious he differentiated between rape and what he was already doing to me. Surprisingly, I never used that word either until years later.

Five months passed without my mom seeing him. He continued to call a couple of times a week "for business" and showered her with cards. In

April 1981 they went to the University of LaVerne and stayed with a friend for two nights with no problem. The next day, they continued to Empire, California, for another seminar, where they stayed in separate homes. But her flight home was out of San Francisco, and he, of course, offered to drive her there the night before. Again, she froze. He always found a way to get her alone. It was Chinatown for dinner, and then he made a reservation at the Holiday Inn—only one room this time. He wasted no time in telling her how he had waited for this night. She had decided, she was going to resist—at all costs.

He went about his normal routine of demanding enjoyment, and she tried to deny him. Outweighing her by at least 150 pounds, he overpowered her, did what he wanted, and then verbally berated her until she cried. He demolished what was left of her soul. "You are so cold, so weak, so unloving, so frigid. You don't even know how to love. You don't give anything to me. What kind of lover are you?" In minutes he had cut her into pieces—reduced her to nothing. To be used like she was and then berated for what she was not. She had been ruined. She could no longer survive.

The flight home was the usual swallowing and preparing for reentry. By now, this was her practice. Each flight home was the burial of one self and preparation of the other—the wife, mother, student. Summer school brought welcome relief. It would be February before she would see him again. It had been over two years of working with him. She had been through hell but had managed to stay alive. The two worlds and two selves were evident, but she managed. She loved teaching and realized that education was her true life calling. She found less and less interest in flying around the country organizing seminars and disasters centers and coping with an abuser. She began to hint that she would soon have to make a choice.

> February 1982 brought five days on the West Coast—La Verne and Fresno, California. For the first time, he called me to ask about "my" choice for housing. I asked to stay with my friend Ruth in La Verne and, hopefully, a family in Fresno. I remember clearly adding the statement, "I will go to California with you on one condition—that you do not touch me. I want to be left alone!"

He complained about my lack of cooperation, but I repeated myself, and he said, "OK."

On the plane, he pumped me with whys. I was able to say that I was torn apart, losing my sense of self, extremely guilt-laden, and so on. Again, I was accused of being old-fashioned, caught up in being "good" rather than having fun. I knew he would never hear my view. He was dominant; he was right. I was clearly the one with the outdated perspective. Then he said, "I'm not getting anywhere with you in this conversation—so just forget it. You'll never be liberated. You will miss much in life."

Truth was, I *was* missing much in life—but I was so numb by now, I didn't know what I had lost. I don't think I knew who I was.

This next incident was deeply painful for her to write about. With a mixture of numbness and physical pain, tears, and whimpering, she dug deep into the caverns of her memory to recall the final straw. A part of me wants to tell it in my words as a way of protecting her from the intimate, horrific details. But I am not telling a story. I am telling the truth, and the truth needs to be told in her words. The truth is about a man who was sick and violent, not one who was having an affair and trying to liberate women. On this occasion, she refused to allow him to carry out his brutal plan. She fought him and won, but I'm not sure she ever really won. Within the complexity of this story, I'm not even sure what winning looks like.

For four nights in California, he had remained faithful to his agreement to not touch her. After several exhausting days of training, they both returned to Ruth's home, and plans were made for the airport in the morning. Mom was tired, went to bed and immediately fell asleep. Then:

On March 1, 1982 at 2:10 in the morning, I was awakened out of my sound sleep when I felt the presence of his heavy body on top of mine. (Again, no bedroom locks.) I was lying on my stomach when I was awakened, my eyes full on the 2:10 of the digital clock a few inches from my face. I began to struggle, and he held me down until I ceased struggling. In a whisper, I kept telling him to get out and reminding him that he had promised—to no avail. He told me to keep quiet. All I remember was that he was heavy, and I was scared. He suggested I roll over. I refused. He asked me several times, and I refused each time.

(As I write this, my body has become numb with some tingling sensations. There is pain in my stomach and abdomen. I am so uneasy—quiet sobs and tears grace my face. This—this moment is the most difficult of all times to reveal. The pain of it all is so repulsive, so dehumanizing, so belittling. A major part of my difficulty lies in the sharing of the worst invasion of my private self. I would do anything at this moment to avoid what needs to be told. But deep within my spirit is the cry for my own personal liberation from a bondage of hell. I want to be well, to be whole, to be free of this brutal memory.

I can't seem to write about it. I stare into space. I cry. I'm fighting for every bit of courage. My hand seems to refuse to write what is in my heart. I'm begging myself to let go—to let go so I can live. Please God, give me the strength to share the worst.)

I was afraid of what he would do. In my refusals, I had angered him to the nth degree. In an instant, and I think it was to be his final blow to me, he released his grip on my arms and placed his hands on my hips. He brutally molested me with his hands as he tried to make room for himself. I could feel the beginning attempt of the final assault. With every ounce of energy in my body, I turned sideways, pushed his body away from me and ordered him out of the room. He sat on the bed breathing heavily. The room was totally dark; my orders were whispers. I repeated them, and he didn't move. I raised up and pushed him off the bed. He stood up and walked to the door, saying something that I never heard. He left my room. I was in a state of absolute shock. I sat, dazed, with my eyes on the door, fearing his return. I finally got up and put a chair in front of the door in case he returned, and I might be asleep. Ha! Asleep? That was something I would not experience for seven months to come. Seven whole months! The rest of the night I lay in bed, facing the door, and remained awake. I was frozen with fear. I couldn't cry or think, I just was. He was *not* going to touch me.

The next morning, I got up earlier than planned and took a long bath. At breakfast, I could not face him. I ate quickly and returned to my room to finish packing. All I wanted to do was go *home*. As I carried my suitcase to the door, I met him in the hallway. He said, "I had to satisfy myself last night—thanks to you."

I paused for a moment but said nothing. I had nothing left to say.

CHAPTER SIX

Leaving

She wrote next:

> *May 6, 1986.* Well, the worst is over. The worst has been to give words and feelings to what has happened in the period of two and a half years. I want to write more, to provide myself the words of the time following this disastrous sequence of events. Following the event in California, I became an insomniac. I soon learned what it was to go to bed every night *and not* sleep. I could not cry. I lost the ability to feel anything. I sank deeper into a period of existence with no meaning.

Within weeks, she led two more training seminars by herself and then was hoping for a break. No such luck. Fort Wayne, Indiana, forty-five minutes from our home, was flooded, and she was asked to organize volunteers. She was sick, exhausted, and had no energy. But out of fear, she responded. She worked hard, alone most of the week, and then *he* decided to come—first to the center and then on to our house.

She didn't know he was coming. And as usual, when he got to our home, he walked right in the front door and met her in the kitchen. They sat across from each other at the kitchen table and cleaned up some disaster business. As he was wrapping up, he looked at her and said, "I really want to take you into that bedroom and rape you ..."

There was more said, but she didn't hear it. She knew what he wanted. Quietly and calmly, she told him she was sick and asked him to leave. He was already angry, but if she raised her voice, she feared he would only become more agitated and aggressive. He paused for a while, contemplating his options, and then left. She locked every door—he would never get in again.

> In April 1982, I led my last disaster training seminar alone. I was really sick by this time but continued to push. When I returned home, I sat down and wrote to him. I informed him that I would no longer volunteer any services in any way to the Child Care Disaster Program. I was leaving it … for personal reasons. He called me after receiving my letter and wanted to know what the personal reasons were! I couldn't believe it—just couldn't believe that he could ask that. I told him I thought he could figure it out. I remember my final words, "If you're not smart enough to figure it out, I'm not dumb enough to tell you!" I remember my own anger at his stupidity.

Sick. She was blatantly ill by this time. Her blood counts were low, and her liver was malfunctioning, but she could not stop. It was as if she had something to prove. Or was she afraid that, if she stopped moving forward, she would die? She taught the rest of the semester and then enrolled in another ten weeks of graduate school for the summer. She desperately needed to be alone. Rest came, but sleep continued to fail her. She studied in bed and pursued no other activities. She dragged herself to classes and did only enough work to get by. In July, she ran into her doctoral chairperson one day, and he immediately reacted to her ghostly appearance.

In his office she admitted to being sick and unable to sleep, study, or simply function. He suggested she drop out for a while and get some medical attention and counseling.

Finally, she resigned herself to what was slowly destroying her body and went home.

> In July 1982, I went home—a very sick person. To the rest of the world, my illness was interpreted as overload from teaching, parenting, wife-ing, and being a student. People seemed to accept my response. I stayed home—rested as

much as I could but still didn't sleep. I thought about life, how empty, how meaningless, how much of a chore it was to even move and exist. I was a nothing—but had not been able to give recognition to the real root of the problem. In some respects, I was as stupid as the man who abused me. I could never say the truth—I buried the cause so well that I lost all cognizance of it.

Slowly, her weary body began to heal. The doctor-prescribed exercise program was propelling her into better physical health. My mother was not an athlete, but I remember her walking and running like her life depended on it—because it did! Her mental health remained a challenge. But at the time she had no idea what this type of healing would look like. After two counselors and eighteen months of therapy, it seemed appropriate (in her mind) for her to stop. She was ready to go back to graduate school, determined to finish. She felt better; people told her she looked better; and she said, "I actually felt some degree of meaning in my life—as much as one can when a 'stone of horror' still remains inside."

The break from school and "disaster" had aided in her recovery. And in the summer of 1984, she completed her coursework and passed her written and oral exams on her first attempt. Her doctoral committee was proud of her. Exhausted but excited, she had a real sense of accomplishment, knowing she had functioned and succeeded with such great odds stacked against her.

In September 1984, I was on the homestretch—the dissertation. That, at the beginning, put me back in touch with him. He so badly wanted to help with my research. When I asked him why he wanted to be involved, his answer was this, "I want to see my name in your dissertation. After all, if it weren't for me, you wouldn't be doing this work. You should really be grateful for my support—for giving you the opportunity to blaze a new trail and gain recognition."

I was perceptive enough to know that *he* wanted the recognition for himself and not for me. I promptly dropped all contact with him and directed my efforts to the American Red Cross in Washington, DC. They were a tremendous help and knew how to work with a researcher.

When I failed to call him about my research, he called me. He thought I had stopped working on it. I told him I was making great progress, and he responded, "But how can you do that without me?"

I fired back, "I am doing just fine without you!" He was angry - I had left him out.

"Just remember, kid, who got you started in the disaster work. Remember who gave you the idea. I think you owe it to me." And again, "I want to see my name in your dissertation."

I knew that I owed him nothing. His name or any reference to his organization does not appear anywhere in the dissertation. I made sure of that. I finished; it was hard. Each page brought memories of him and his destructive power over me. When I completed it, I shelved it. I didn't want the memory. Yes, there is valuable information there, and it needs to be disseminated. But I don't have the personal resources to return to work on it.

This chapter in her life was finished. No more disaster work, childcare centers, or travel. No more graduate school to escape to. In fall 1984, she was granted a full professorship. And in spring 1985, she graduated with her EdD and walked for commencement in her cap, gown, and hood. She was so proud—it would always be one of her greatest accomplishments. Her doctoral hood was one of the few things she specifically requested to be on the altar at her funeral. It now hangs in a closet in my home. I cannot bring myself to part with it. Her journey to achieve it gave her meaning and worth during a time when she felt she had neither. When she was not capable of anything else, of simply living, she could be a student.

But I will always struggle with the cost. I am finding tears as I write this because the cost to herself, her health, and her family was so great. I find it difficult to separate the abuse from the education. They are so closely intertwined, though neither one was a direct result of the other. The degree in higher education was not a motive for escape, and the need for escape was not her choice. But for five and a half years, it gave her the welcome opportunity *not* to be a mother. It took me years after her death, but I was eventually able to find some peace in forgiving her for something that was never her fault. Without this escape, she may not have survived.

CHAPTER SEVEN

Where Am I Now?

School behind her, she looked inward:

May 7, 1986. Where am I now? Aware that I have been able to survive the worst. I have faced the experience. I am propelled to find the Karen who has been slowly destroyed. Somehow, throughout the seven years of humiliation and destruction, I've hung on to the last thread of life. I have been robbed and beaten—physically, spiritually, emotionally, socially, mentally, and morally. There's no part of my being left untouched. I've lost the ability to love and give—to friends, family, and students and to God. I'm not aware of God. I'm not aware of love. I am aware that three people have committed themselves to support me. That alone has provided the courage to reach out and to reach within myself.

All I ask is that, as these many pages of words are read, you believe me. I don't want sympathy. I want support to continue my search for meaning and growth in this human experience. I want your patience as I continue with the struggle of learning to love, trust, and give of myself. I continue to feel guilty that I've asked you to share this pain. Somehow, it seems we should all be spared that. But pain is a given in life. I continue to think that I can find myself. My journey now is one of hope—that I can rebuild relationships with my beautiful family who I've hurt desperately; that I can rebuild myself, to sense my own beauty, talents and gifts in place of quiet anger and fear that destroys; that I can rebuild a meaning for existence. I feel alone now, wondering if I am capable of being trusted and loved. I feel alone in my family. What will their response be and what will our response be together? Yes, I feel alone. But somehow I feel "right" about the direction I'm going.

What I've written is long—maybe too much, too many words and too many details. I wonder if I've been right in that approach. Yet, I feel the need to have at least *one* other person in this world know the extent—the width, the breadth, and depth—of this experience. Then, and only then, will I cease to feel alone. Maybe I have written too much—made too big of a deal out of this—but to me it's been a "big deal"; it's been my life for seven years. I want someone else to grasp the immensity of it all with me.

Somewhere, deep within my being, is a new spirit waiting to be born.

May 8, 1986. I reread it all. It's too much to handle. The words hit me hard. It really *all* happened. I hurt. I'm alone ... I need an arm or a hand to clasp mine. I need someone, someone who knows. God, are you here? It's too much to realize alone. I'm alone, and I cry. Oh God, once more I plead—help me to sustain myself through this moment of truth.

Two days later, with the help of our pastor and his wife, she told my father the entire truth. Our pastor did most of the talking and telling as she huddled, scared, nervously awaiting his response. (At some point during the last seven years, she had vaguely told my dad she'd been raped. The who and how often had never been disclosed until this point. The sexual pillar of their marriage had suffered immensely, and she frequently cried during their infrequent intimate occasions. She had to give him *something* to explain her behavior.) The worst had been exposed, and she learned that my father had suspected him all along. He was angry—but not at her. He was angry at *him*, at what he had done to her that had inhibited and prevented their growth together.

To this day, my father is the single most nonconfrontational person I know. It's not a bad thing; it's just the way he is. He does not raise his voice or argue; he just speaks slowly, quietly, softly. He is the peacemaker. If my husband had just learned this information, *angry* would not be the word I would choose to describe him. But for my father, it fit. I'm sure he was simply angry—angry about what had been done; what he could not change; and what he, she, and they together had lost. I'm confident that my father's gentle nature is why she survived this season of her life. She did not need him to be angry; she needed him (now that she was willing to let him) to love her.

I can't imagine seven years of her withdrawal from life, from their marriage without pushing for more answers. Maybe he had an idea and just didn't want to know the truth. The mind is a powerful instrument. For my mother, it was able to entomb the events and details she was not able to handle. And for my father, I believe it prevented him from asking the questions to learn the answers he did not want to know. It protected him, and he just kept moving forward. Had he probed her for answers during this time, I think she would have pulled away even more. I'm not sure that, even if he had pressed her in the gentlest of ways, she would have been able to find the truth while it was happening.

And so, he continued with his life as teacher and father, and we kids didn't know any different. My father saved us for many years, although we didn't know we needed saving. As far as my brother and I knew, we had an extremely normal childhood. Had my father had any job other than a teacher, life would have been very different. They both taught during the school year. And while Mom was gone for ten weeks each summer, we went camping and played tennis and basketball. My brother played Little League, Dad and I became evening running partners, and we always spent a week at church camp. While some of our friends began to experience divorce, our parents were still together in a discombobulated kind of way. We did not appear on the outside or the inside to be dysfunctional.

CHAPTER EIGHT

Summer of Nothing

For Mom, the summer when she would no longer be away was a new start:

> *May 26, 1986*. Here I sit, the first day of my three-month vacation, almost numb. I don't remember when I've had "nothing to do." It's a gift I've given myself. I've actually mused in the last couple of years that maybe I'd never live this long—to feel a day with nothing to do. Thanks to God, I've made it.
>
> I want the summer of 1986 to be a significant summer—one where I can sense a permanent return to health—physically, emotionally, and spiritually. I want to really experience the meaning of rest.
>
> Last night, I poured myself the question, "Where do I want to be by September 1?"

I absolutely love the imagery here, enough that I needed to break into her entry to say so. I can picture her holding a glass pitcher and pouring these words into an amber goblet as she contemplates the next few months. She had always had professional goals, but this was where she began setting personal goals for her summer, the upcoming year, and the remainder of her life. Every New Year's Eve from now on, she would write out her goals for the year to come—where she wanted to see herself flourish in the next twelve months. Ironically, on her last December 31 on earth, she was empty; the plans and goals did not come.

"Last night, I poured myself the question." It almost forces you to visualize, to ponder, and I feel like I just read it for the first time. My mother was a brilliant writer. As I read and reread her journals, I am amazed by her composure amid her anguish. Her word choice and inflection were immaculate and accompanied by flawless grammar and spelling. I have occasionally had to look up words to double-check their meaning and validate the point she was trying to convey, and she was never wrong. Who uses the word "mused"? My mother does! I have found myself giggling occasionally, as she would correct her handwritten pages by slashing out a wrong letter or place an "sp" with a circle around it if she was unsure about her spelling. She was the ultimate perfectionist. I get it honestly! We read on:

> By September 1, I want to be able to feel who I am. I want the circuits unloaded and a sense of peace flowing through where, for so long, confusion, clutter, and despair have traveled. I want to be in touch with my soul—to be able to bid farewell to pain and welcome joy and a sense of purpose to my life. Too much of my life has been the race to get "such and such" over with. I'm sad that is my life—or has been—for that isn't life! I want to sense the joy of living and doing and being. Somewhere beneath my cluttered soul, there is a reservoir of potential yet to be tapped. I wonder what's there, what I really could do and be? I wonder what I'm willing to risk to emerge.

She eagerly wrote a list of "Some things I want to do." If I'm being completely honest, it hurts that spending time with my brother and I was not on this list. She had been unavailable for seven years—physically, she was there off and on, but emotionally she had not been present since fall 1979. We were so young and formative during those absent years, but repairing those relationships was not at the top of her list. We were teenagers and had our own lives. We were not a critical part of her healing process for now. She would read, return to the piano, exercise, sew, cook, spend time with my father, relax, and learn to love again.

She also began counseling with our pastor and was presented with the act of anointing as a part of her healing. She was restless with the idea and wrote frequently about her struggle. While she was still so empty and in need of healing, she did not want a "quick fix." During the anointing process, the participant is asked whether anything in her life might prevent healing. This became a barrier for her. She had unresolved anger and felt unworthy of the act. Were there things she still had not admitted? Did anointing require forgiveness on her part? Would it enable her to forgive? There was also a confession component, and she was afraid, unsure of what she would need to confess to open up the gates of healing. There was resistance, and she conversed with God about why he was holding her back. What else did she need to go through? Was there more to the story, more yet to be uncovered? She resigned herself to His direction. God was providing the holdup because she had yet to surrender her control.

> *June 10, 1986.* JD [our pastor] is coming to talk with our family. It is a time of great apprehension for me. How will the children respond? At this moment, I am trusting God to be with us, to be present in our pain, to help us endure and understand, and to grow. I want growth in our whole family—a growth toward closeness, empathy, and sensitivity. It is possible, and I trust God to be with us in a quiet way to help us through this time.

This was when we learned the who, the where, and for how long. But frankly, I don't remember the conversation. I don't remember any plea for growth and wholeness within our family. It was a lot of uncomfortable information for two teenagers. Of course, I had no perspective at that time. But her desire for empathy and sensitivity was selfish, and I mean that in the best way. She so desperately wanted us to be an active part of her recovery, to feel her pain and to walk this journey with her. She did not have the capacity at the time to see that we were hurting as well and we, also, needed to heal from the last seven years. Our needs were not always congruent.

Further, as close as we were, I do not remember *ever* having a conversation with my brother about what happened—not the rapes, the person responsible, the aftermath, anything. Nor do I remember any sit-downs with my father about how Mom was doing and how we should treat her. Even though we all knew what had happened, we didn't talk about it. I have since found it puzzling that Mom did not journal about the blowup with Matt one month prior, and I did not write about the June 10 family meeting. We both dated our entries, and nothing matches up.

Her summer of nothing slid into a constant battle between healing and hopelessness. She continued to question the idea of confession. Didn't God already know what had happened to her? Was it pride or denial that it had really happened? Was it her desire to be perfect, and her story was too much? Was she too good, too smart to have been involved in something like this? But healing comes not from being perfect but from being forgiven, and forgiveness comes out of being honest.

> *June 18, 1986.* One day at a time. The analogy of the ice cube tray—to subdivide my despair and take one small compartment at a time. Help me, Lord, to be content to handle each day—and only that day—and to rest in the peace that each individual day fits in with the rest of my days and that each is connected and supported by the framework of the total span of time.

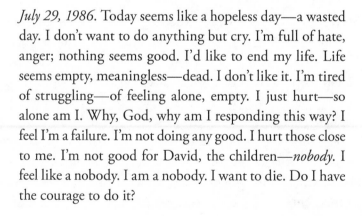

> *July 29, 1986.* Today seems like a hopeless day—a wasted day. I don't want to do anything but cry. I'm full of hate, anger; nothing seems good. I'd like to end my life. Life seems empty, meaningless—dead. I don't like it. I'm tired of struggling—of feeling alone, empty. I just hurt—so alone am I. Why, God, why am I responding this way? I feel I'm a failure. I'm not doing any good. I hurt those close to me. I'm not good for David, the children—*nobody*. I feel like a nobody. I am a nobody. I want to die. Do I have the courage to do it?

> *July 31, 1986.* A different approach to life today. I feel encouraged to live …

On September 23, 1986, I wrote the following in my journal (I was still only fifteen years old):

> Everything is so weird here at home. Ever since Mom and Matt had that fight last May, things just haven't been the same. (I'm not sure they ever will.) It's really scary, and I'm not sure how to deal with my feelings. I want to reach out and tell someone how I feel, but I can't. The only people who know about the situation are our family and a few other very close friends of my parents. If only I could tell someone else what I'm going through, maybe I would understand it more myself. My feelings are so confused that my head feels like it's spinning. Sometimes I just feel like running away from it all. I want to get away where things are normal. I hate having to cope with Mom's moods. Sometimes she seems OK, but a lot of the time, she's tired, depressed, or upset. It's hard to be careful with what I say and do because the smallest thing can set her off. I'm tired of Mom crying all the time, she and Dad whispering, and the awkward silence that is often felt. It makes me mad when Mom's eyes are swollen, and her nose is red. I just want to leave and escape the pain. I hate feeling this way but it's so difficult having to be so sensitive all the time. If I could, I would package up all of the pain and despair in our family and blow it up.
>
> I know it's wrong to hate, but I've never hated anyone more than I hate the person who caused us so much pain. I feel so much hostility toward this person that I could just beat him to death. That is such a horrible way to feel, and I'm ashamed of myself for feeling that way, but this person has done something that is irreparable.
>
> I can't imagine all the pain my parents are experiencing, but I am aching too. When I'm at school, I try not to think about it, but at home it's hard to ignore something that is constantly there. Putting on a front may not be the best thing to do, but anymore, I'm not sure what the best

thing to do is. Damn, I wish it would all disappear. Most
of the time, all I want to do is cry and hide until it's all
gone and it's safe to come out.

Wow, if that isn't a cry for help! I'm jumping ahead a bit in my timeline, but I wanted to reiterate that we did not talk about it as a family, and we were apparently told at that point not to tell anyone else. Surprisingly, I must have obliged my parents by not going back to Sara with the truth from that first day. My journal was also read by my English teacher (as a weekly assignment). So I could not divulge too much information there either. As much as I loved and trusted her as a teacher, I waited patiently until I was given permission to tell her the rest of the story. I'm not sure of the significance. But it was January 1, 1987, when I revealed the truth—after an entire eight months of keeping silent.

The comment about her swollen eyes and red nose haunts me to this day. I can vividly picture her in her nightgown and robe, coming down to the breakfast table. We ate breakfast together as a family every day, and our menu seldom changed. On Thursdays we had French toast, Friday fried eggs, Saturday pancakes, Sunday hard boiled eggs, and so forth. Sometimes Mom would not come down right away. No one asked questions. We just prayed and started eating without her. I'm not sure when it started or how long it lasted, but it was clearly happening between May and September.

And then she would come down, and she was so painful to look at. She was deathly pale, undoubtedly exhausted from a lack of sleep, eyes swollen like she had been crying for hours and nose red as if she had been out in subzero weather. It was excruciating to see someone that weak and fragile. I began to wonder if there would ever be a morning when she would not come down at all, *ever*.

Well into my forties, I would have nightmares about my mother in an upstairs bedroom and having to check on her to see if she were still alive. In my dream, I was always a child, coming home after school and climbing the stairs, not knowing what I would find.

CHAPTER NINE

Confrontation

Late summer 1986 was rock bottom. Night after night, sleep continued to remain at bay.

> *August 5, 1986, 2:00 a.m.* Sleep is precious to me. I long for it—peaceful, continuous, full sleep. I don't understand why I don't experience it. I plead with you, Lord, please— for sleep. I lie in bed and weep—weep for many reasons— but sleep lost is a source of sorrow. My soul continues to cry through the night. I feel the hurt, the pain of an unresolved crisis. I continue to feel alone, floundering like I want to give it all up. I now feel so sick of hurt and pain, so tired of struggle, so dismayed at little bits of progress, so hopeless. Again, I ask for strength to hold on, to keep going.

I believe that she wanted to die. Death, the eternal sleep, would have been a welcome, simpler choice. We all might have even understood if she had taken that step. But my mother was never one to take the easy road. She was a farm girl, and there was an assumed work ethic, no matter the task. She had it in her to save her own life. But many days, she felt her will to live was buried too deeply, and the work required to find it was much too difficult.

In addition to her in-person therapy she began to read. Surprisingly for that time, she never seemed to have a shortage of self-help books dealing with abuse, trauma, and healing. Her faith played a major role in the beginning of this "digging out" process as well. Reading entailed underlining, highlighting, and writing in the margins. She would read, journal about what she had read, and then pray in writing for God to guide her through what she was learning. Little by little, she was educating herself into the healing process. It was what she knew how to do.

I think the initial step in her self-help process was to relinquish control. For a highly educated, organized, type A person, having control is critical. There needs to be an element of surrender when you dedicate yourself to the healing process, not knowing what exactly it will require of you or how long it will take. It stipulated unlearning her style of mastering the world and allowing herself to be led by her faith through the unknown. She was a goal setter and typically had a timeline for achievement. There were so many components to this journey, so many steps to recovery. No one knew when health would return or what it would even look like.

Continuing from August 5, she wrote:

> Tonight I read from *Transitions* by William Bridges: "The healing process must include the courage to unmask the anger, bring it out before God and put it on the cross where it belongs. There will be no healing until it is acknowledged, confronted and resolved. Resolution means forgiving every person involved in that hurt and humiliation; it means surrendering every desire for a vindictive triumph over that person. It means allowing God's forgiving love to wash over your guilt-plagued soul."
>
> Anger and resolution of that anger—help me, Lord. Help me to face it, not escape it.

Because of her repeated abuse, she did not know how to find anger within her being, let alone express it. Her ability to show anger was silenced, along with her voice. Her fury revealed itself in sleepless nights, tears, flashbacks, and endless tossing and turning—to no avail. Oh, she hated him with a passion. She hated this season of life, where she felt robbed of everything good. And she hated the expectation of the world that she would live through it. She wrote about giving herself permission to let the feelings out, about wanting to scream, but her hatred had no sound. She had yet to find its voice. She had never screamed!

Through another book titled, *The Hiding Place* by Corrie Ten Boom, she discovered the illness of indifference. It's a disease that inflicts when one can no longer stand emotional pain. It progressively paralyzed her, and she became indifferent—to joy as well as pain. She admitted to gradually being overcome by the disease as it enabled her to survive, but the survival was not a healthy one. In order to cope with feelings of helplessness, she turned off the feelings brought about by abuse and, in turn, unknowingly deadened her capacity to love. She stated she could no longer love or feel the love of others. Even when you are cognizant of your disease, how do you relearn to feel? To love?

> *October 6, 1986.* I'm down—out—empty. Yet, I'm called upon to proceed with life—to give. I hurt—physically and emotionally. I'm tired—my body needs sleep—yet I go on. Life is complex. It seems I do what I feel I can't do, and I'm called upon to do more. Yet, I'm reminded that the Lord doesn't ask more of me than he knows I can handle. But, Lord, today I just want to scream at you, "I can't do this!"

Ah, anger—even at God—is a good thing.

Another essential step in her healing was the decision to confront her abuser. Remarkably, she was willing to do this early on in her therapy. I believe it was a means of taking back the power that had been stolen from her. She was not willing to face him in court, to relive her story in front of a judge and jury. But she would tell her truth to the people who employed this man to travel the country with her; she needed to do that. The necessary person was contacted, and the initial meeting was set in late October. She, my father, and our pastor met with him alone, and Mom was able to tell the critical parts of her story. She was listened to, believed, and met with overwhelming support. She was ready to act, and a date was set for the confrontation.

On November 18, 1986, more than seven years after the initial incident my mother was given the opportunity to confront her abuser in a safe environment. There were five other people in the room, and he proceeded to sit in the chair beside her! After the employer addressed the issue, Mom told her side of the story, and then he followed with a quick denial of rape.

He then proceeded to state that he didn't know the difference between rape and an affair. Mom promptly explained the difference, followed by describing the first incident in Florida and the last in California, more than two years later. He was subdued.

She wrote:

> He did not present himself well—physically or verbally. The entire eighty minutes was a difficult and sad scene—a man who obviously did not perceive his behavior as devastating. In a way, I felt triumphant. I was able to say what I wanted to say about the hurts, the pain, the losses— and able to say them with civility and emotion. He said he felt "raped" by me when he read my dissertation, and I gave no credit to him or the church … Power, he wanted power over me.
>
> I finally turned to him and said, "Can't you believe that I have the ability to pull off a research project on disaster without you? Let go of me. Why can't you let go???"
>
> I went back to the rape scenes and described in detail how the first one occurred. He argued that there was no sex the first night. I argued back, clearly remembering him putting on the condom. I can hear the paper being torn … God, it's like watching someone sharpen the knife they intend to use to stab you. I remember *everything*. I hated him at that moment—and I still do! In today's meeting, he said he recalled caressing my feet and accused me of being the initiator! Good grief!

She closed the meeting by asking him *never* to bother her again. She questioned his sincerity, and he reaffirmed that he would leave her alone. He extended his hand, and she began to sob. She paused, dropped her arm, and gave him a brief handshake. Was this a peace offering? Would anything ever bring her peace? Is there freedom beyond injustice? Was there a consequence that would bring any form of justice?

He was to call his wife and his pastor before going home and it was recommended that he enter psychiatric testing and intense therapy for his deeply rooted issues. I have always wondered about the phone call to his wife and any conversations with her that would follow. Our families were friends. I can picture her in my mind today. How did he tell her that, on all those trips, almost every disaster, every workshop, every training seminar, he was forcing my mother to share a bed with him, and he was raping her? Did he use the word? Or did he present it as an affair, an inappropriate relationship? Would he ever truly understand the difference?

I remember her coming home from the confrontation slightly lighter than before. It had been a positive step forward. She had succeeded in telling her truth, not only to him but also to several other significant people. During the three years of abuse, she had tried to have a conversation with him about what was happening, but he never wanted her to analyze their relationship. She should just relax and enjoy it. I believe that he approached her in 1979 not only because of her expertise but also with the intent of creating an opportunity for himself. She was intelligent, attractive, and small in stature, and he was a sexual predator. They already had a friendship outside of the proposed position so there was an existing level of trust. He was expecting an affair to take place, but she did not cooperate to the extent he had hoped. She did not participate. But neither did she fight him off. So he continued his quest, hoping she would eventually come around. In his twisted mind, they were having an affair. He was seducing her, and she continued to come back. No one returns to be raped.

My mother was a woman of strong convictions. I have been asked on more than one occasion why she continued to go back. Why would she place herself in the same situation time after time, knowing what had happened on previous trips? I do believe that, each time, she convinced herself it couldn't possibly happen again. But more importantly, she believed strongly in what she was doing. She had created and perfected a program that would change the scope of disaster relief for families and children and she was not willing to raise the white flag before it even got off the ground. She selflessly pushed her trauma to the depths of her soul so she could continue to thrive in this role.

I remember her suitcase, the "Kit of Comfort," and how carefully she chose and packed each item for a specific purpose. There were puppets and dolls and markers and Play-Do and a host of other things to encourage creative play and conversation about what the children had been through.

This was her dream, and she would not abandon it. To this day, her program still exists and is implemented in conjunction with the American Red Cross in nearly every natural disaster in the United States. It is an incredible part of her legacy, but I will always weigh the cost.

CHAPTER TEN

Therapy

Therapy was the next step:

> *November 26, 1986.* Another difficult day—why do I
> fear it so? A trip to Indy for a session with Greg, and I'm
> uncomfortable. I fear him because he evokes so much
> from me—and I feel it's more than I want or deserve. I'm
> still afraid of my own anger. It's interesting that I fear
> this session. Why can't I see beyond it—to the health it
> will bring? I'm too pessimistic at times. I dwell on the
> difficult more than the power that comes from working
> through the difficult. Where is my courage today? Where
> is my hope?

Greg was a new therapist. To this point, pastors and counselors had
only been able to uncover the story. No one had succeeded in unpacking
her anger. She was clearly afraid of the rage that resided within her but was
equally fearful of keeping it hidden and not allowing it light. At Greg's
request, she began the construction of a doll. The doll would represent her
abuser and become a pivotal part of releasing her anger. She chose an ugly,
gray, abrasive fabric and gave him no ears or eyes. He had never heard or
seen her. She created him carefully so she could later destroy him. Along
with beating the doll, in Greg's therapy room she donned boxing gloves
and punched a wall of foam. She pushed Greg's shoulders and kicked him
while lying on her back, all while screaming the word "No!" It was hard, he
was heavy, and she was exhausted. She hated it and the memory it brought.

Her November 26 continued:

The session with Greg was a surprise. After a beginning dialog between David and me, Greg decided to work with David. In fact, one and a half hours of the time was spent on David. He had him express fear and then anger. And David moved into the anger so easily. I was frightened as well as surprised by his anger—really rage! I thought he would attack Greg! I saw David kick, hit, swear, yell, and literally *look* enraged. I have never seen him look that way before. I felt relieved that David was enabled to be liberated of his anger, although Greg says there is still some there being blocked. But David has been able to let much of his go. Bless him! I love him so. I have to admit I envy the ease with which he could let go. I questioned, Why not me? Why can't I let go like that? And Greg reminded me, that for seven years, I was successful at storing my anger—it was my survival. I stored it so well that it was difficult to return.

Greg then worked with me. I hit and yelled. He held my throat and helped me unlock those muscles—my yell became lustier and healthier. I could really sense the difference and felt better afterward. Yet I returned home with my belt of anger and back ache. My deeper pain had not found any release. I had built up my anxiety for a grueling day, and it never came. I was more the observer. As I reflect, I find it hard to have to wait another one and a half weeks, to carry my anger for longer. I want to release, and I need to release; as much as I fight it, I know the release is behind the expression. My morning devotions spoke to me of waiting and anticipation. I continue to wait in solitude. Is there some divine mystery, which can only be received and carried out in waiting? I trust, Lord, that in waiting, I shall know.

December 6, 1986. Another session with Greg. I was so scared to go—visions of my last meeting with him and then David's session brought more to mind than I wanted to see. I was able to voice my fear to Greg—as well as my anger, but also fear of my anger and what he would have me do with it. To my surprise, we worked on "soft" things. I began to cry, and we worked on grief. I cried for a while, and then Greg had David hold me to cry some more. My cries are quiet—soft, muffled. Greg kept urging me that it would be good to give sound to my cries—that is still buried. My body was in pain, my back and abdominal area.

Greg proposed that I take a leave in teaching. Oh no! How could I do that? David and I talked about the implications, the need to give my body time for healing.

The second part of the session was focused on the telling of the story to my parents. Oh, God, do I have to do that? Greg says yes, but what does God say? We spent time visualizing telling them ... Why is it so hard to go home? Is it due to being a good girl and I don't want them to know something bad—dirty, ugly—has happened to me? Is it because I'm afraid they won't understand? What if they reject me? Or will it be the catalyst that helps our family break through to intimacy? What will happen?

On December 13, Mom went home, just three miles outside of town, with my dad and our pastor to tell her parents. My mom was a tough girl. She was raised on a farm with chickens, cows, pigs, and crops. She had plenty of chores, dogs, and 4-H animals. She always did what was expected of her. She went to college and never came back. She met my father and married him at twenty-one, after her junior year.

The "telling" went surprisingly well. As our pastor carefully told the story, her mother, shockingly, had no tears but seemingly gallons of understanding. Her father, a man of few words, sat quietly giving periodic affirming nods as the story, laden with feelings and occasional tears spilled out. What could possibly have been going through his mind?

How painful to have to reveal such unspeakable hurt to the people who gave you life. The story was out, but the real hurt was not evident.

Steeling herself against the true pain, not allowing her true feelings to be known, she had done what she needed to do. They assured her she was loved and could come home at any time. She was hugged and kissed by her father—the first time she could ever remember such affection. She had accomplished "going home." But how far home had she gotten? Had the message been clearly understood and entirely absorbed? How could it be? It was so much information for any human to absorb in such a short period of time.

> *December 23, 1986.* To Indy again to meet with Greg.
> I wasn't anxious today. Why? Becoming comfortable or more steeled? I don't know. Spent time trying to get to my pain again—with not too much luck. I could feel Greg pressing in on the pain in my stomach and encouraging me to cry, to moan, to make sound—to not swallow. Each time, I swallowed, I repressed the cry and the pain. I cried for a while but not audibly. The pain is so, so deep. Deeper than I know. Gosh. I know Greg wanted me to cry out, but it didn't seem natural for me to do. Maybe someday, hopefully soon. After doing some "softer" exercises for a while, we discussed plans for January. I had agreed and been granted permission to take the month off. I would work with Greg twice a week, bring people of my support group, and he would possibly come to our home. He also suggested we bring the kids to a session.

Inasmuch as we don't want our parents to see our true pain, I am pretty sure we don't want our children to see it either. This may be the most difficult section of the entire book for me to write—the most pivotal point in my own story. For nearly eight months, I had tried to be the good, easy child—walking on eggshells, not ruffling any feathers. But for the most part, I had tried to escape it all. I tried to be busy, absent if possible or simply not to lift my eyes to the ghost at the breakfast table. It was frighteningly painful and difficult to be home. I would make up lies and invite myself to spend the night with friends—anything not to be home, anything not to be a witness to the pain that was milling around our family.

And now she was asking us to go to a therapy session with her! My brother quickly declined. He did not want to go, felt the whole issue needed to be forgotten and that the therapy, at fifty dollars an hour was not needed. He had enough problems of his own; he didn't need to worry about her as well. The ignorant words of a seventeen-year-old boy had hurt her deeply. I had no choice; in my mind, I had to go. I was scared. I was afraid of watching her cry and not being able to walk away. I was afraid of seeing her in so much pain. I was afraid of what went on in her sessions but figured the only way to overcome that fear was to go. I could not hurt her by not going. She wrote very little about that day from her perspective:

> *December 29, 1986.* Another trip to Indy. Heidi went too.
> I had mixed feelings about that. I don't want her to have
> to deal with adult things when she's only fifteen years old.
> When it hurts me so much, I hurt additionally when she
> knows too. But I was able to tell her about the repeated
> rapes and about my feelings of worthlessness. I really don't
> want to write about it. I hurt; my head spins. I felt lower
> today when I left than usual.

What I remember and wrote in my journal a few days later changed me forever. I wonder if she knew what that day had done to me. She seemed troubled by the day and what she had exposed me to, but I wonder if she ever understood its lasting effect. I enlightened my father a few years ago, and I'm not sure it had ever occurred to him. On January 1, 1987, I wrote a ten-page entry in my journal spelling out the whole story and what I had learned and experienced since the argument in May. In response to attending the therapy session, I wrote:

> It was a difficult day for all of us. We spent one hour just
> talking. I found out more about the rapes. Plus Greg had
> me do an exercise with Mom that I did not like at all.
> I had to hold Mom on my lap and pretend that I was
> her mother, and she was my hurt child. This scared me

because Mom wrapped herself around me and cried. This made me uncomfortable because I felt so much bigger and stronger than her. I didn't like this feeling because, if I had to protect her, then who was to protect me? In the second hour, I observed her therapy, where she looked inside herself and then responded by screaming, kicking, and hitting. During this part, I got up and left because it was so hard for me to take. I saw my mother as a little child, and I didn't like that.

If I had to protect her, then who was to protect me? If she was the child, then who would be my mother? I understand that this was her therapy and not mine, but a child should never be made to feel unsafe. On the surface, I somewhat let it go at that age because I felt like the therapy was helping. But in my soul, I would feel this day forever. She was making strides with Greg, and I needed her to get well. This was not about me, but this was my shift, my disconnect. I no longer felt safe within my own family. My father, bless his heart, was a good, strong man. But it took every ounce of everything in him to save my mother from herself.

Subconsciously, I would spend the next twenty-five years searching for a world where I felt safe. I was in my early forties when a marriage counselor urged me to dig into my mother's story and deeper into my relationship with her before I uncovered these feelings of abandonment and yearning for protection. I spent years steeling myself, working hard, and becoming independent. I was trying to convince myself that I could protect myself, while all along, I was longing to do what she did—to crawl into someone's lap, curl up, cry and feel safe. I needed to have the chance to be that scared child once again and, this time, have someone hold me, protect me.

Outside of her therapy sessions, Greg wanted Mom to be held as often as possible, for at least thirty minutes with no verbal interaction. I never volunteered for this job again, until the last few days of her life. I would crawl in bed beside her, hold her hand, and run my fingers through her hair. Then, all I wanted to do was hold her, to protect her from everything.

CHAPTER ELEVEN

Former Assaults

Therapy continued through the month of January. And toward the end of the month, Greg suggested Mom do a two-day marathon session before going back to teaching. She had the time to invest and the time to recuperate, but the thought terrified her. She was scared of the intensity, scared of the unknown. Was she ready for what might lie ahead? Initially she said no because it was her decision, and she needed the power. But then she let go of the control, knowing she could not consciously make the decision on her own, and she prayed:

> *January 24, 1987.* Lord, I have a decision to make. Yes, I will go, or no, I will not go. I'm scared—of both decisions. If I say yes, where will that lead me? It would be easier if I could just see around the corner. What I really need is enough trust in the light for the next step. If I say no, what will I miss? I wish I could see around that corner too. I'm scared, Lord. Scared to let go, to break the ice and crumble the walls. It seems safe inside, although lonely and full of pain. It's tough to let go of a pain that I've worn for so long. It may seem incredible to admit it's comfortable—it's so much a part of me that I can't imagine living without it. To give it up is to face death. To decide no is to say yes to death. To say yes would be kissing death goodbye— opening the door and pushing him out. To say yes would be to clean house, to dust off the filth of the past, to sweep out the cupboards of pain. To say yes would enlarge my space for the sweetness of life. Lord, when it seems so easy

and clear, why does it remain so difficult? I have a decision to make.

"Your fear is bigger than the actual experience," Greg had told her.

After two hours of shaking and trembling she was convinced he was right and was able to move into a state of deep peace. Still unable to connect with her own pain, she was able to establish a sense of goodness and a place of personal safety. She had work to do—preparation to meet that which she most feared before going back to see him. She was learning to feel again; it was a step in the right direction. But as the numbness wore off, the feelings were intense and sometimes unmanageable. The death wish returned. The desire and pull to die were strong, welcome, and comforting. It seemed the way to resolve everything.

Nearly four weeks later, she returned to Greg and was able to touch more pain. For the first time, she could visualize the inside of one of the hotel rooms; she could see more detail and feel more fear. Death was still looming, and her mission in life was not understood. Sometimes she felt her mission was to die. She expressed to Greg her overwhelming awareness of death, even wanting to plan her memorial service. Dying was a part of her daily conscious. According to Greg, she was currently in death—a process of the old Karen dying—and she had not yet arrived at the new. She was on the edge—a dangerous, frightening edge—and very uncomfortable.

> *March 12, 1987.* For some reason, I keep going—going somewhere, in some direction. And I hope and pray it is the right direction—a direction of promise, of recreation, of new life—for I am dead. I long for the good life for me, that as of yet, does not exist. My patience runs thin. I dislike the wait and the journey. I dislike the past journey, and I am afraid of the road ahead. I still feel on the road to death—full of many uncomfortable pebbles and stones, a rocky journey.
>
> I feel the need to talk about my story—to tell it over and over again. I need to know, to feel, to claim this story as truth in my life. But it hurts. God grant me the courage to speak and to no longer protect him.

During the month of March, she worked with a close friend and colleague at school to establish a support group of faculty women. There was a need for her to feel safe and supported while on campus. There were seven women in addition to herself, and she was able to share—not in great detail, but generally about the rapes and more of her hurt, pain, counseling, fears, and need to be supported and cared for during this time. She was heard, well received, and supported.

In a second meeting she was finally able to reveal more details and, most importantly, his name. None of the women were surprised, and one shared of difficulty she'd had working with him in the past. Mom was embarrassed and distressed to reveal parts of her truth but felt strengthened and affirmed by this group. She finally realized the energy it had required to exert control over that information, to keep her past a secret. It was a step forward in her healing. But who else needed to know?

Continuing with Greg, she began to self-direct her therapy. If you knew my mother, this should not come as a surprise. She began going to her sessions alone and told Greg that her immediate need was to tell and retell her story. She began to feel a shift and needed to move through the blockage to reach the inner core. She voluntarily returned to one of the scenes and was able to move around and find significance in certain areas. Being able to replay the attack brought about the reality of being the victim and releasing any ownership of responsibility.

> *March 23, 1987.* I started reading the book *I Never Told Anyone* by Ellen Bass. For the first time, I was able to read words and descriptions of the horror that happened to me. And suddenly, I became aware of a former assault—prior to the rapes. God, how much can I take? How much can I endure? How much can I know? How much can one woman's body withstand? Oh God, I wish I could cry! I wish I could cry! And now I seriously begin to wonder about an assault earlier in my life.

> *April 1, 1987.* It's 1:00 in the morning. I awoke after being asleep for a couple of hours. I feel so strange. What I feel is hard to describe. It would be easier to describe if

I could grasp it. I'm going to try. I'm afraid. I'm afraid of the way I feel. It's like a strong message is trying to break through my tough resistance. I don't understand, and that's why I'm afraid of the unknown. I'm afraid because I have the strange feeling about me that my end of time is near. I want to scream and shout at the rest of my sleeping household—to get them up from their trouble-less sleep and invite them to spend these moments with me. My head hurts. I want to believe I'll be here tomorrow—and the next day. I want to believe I'll be well again. I want to believe in my chance for wholeness and wellness, but I'm overcome with the feeling that those aren't for me. I want to scream out in anger, "Not now, Lord, not now. I'm not ready to go. I'm not ready to die." But I feel strange—out of place—like I don't belong here. Maybe I would be happier elsewhere. I feel on the edge, like I'm letting go of something and being beckoned to move on. I cry. I don't want to let go, for I don't know what's ahead. I am so afraid. I want to stay—to taste tomorrow in this life.

If I should die, I want my story to be shared—the reason for my suffering and pain. I want people to know that rape destroys and kills—takes away the goodness of life.

I want to be buried in my pink gown and robe. On the altar, place objects of my life—my doctoral gown, books, sewing, homemade bread, roses, and so on. You know some too.

Who were these words meant for? She wrote and spoke many times of wanting to be laid to rest in her nightgown and robe. If she was going to sleep forever, she was going to be comfortable! And over the years, her list of altar requirements continued to grow. But who did she want to tell her story? To my knowledge, she never verbalized this request to anyone. On this day in 1987, I thoroughly believe she thought she was dying. And if her story had no more breath than it had on that day, she needed someone to stay the course. By the grace of God, she lived for another fourteen years. She never shared the intimacy of her journals with anyone, but we all knew she continued to write. She numbered them, dated them, and stored them in order in a canvas bag in her closet with no instructions.

Back to April 1987, she was still experiencing "visits" from death. However, they no longer scared her. The feeling became familiar, as if she needed to burst, or she would die. On the inside, she harbored another horrible story. The memory of another assault, an earlier one, still existed but could not be touched. She had a deep fear of the unknown—not the unknown of what might lie ahead but, rather, the haunting of what remained in her past; her body continued to store something away from her—something that wanted to press forward and rise to the surface. She leaned toward hypnosis as the only key to the padlock on her inner experience. Horrified by the unknown and haunted by the black space, fearfully, she wanted to know what was holding her back, and she wanted to know immediately.

May 7, 1987. I discovered more of the secrets of my soul today. I went to see a psychologist who does hypnosis. I had a two-hour session. We talked in general at first while I provided my history regarding the rapes. She went through the relaxation process from toes to head. I could tell I was not relaxing well—I just felt too much tension. Then a visualization—a pleasant place (I picked a sandy beach)—I could feel the sand between my toes. She asked me to walk down the beach to a cove some distance away while she counted to twenty. I never made it to the cove. A large "black thing" was in my way, and I could not proceed. I was stuck where I've been many times before and could not get away from it.

I finally saw myself as a little girl standing in front of this black thing. I had on a blue dress, and I still had my pigtails, so I was somewhere around three or four years old. I stood crying, alone, head down, and no one came to rescue me or comfort me. "It" was so huge. I was dwarfed by the size of it. I described it as grayish-black, furry, and pebbly—not smooth. I took a flashlight and examined it closely, and suddenly I knew what "it" was—a scrotum.

To any little girl, a scrotum of an adult male would be enormous. She asked me to reach out and touch it. I refused; there were memories of slimy, wet stuff, and I didn't want to hold or touch it.

This makes so much sense. I cried, and she held me. My body shook with sobs. She comforted me with her words to the little girl. "It's OK, little girl, to cry. Adults make big mistakes, and it's OK to be sad. Cry sweet girl, cry." She then asked me to yell at the black thing—to kick it out of my way. I lost my voice. I couldn't speak. I was afraid and felt threatened—fear of what would happen if I said anything or asked anyone for help. She yelled at it for me—told it to get out of my way, to not bother me anymore. She kicked it to move it. It moved slightly to the left, but I still feel and see its presence in the path. I can see more of the beach now.

I then had to ask the little girl what she needed to help her feel safe. She responded, "I need to cry and to be held."

As she recounted this part of her story, she recalled conversations with each of her parents, one as a child when her dad ran over her kitten with the lawnmower and one with her mother, just a week prior, in reference to her brother's pending divorce. On both occasions, she was told not to cry and not to ask questions because, if they forgot about it, it would go away. If this was their philosophy, was her father responsible for violating her as well? Had he told her—and similarly asked himself to forget about the act—so it would just "go away"? Did this "thing" still reside within her? This feeling of bursting; it must come from something in a space where it doesn't belong. She wanted it out. The therapist told her to practice being angry for when that day came.

CHAPTER TWELVE

Anger, Trust, and Confession

Mom wrote about her anger:

> *June 3, 1987.* I am so angry—my anger comes out in inappropriate measures. Angry at Heidi for asking for money to go eat instead of eating here at home—angry at myself because I gave it to her. Angry at Heidi because she wanted to stay out until midnight. I did not give in to that one—but who does she think she is to ask, to beg beyond reason. Damn her! I'm angry! I even hate being her parent. I don't like having to parent her right now. I'm just angry!! Angry as hell.

Oh, I gave her plenty of opportunities to practice being angry. My brother had recently graduated high school and was not around much, so I seemed to be an easy target and knew how to push her buttons, sometimes without even trying.

One of the hardest things to read about was myself, the anger and disappointment she felt towards me but that we never discussed. I understand now that this was a byproduct of her abuse. She did not speak the language. Nor did she know how to give it a voice. By the time I read about myself and how she'd felt about me at certain times, she was gone. I had no recourse, no opportunity to defend myself, and I found myself hurt and angry at someone I could never speak to again. It was painfully difficult to be angry at my dead mother, but at times, I couldn't help it. Knowing what I know now, her reaction to me was often connected to a greater source. I was just good at touching the tip of issues such as trust, boundaries, disrespect, personal space, and freedom. She was still deeply afraid of her own anger and the magnitude with which it pulsated inside her, but she tested it out on me frequently over the next few years. I think I eventually became numb to it. Her wrath was ugly but more often worth what I had done to deserve it. I frequently came home late at night, expecting her to meet me at the front door, and I was no longer afraid.

She made another trip to Greg, hoping he could help her freely let go and express her anger. The session was good, but the main topic became trust. He needed her to trust him with her darkest moments. He wanted to be the one to bring her through this trauma, but she didn't trust him. Greg confronted her about orchestrating her own therapy and flying solo for the last two months without him. At first, she took this as a compliment but then perceived his words as a voice of concern. She had reverted back to "solo" as a means of survival. She no longer needed a man she'd once trusted to lead her astray. She would not risk being hurt again. He was amazed and astounded that she'd survived the last two months with the heavy burden she had carried. There was nothing courageous in her mind; she simply needed to survive. She had become an expert on survival, but this task of becoming well, this was not something she could do alone.

> *June 10, 1987.* The issue is, I don't trust. I don't trust anyone—not even my own husband. I don't even trust God. Furthermore, I don't even know *how* to trust. I don't know where to begin to turn mistrust into trust. To think of trusting is an extremely scary idea. I'm afraid to do it. How can I do something I don't know how to do? To let someone else lead me means I lose control. Am I able to surrender control enough to trust someone else to lead me into healing?

After reading a book on spiritual journaling, she followed the author's recommendation to write some undelivered letters. As a means of releasing truth without confrontation, she began with a letter of confession to God. Even though these letters were never intended to be sent, I think God was still the easiest and most significant recipient. Putting her truth in writing to God was completely different than praying to him aloud. She had always felt that confession was a terrible thing to do, a sort of dragging yourself through the mud. If she confessed, she would surely be struck down by a wrathful God, because she had been taught early on that God expected her to be good, and somewhere along the line she wasn't.

The issue of trust remained:

June 21, 1987. Is part of the reason I don't confess because I don't trust God to forgive me? There is tension between good and evil within me—but I'm afraid to deal with that tension. I've suppressed my feelings. I've suppressed the conflict between the two selves. Oh, how many times I've referred to my own internal tension as a feeling of being at war. When something bad was experienced, I've pushed it under to the subconscious level. I've done it so much that I've lost track of the truth—and numbed myself to the conflict. Behind the fear of admitting the tension is the false notion that to admit sin is to admit weakness and failure, to risk being accepted by God and others.

Why do I fear change ... for the good? Why don't I trust God to hear my story? Do I enjoy feeling ugly, dirty, powerless—sick of heart and mind? No, I want health and healing. I want, yet I'm afraid. Can I really have health? Can I be healed? Can I trust God? I'm keeping that huge black space inside of me. *I'm* doing it—all because I'm not able, or willing, to confess. I'm the one preventing myself from getting well. I'm ready to start trusting. I'm going to start by writing a prayer to God:

Dear God,

I feel like an infant—taking the first shaky steps to trusting by confessing. I'm scared, Lord. Hold me tight in the palm of your hand—and don't let go ...

For the next seven pages, she confessed in detail a story from her past. It was a story where once, again, she held no personal responsibility, but the memory kept her soul shackled in a bondage of darkness. She wanted

God to know her completely; she needed these chains to be loosed. She was learning that confession meant facing and naming her darkness, crying out the grief that had marked her with a concrete exterior.

> I realize today, the hurt, the coldness, the distance is still very much a part of me. I hate it. I hate myself. I want to be free. Yet, I read that the journey to freedom is not away from God but, rather, towards God. It all begins with confession. I've told this part of my story. I confess my guilt and wrongdoing. I confess my sin. God, please hear me tonight. I want to be forgiven and set free from the muck and mire in my life. Please hear my plea. Amen

Her second undelivered letter was to her current pastor, the friend and confidant who had stood by her side since day one of breaking her silence but who had recently confronted her with the question of whether she truly wanted to get well. Had she become comfortable with the pain to the point of tolerating it as a part of normal life? Was she able to let go of a sickness she had worn for so long? Could she envision what life would look like without it enough to put in the work? Could she be strong enough to get out of her own way? To recover meant to become someone she had never been; it required change. This was a hard truth and even more so when presented by someone you trusted. It was devastating for her to hear but necessary within the healing process—as if he had told her she now had something to prove.

> *June 23, 1987.* My anger is so high this morning—anger at you. For the first time, I feel so betrayed by you. I am working at trusting men and people I thought to be friends, only to have you defeat me yesterday by telling me you aren't convinced I want to get well. Damn you! How could you say such an ugly thing to me? You hurt me to the core. I feel stripped of the self I've worked so damn hard to rebuild. Don't want to get well?? Why, then, why, I ask you, would I spend so much time painfully examining my own life—uncovering layer by layer of the

painful memories and experiences; missing work; paying $2,500 on a self that others, including you, have said had promise, courage, and hope. Now I don't believe any of you, especially you. Again, I've worked hard to get to this place—a place several have said shows incredible progress—and then *wham*! And you ask me to trust?! How can you expect that? I am hurt, disillusioned and deep in despair. I want to quit, give up and never trust anyone again—ever! It only brings more pain. Why live?? Why try? Why put forth more effort? I'm to the point where I no longer want to work on this issue; there is no use. I really would like to die.

This day was significant, perhaps a turning point in her journey toward healing. The ability to express and verbalize anger is instrumental in the process of moving from victim to survivor. Victims of sexual abuse, whether children or adults, are hushed from the very beginning. They are told not to tell and not to fight, or there will be consequences. The inability to become angry can become lethal. Unexpressed anger is internalized, and the byproduct is depression. Anger is essential for life.

Someone, one of the most significant people in her journey, said to her, "I'm not convinced you want to get well." Maybe it was the inadvertent challenge in that statement—"prove to me that you want to get well"—that shook her up. And she got angry.

After the letters, she cried. Buckets, she wrote. And then she went to the basement to express herself physically. The basement of our house was somewhat of a dungeon, but she found it a safe place for her anger. The squeaky steps led way to concrete floors and walls. There was an ominous, octopus-looking gas-forced air furnace, and the only shower in the house was straight out of Gilligan's Island, with a bamboo mat and a wraparound curtain. Dad had a workbench. There was a canning storage room and a room that would later become a TV rec room. As children we were allowed to roller skate from room to room on the concrete, and it was a glorious, sacred space. It was dark, damp, and completely underground. She could yell, scream, and beat on things, and no one would hear her.

She beat the doll she had created for this very exercise. She beat it with a tennis racket until the racket split in half and one side completely broke off. The doll lost stuffing, and its shirt was torn. She hit, swore, stomped, and yelled hateful things from a deep guttural place within, all feeling and sounding authentic. The action must proceed the feeling, she told herself. "I must *do*, and then I will *feel*." All this time she had been doing this in the reverse order. She had been pushing herself to feel, hoping it would bring the anger to the surface. But when she enabled herself to become physically angry in the safe confines of her own home, the rage boiled and exploded.

CHAPTER THIRTEEN

The Little Girl

She recorded this release of anger:

> *July 2, 1987.* In the evening, everyone left, and I went to the basement, doll and racket in hand. I hit the doll. I cried. I let go of angry words. For the first time, I could let go of anger towards two individuals. First, the young child in me could shout, "I hate you, Daddy. I hate what you did to me when I was too young and too innocent to know or understand. I hate you, Daddy!" The words seemed to fit. When I've said I don't know "who"—I begin to understand that I do know the "who." It's coming to my consciousness. I was also able to say, "I hate you, God. I hate you for allowing men to violate young children. Why can't you stop them, God?" I continued to hit and beat and to literally fight back—for the first time! I was the young girl fighting back at her daddy. It felt good and felt right. For the first time, I felt the freedom to fight back at a parent. After forty-some years, I could unleash my anger at my father. What a revelation! How liberating! What a release!

The next day brought a different scared little girl. I gave my mother the uncomfortable opportunity to be my parent. It was an experience she never wanted but one that taught her she still had the capacity for compassion and the ability to love under all circumstances.

July 3, 1987. What a night. Heidi came home at 10:30 and asked to go to the college with some friends from work. We foolishly gave her permission to stay out until 1:00. What a mistake! When I went to bed, I could not relax and go to sleep. I was stirred over my venting of anger and felt uncomfortable about Heidi—mothers seem to know when their children are in trouble. At 1:15, the police called and asked us to come to the police station. Heidi and two boys had been arrested at the college ball diamond. Heidi was arrested on two counts—curfew violation and consumption of alcohol as a minor! She was taken to the county jail and spent the night there. It was a difficult night for all of us; it's tough seeing your daughter being taken away by the sheriff, alone, scared, and guilty. As a parent, I felt hurt for her. But I also felt she deserved the consequences of her behavior. Some lessons in life are difficult to learn. Yet the value in them is beyond anything taught in any other manner other than direct experience.

At 10:30 in the morning, we went to get our scared daughter. Jails are cold. We never dealt with anyone directly except the man who took the bond money. In the waiting room, we were surrounded by one-way mirrors and dealt with the release of our daughter by intercom. She was finally released out a side door, and we were instructed to meet her outside. There she came, in tears—scared, feeling guilty and ashamed, "like shit," the worst she could feel. We hugged her and brought her home. She cried and began to unfold the story. I remained calm but firm. I realized that, when a parent is hurt by a child, love continues to pour out.

I also realized my own increased sense of personal worth. A year ago, I would have been shattered by this experience. This year, I realize my newfound strength and inner calm in the face of crisis. I was disappointed and hurt, but I could really feel for Heidi. I felt supportive of the police action. We have given our children the freedom to make many decisions for themselves. If they choose to act or behave wrongly, then they also had to take the consequences. The truth and reality hit Heidi last night, and she took her consequences. Throughout all of this, I believe both of our children realized that, in time of need, parents are there to support them. They have learned that we don't approve of such behavior, but in spite of their behavior, we are with them and continue to love them.

I remember this night clearly. After finishing my shift at work, a few of the older, male coworkers invited me to meet them at the baseball diamond for a few drinks. With my parents' permission, I met them on campus, and we sat in the dugout with our drinks. I was sixteen. They were both a few years older but not necessarily of legal drinking age. I had never had alcohol outside of a few sips at the dinner table. I have no idea what I drank or how much I had consumed. But when the police officer pulled into the parking lot and shined his flashlight on us, I knew I did not have the wherewithal to run. I stayed where I was and allowed myself to be handcuffed and placed in the back of the police car.

Once at the police station, I assumed they would call my parents to take me home, but that was not the case. They were called to come see me, maybe for the visual that I was physically unharmed, but I was not released to them. They escorted me twenty minutes down the road to the county jail, where I was processed and placed in a small rubber cell alone because I was a minor. I was allowed to remain in my own clothes, red cutoff sweatpants, a white Mickey Mouse T-shirt, and white canvas Keds.

I did not sleep. Nor did I cry. I just sat on the floor. The guard was not happy when I refused his lovely offering of breakfast in the morning, but I didn't care. I just wanted to go home. Days later with all of us back at work together, one of my "friends" paused and whispered in my ear, "It's too bad we got caught the other night. I was going to get you drunk and rape you!"

I stopped in my tracks, horrified. How could he use such an ugly word so callously? The night in jail had, indeed, been a blessing. Had this happened to me, I, too, would have told no one. Sadly, there would have been no capacity in our household for the trauma of another rape.

Looking back, I recall that my parents did respond to me in a

73

surprisingly calm fashion. There was no yelling and no blaming. I had made my choice and paid the consequences. This was how my parents disciplined. It was more about instilling a good decision-making process. What I don't remember is either of them asking why. Why had I been willing to put myself in that position? As a parent, wouldn't you be concerned that your sixteen-year-old had gone out with the intention of drinking? What were you missing in her life that she was being drawn to that avenue of potential danger? Was this another cry for help that was missed because of the overwhelming cries in our household already?

I went to church camp immediately following my court appearance. It was the best week of support and healing, but the slight trauma of the experience did not seem to discourage me from drinking again in the near future. I never got caught again. My physical safety was never compromised because of alcohol, but I was surely filling a void. I seemed to be soothing my own pain, escaping my own reality, and finding comfort in this external substance.

For my mother, the little girl with the light blue dress and pigtails returned. She appeared in dreams and in therapy sessions with Greg. She was spontaneous, dancing, and frolicking about the barnyard. She was free. But what happened to this child? Where did she go? She had died. Her free spirit was taken away.

When my mother was young, she had blond hair. As a farm girl, she had frequently worn her hair in braided pigtails. Shortly after her fourth birthday, my grandmother banded both ends of the pigtails, tied ribbons around the curly tips, and cut them completely off. My mother was heartbroken, and then, oddly enough, grandma placed the braids in a picture frame and hung them on the wall—constant reminder of what was no longer hers. I'm not sure about my grandma's motive at the time, but the timing seems significant in marking the end of her childhood. Her mother no longer wanted her to be a cute little girl. Was there a reason for this?

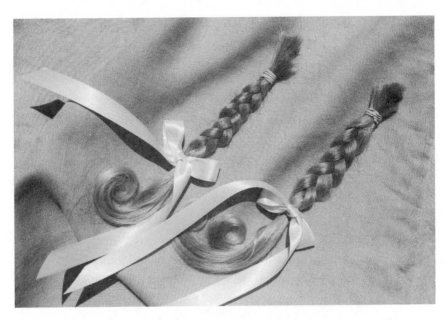

There were no memories past this age other than ordinary work on the farm. She was alone. The desire now was to reconnect with this child—to talk with her, invite her in, and see what she knew. What was there to learn from her four-year-old self who had been robbed of life at such an early age? What secrets did her body hold? But Karen the child was very distant and the reunion unlikely. Did she know the adult version of herself was desperately searching for her? Was she running in the opposite direction because the truth was too painful? Adult Karen caught a glimpse of the child inside herself, but the blackness prevented her from going any further. Who or what was the blackness in the way? She longed for the day when the two would be able to see each other clearly, turn to each other, and embrace. For many years, her writing contained letters, conversations, and visualizations of reunions between the two Karens. In her adulthood, she was determined to restore or possibly recreate the childhood of the little girl with the pigtails in the blue dress.

On August 5 and 6, 1987, there are entries about a dream. In the dream, she was standing outside experiencing a dense fog that lifted suddenly from one glance to another. The atmosphere became crystal clear. She questioned the possibility of her confusion clearing and understanding setting in, with the emphasis on suddenness. Was this another promise?

Almost two weeks later, my mother had lunch with her sister-in-law, Lois Kay, and my grandfather's younger sister, Isabel.

> *August 17, 1987.* The breakthrough from the fog (recall the dream of August 5). Lois Kay and I took Aunt Isabel to lunch. Lois talked a lot about her separation from my brother, and then I got to tell Aunt Belle some of my story. I finally told her about my counseling for rape and Greg's hunch that I was sexually molested as a young child. I asked her if she knew about anything that may have happened to me as a child. She pointed to herself and then told me that my dad had molested her repeatedly as a child, starting around six years of age. He had intercourse with her—against her will—many times. Aunt Belle was traumatized by it all. She never was touched by any of the other brothers. God, I felt jolted. We all cried. I could not believe it—or didn't want to believe it. My father! Suddenly my body knew that it was he who was responsible. My father—a man this community respects so highly. *Bullshit.* I have no respect. Nothing tonight but bitter hate!

Two days later, my mother and I had our first mother-daughter late night talk. She told me of the revelation about her father out of concern that I might have fallen victim to him as well. My grandfather had been my caretaker during the year I was in kindergarten. I went to school in the morning, and Grandpa would pick me up and take me to the farm for the afternoon. It was a special year for me, and in every crevice of my mind, I know he never hurt me. We would go to the barn, work in the garden, and pick flowers. And when Grandma got home, we would go to the grocery store, and I would help her cook. He called me "Shorty" because I could walk under the kitchen table, and there were constant games of dominoes and checkers. What a relief to feel confident I have nothing but good in my heart for this man! But what a contradiction to know that he had hurt his only daughter and sister, the people in his life who he should have fought to love and protect. I clearly remember asking her if she thought she would

be relieved when he died. For some, this is an uncomfortable but natural question to answer.

And now came the journey toward another confrontation. What would she say? Maybe it would be easier to write a letter first and follow up with a visit. What were the consequences and risks of confronting him? He would not admit to anything or ask for forgiveness. He would simply drop his head and refuse to discuss the issue. Would he become suicidal? For my grandmother, one of two reactions seemed likely—(a) devastation or (b) relief, a time of release. Had she known all along?

My mom prepared and decided to tell her mother first. But she walked away feeling like she had not been heard.

Within a matter of days, my grandmother confronted her husband with Aunt Belle's accusation and my mother's story, as she presumed it would have happened so many years ago.

His response? "Absolutely not!"

CHAPTER FOURTEEN

1988: A New Year

Looking forward to 1988, Mom began the next journal with several lists. The list of what she was looking forward to consisted of continued counseling, extending the emotional distance with her parents, playing the piano, examining her relationship with God and the church, and going off all medication. A slightly different list of what she hoped for described more vacation time, a renewed sense of energy and creativity, an awakening and enjoyment of her sexual self, crazy happiness, and laughter. As changes she would like to make, she named several cosmetic upgrades in the house and increasing her vocabulary.

Goals were somehow different still, especially to someone like my mother. They had to be realistic and attainable but challenging. She listed reading, mastering more on the piano, and cross-stitching. The other three seemed very significant, derived from another place entirely:

1. *To let her hair grow.* This was symbolic and, perhaps, necessary for the eventual reunion with the little girl in the blue dress and pigtails. I think it also showed that she was committed to getting in touch with her feminine side. For years, she'd described herself as cold, rigid, unfeeling, and unloving. Becoming pretty and soft might lend itself to being able to care and love in a completely different way.

2. *To not go to church.* To examine the meaning of God in her life in a new way. To give herself permission to question God and her faith. She had been hurt so desperately by men who represented the church, and she needed a chance to reevaluate her faith. She questioned the institution of the church and how it could let men, held in high regard, remain as leaders in their

congregations following various acts of violence and abuse. Her severed relationship with God made it difficult to attend and sit in His midst on Sunday mornings. So, she allowed herself the freedom to stay home, read, meditate, and worship in her own way.

3. *To write more.* To study the nature of herself and the meaning of her story. To consider publishing a book—a memoir of sorts to tell her story in full and a narrative of hope for other victims. As with most of us, she questioned the who, where, what, and how of getting started but never did. Every time I come across her words, her desire for her story to be told, I pause and take a deep breath. This was her request, and I am honoring her as the messenger.

That year, 1988 begins as one of great revelation. Dreams were analyzed, and visions of her past begin to fit together like pieces of a puzzle.

January 31, 1988. I relive the counseling session of yesterday ... I was the child wanting to be held. I felt a desire to cry but couldn't at first. Slowly, the tears came. I squeezed my childlike eyes shut and allowed the tears to soak my pillow. And then, in the darkness of closed eyes, I saw him—my dad—young, sleek black hair. But I could see him only from the chest up. I began to know; I had moved into a knowing that had remained deeply submerged. His image became unmistakably clear, and suddenly, I knew where I was. I was home in my childhood bedroom. It was totally dark. Yet off to the side of the bed, I could see my father. He was young! I could see my entire room; it was incredible! Unbelievable! My dad didn't do anything. At least my memory was not yielding it at this moment. He just stood there—close to my bed, very solemn and stern-looking. He was close—maybe one to two feet away. I wanted to close my eyes, but no matter how tight I squeezed them, he didn't go away.

I sat soaking up the image, and then suddenly the room was flooded with light, and he was gone. My room, the arrangement was in full view. I could see it clearly aided by the morning light coming in the east window. There I was, young, blond hair, lying curled up in my bed, not wanting to get up. I was curled up, frightened, and wanting to stay—to not face him at the breakfast table.

It made sense. I never wanted it to, but it did. My grandpa rose in the wee hours of every morning to milk the dairy herd. It was always dark, but he could easily navigate his way into her room without light. She may have never seen his face because, by sunrise, he was gone. I wonder if the four-year-old child ever truly knew it was him. My mother frequently told the story of being afraid to go to bed. All three bedrooms were upstairs, and as the youngest, she was always sent to bed first, alone. She would dramatically reminisce about checking inside every wardrobe and under every bed before finally settling in. She was looking for the monster, most likely the one who would visit her bed in the mornings. Did she not know he was simply downstairs?

To this day, I struggle with the reality of this part of her story. I never doubted her when she came forward with what she thought to be true. And then later, as the pieces fell into place, it was hard to deny any of it. My struggle is that my experience is so vastly different from hers. My grandparents were two of my most favorite people, and I loved my time on the farm. I loved the narrow staircase that led upstairs and the smell, whatever it was, that permeated everything up there. I loved to spend the night at the farm, to sleep with my window open and listen to the frogs and crickets in the swamp. I always slept in the back bedroom, never my mother's, because I loved the "high bed." The pineapple-carved four-poster bed made me feel like a princess, and I would snuggle deep into the middle so I would not fall out! I was devastated when they decided to sell the farm in 1989, but my parents bought me the pineapple poster bed as my graduation gift.

When I set out to write this book, I wasn't even sure I wanted to include this part of the story. My uncertainty was not out of protection for anyone or family shame, just a love for these people, many years gone, who were influential in my upbringing. But people change, and sometimes they get it right later in life. I often tell my daughter that she got the best of my mother.

Several months into the year, my grandfather still denied any wrongdoing with my mother and Aunt Belle. He continued to plainly state he was not guilty of what he was being accused of. So where did this leave her? She was trapped. She was trapped between a man who said, "I honestly did not do that," and herself, her body, that said, "This happened to me."

> *April 6, 1988.* Trapped. How do I move out and through such a situation? I belong to a powerful family in this community. Yet, I desperately want to break out of it, not succumb to the pressures of it. I want to be me. I believe in me. I want to be free …
>
> A thought—as I reflect on ways to find reconciliation between my family and me, I realize that the time has come for me to let go of the childish notion that my parents and I will ever come to terms over acknowledgment of my sexual molestation. I once thought that was the only way to achieve wholeness. Now I see that there are alternatives to seeking wholeness without my dad and me coming together. I'm ready to consider alternatives. They may be unwilling or unable to establish a positive relationship with me. So, it is up to me to nurture myself and stop waiting for them to change.

> *July 23, 1988.* The Serenity Prayer—to accept what has to be, change what I can change, and know the difference between the two. I can now accept what two men have done to me—that's a given in my life. I can also accept that I can move beyond the anger and rage of those experiences. That's the changing I can do. I can move way beyond this experience—move and grow from it in a positive direction. I can change my attitude from hurt to love and growth.

This was a year of significant personal growth. Although she did not begin to write her personal story, she started with writing exercises that brought many important realizations to light:

Where am I now? I no longer feel bad, dirty; yet feelings of shame still exist. I no longer sense the powerlessness of the victim; I sense, to some degree, my own power. I still feel different from other people, although I recognize my sameness. I don't feel something is "wrong" with me but feel I'm different way down inside. I no longer feel self-destructive or suicidal. I do not want to die. I have been blessed with glimpses of the promise of wholeness. I want to live. I do not hate myself. I do not hate myself for hating others. I do not have a hard time nurturing and taking care of myself. I do not find it difficult to trust my intuition. I am not sure how I would protect myself in a dangerous situation, yet I feel I would fight for my life. I only feel the repeated victimization when I am subject to invasion of my space. My sense of my own interests and talents are far more apparent to me than ever before. I no longer struggle with motivation. I do not fear succeeding. I can accomplish things I set out to do. Sometimes I err in choosing to do too many things. Perfect? Indeed, no. I have become more content with my realization of imperfection. There is more balance in my life today. I can recognize feelings and tell the difference between them although I still have trouble with expression. I am becoming comfortable with anger. Sadness is difficult to handle. Am I comfortable with happiness? Not exactly. It scares me—like being out of control. Recently I've achieved a sense of calmness. Confusion is not present to any measurable extent. My range of emotions is greater due to the fact I can feel. Depression—still to some degree but light or periodic.

August 2, 1988. I need simply to take pen in hand and begin to write. I need to believe I do have the spark to call forth the diamond from my own deep, dark abyss! I want to believe I have the ability to write, to think, to create. Dig deep, Karen, and believe.

August 5, 1988. Tonight, I sit down to begin writing an article. I thought I was ready for this, yet when I put it on my "to-do" list, it is the last item I gave my attention to today. I've wanted to write for a long time, or so I thought. I thought I could do it, yet I seem blocked, almost overwhelmed. Writing is a time when I can use my own words, develop my own style, say it like I want to, yet I seem so reluctant. Is it the power of my words or story? Is it the vastness of my reading audience that will tell my soul, "Your secret will be no more?" Is it the unknown— not knowing who will read it, how they will respond, what they will do with the information, and where this act will lead me? Or is it my inability to believe in myself enough to believe I can do this?

I am not sure what direction the article will go. I can't "see" it in finished form. I'm not sure what will come out of the end of my pen—if anything. Is it a need to let go—to write, to do something I feel very passionate about? Do I need to let go of the fears of what other people will think? Can I now realize this is my time to come forth, not only for myself, but also for all women who've shared an experience similar to mine? Can I move beyond thinking what this will do for me and consider what I, or my story, can do for others? This is an awesome responsibility, and I feel so ordinary. Can I possibly reflect the divine—reach inside my dark cavity and pull forth a sparkling gem? Can I believe enough in myself to pick up the pen and know the words will come? To do so is an act of faith. God, guide my thoughts and my pen as I proceed.

As I read this last entry, I realize that thirty-three years later, these are the exact same fears and desires I have for this book. I have always felt called to write about my mother, and she is by far my favorite subject. Words of honor and admiration come easily, but the true story in its entirety is overwhelming. I rest assured that I have her permission to write it, but some may say it's not my story to tell. But it is. For the thirty years she and I coexisted on earth and the twenty that have followed, her story has governed my life in some way. The abuse, the rapes, the detachment, the disappointment, the healing, the illness, her death. Most of the time I had no choice but to experience all of this with her from the outside. It was impossible for me to put into context until, one day, someone called me a secondary victim, a secondary survivor. My story is just as important, for I know that the number of children, spouses, and family members who have traveled this road is unfathomable. As my mother stated, I am ready to move beyond what this will do for me and consider the impact on others.

CHAPTER FIFTEEN

Worried about Heidi

Safety is a subjective, perhaps ambiguous term. Safety means different things to different people. For my mother, safety meant quietly being held in the arms of another person. For a few years, I searched desperately for that sense of security and safety. My search always involved a boy, but the relationships never lasted because the emotional component was never met. I needed the physical security. But after years of being shut down emotionally, I needed to talk, and I needed someone who was willing to listen.

Enter Tyler, my knight in shining armor. For three years, he existed as the best and the worst person in my life. On October 14, 1988, I wrote in my journal, "I am amazed at how quickly two strangers can become friends ... We began to talk ... he seemed interested in my situation ... He asked me questions that really made me think ... He really understood and seemed to care ... I could freely explain myself and do it clearly."

He was a college student, three years older, and we worked together several times a week. For the first time, someone repeatedly asked me how I was doing. It was genuine and unprovoked; he truly cared. Then one night, he asked me for a ride home, and our conversation turned to how we felt about each other. He was attracted to me. This was all new. I had silently fallen head over heels but never assumed he felt the same way. The hitch? He had a girlfriend at another school. He wanted to be fair to her but was having trouble finding the answers.

Subsequent entries in my journal included things like this:

> Once again I set myself up to fall and I fell hard. I knew this
> was going to happen, but I let it continue, and now it hurts.

For five days I was happy, and in those five days my feelings for Tyler continued to increase.

I feel helpless. I don't know where to go from here. I don't want to lose your friendship, and it would hurt terribly if you purposely tried to stay out of my life. I think we continue and set limits as long as we can stick to them.

For the last six weeks, I have been chasing something I knew I could never have. Every time I got closer; I was pushed further away.

Why do I continue to feel the way I do? Why does a simple smile make my day and a single touch awaken my heart? Why do I want so badly something I cannot have? How can he make me so happy and at the same time so sad? What am I holding on to, waiting for, really wanting to happen? Why am I so drawn to him by a force impossible to compete with?

Some things are worth a little pain—and so are some people. You have done so much more for me than you realize. You are always there with open arms, listening ears, good advice, and a shoulder to cry on.

He was my safe place and even if I could not have him completely, I needed him in my life. Our relationship was desperately unique. It was fiercely magnetic and then cold, fearlessly loving and then peacefully quiet. It was exciting and adventurous, painful, and sad. He would never be available to me in the way that I wanted, but for years I accepted him in any capacity. For the first time in my life, I understood how it felt to be held. Regardless of the circumstances of our relationship, when his arms were around me, I was content. Safe. Whole.

But I was suffering, and for the first time, my pain caught my mother's attention. How many mothers have prayed this prayer?

> *January 13, 1989.* Oh God, I don't know who you are or what you're about, but something inside me tells me you're there when you are needed. I need you. Please listen. I'm worried about Heidi. She's acting as though she's upset. She's out late, she sleeps late, she's not eating regular meals, she's not talking, and she's hardly at home. She's avoiding David and me. I'm scared, Lord, when I'm out of touch with Heidi. I see her feeling upset, and I want her to be happy. Oh God, please direct me in the best way to approach her. I want to help—in an appropriate, loving way. Oh God, help me to reach out and to know what to do. I pray to you to especially enfold Heidi in this time. With your loving, warm and safe arms, cuddle her close to you and keep her safe. Help her to make wise decisions and choices now. Keep her safe from costly mistakes. Guide her carefully, oh God, don't let her go. Amen.

> *February 9, 1989.* A deep feeling of gratitude today— Heidi slid into a ditch yesterday after spinning around on the bypass. Fortunately, no one was close, and no one hit her. She was enfolded by God's loving arms. Thank you, God.

These were the days of no cell phones. I had hit black ice on a shaded curve, spun one way and then the other, and missed a concrete fence post by mere inches. Shaken but completely unharmed, I walked away from my car and up to the road, where I hitched a ride from a friend who just happened to be driving by. I did not go home, not to my parents, but to my safe place and sobbed in his arms like a child.

Words are empty without action. There was no reaching out, no loving or appropriate help. That spring of 1989 was my senior year of high school. Today, I look at what has just occurred in my own life. My youngest child recently completed his senior year of high school. My life was consumed with all of his "lasts." There was the last soccer game after fifteen years on the field, the last track meet and sports banquet, the last morning trek to school, and the last packed lunch. Senior pictures, tearful Facebook posts, prom, graduation, college visits, acceptance letters and commitments filled my life. For an entire year, as his mother, my life was dedicated to my son. From February 1989 until January 1990, *my* mother wrote one entry in her journal about me, and she was angry at me for coming home at 4:00 a.m. Nothing else. No pride in her daughter for taking two college courses spring semester, graduating with honors, and making a college decision. No comments about my prom dress or that Tyler and I were voted the couple having the most fun. Did she even know? I didn't seem to exist.

What existed was her anger—anger at my grandfather and men in general. She was angry at her abuser for a multitude of things, but on the forefront was her aversion to sex and the fear and anguish it evoked in her. And she was angry at my dad, who often tried to stifle her outward expression of fury, forcing her to, once again, extinguish her voice and pack it away. Entry after entry described in great detail her anger, hatred, and bitterness. It was an ugly season for all of us.

Sometimes we feel like we're invisible, nonexistent, but to be ignored in her writing for an entire significant year was pretty powerful. Where was her desire to be in touch with me, to guide me, and to ensure my happiness? My saga with Tyler continued. And in September, without mention, I moved a few blocks away to a dorm on campus. Strangely enough, being out of her home and present on the same campus placed me back on her radar, in not such a glorious way. Being a student on the same small campus where my mother taught felt like being the child of the principal. She seemed to know everything I was doing, more so than she had when I was living at home. Was I drinking, staying out all night, sleeping in my own bed? All of a sudden, these things mattered to her, and it was suffocating. Her answer was counseling. Apparently, she felt alcohol and Tyler were at the root of my degenerate behavior; it was certainly not a result of the last several years of my life. Reluctant and exhausted, I came home for the month of January and began counseling. I went through the motions to satisfy those who needed to be satisfied but never touched any real issues.

Having me home again must have prompted her to write. When I came into possession of the journals shortly after her death, I discovered an entire journal dedicated to me. It inspired me and shattered me at the same time. She was trying to trust me, understand me, even love me at many times. Her ultimate decision was to let me go, to protect herself by not taking responsibility for my decisions because they were too painful for her. If she separated herself from me, then my pain could not reflect on her, and she could no longer be hurt by me. She was insulating herself from her own creation.

Now it was my turn to be angry—angry at my mother, who was gone. I was angry at my mother, who had been unavailable physically and emotionally for so many years of my life and then decided she did not like who I had become in her absence. It was so unfair, and again, I had no recourse against her. She had made a conscious decision to absolve herself from further pain by placing moral distance between us. She had abandoned me in so many ways, had not taken part in my emotional growth and had then released herself of any responsibility.

> *January 3, 1990.* Tears—of concern for Heidi. A young life with so much potential. It hurts to see her want so much—clothes, money in particular. I feel it's a sign of insecurity, of not knowing who she is or what she wants. Maybe an empty feeling ... I look at Heidi and cry. I want her to be whole, complete, not empty. I would like for her to come face-to-face with herself and ask, "Who am I and what do I want/need?"

> *January 9, 1990.* Heidi and I had a good talk after her first counseling session. I am happy she's willing to share— her sharing branches out into other sharing, but that's OK. We share, we move into one another's spirit, and the closeness is felt. I love her.

I have decided to write notes to/about Heidi as she journeys through counseling. I want to share with her in this way. We both appreciate writing and journaling. I think this would be a neat thing to share between mother and daughter.

∞

January 20, 1990. It's so hard at times to see Heidi upset, to be able to see things in a way different from her and know she's not ready to deal with them yet. I raise questions about her, questions I'd love to ask her and, yet, feel she's not ready to hear. Could it be your own holding on to Tyler is what causes you inner turmoil, not only now but in previous times? Can you care about him enough to let him go when he's asking you to? Do you continue to live with a false hope yet fail to recognize it for what it is? Can you risk the pain of letting go in order to take care of yourself? Can you stand aside and view what this relationship does to you? Could you be the perpetuator of your own pain?

If only she had given these notes to me or asked me these questions directly. If only she had pinned me down with a "come-to-Jesus moment," instead of writing these thoughts in her journal and never sharing them with me. She could see what I could not. Her eyes were wide open, but her heart was so torn, she was afraid to tell me what I desperately did not want to hear. Tyler did not destroy me, but I allowed him a power over me whether he wanted it or not. For twenty-five years, through difficult periods of two marriages, I quietly left the door open. Through moments of vulnerability, I still sometimes felt that he was the only one who understood me. I had the reverse of white knight syndrome—this irrational belief/desire that he would eventually see me, sweep me off my feet, and rescue me again.

January 28, 1990. I had trouble seeing Heidi leave for school. I feel uneasy with her and about her. I'm uncomfortable with her behavior ... it's those adolescent years and the normal behavior of being an adolescent. Somehow, I get feelings triggered by my interactions with Heidi ... could it be that my own confusion and distrust in my mother-daughter relationship plays a role in my own daughter-mother relationship? I feel the sadness, the loss, yet the wanting to hold on ... because I miss the closeness of my own relationship with my mother. I find it hard to accept Heidi's behavior, even when I know that most of it is normal. This is a difficult time—a time I need to sit back and wait (and trust) that she will move through this time and that I will endure. It's hard to let go, let be, and let grow.

Oh, Heidi, I just ache—for me and for you. Your behavior is not ordinary. What is it you want to say?

A mother's grief—how long, Heidi? How long will you continue to act this way? The grief, the pain is so hard to bear. Sometimes I wish I didn't know you. To love you tonight is only returned with pain.

Inside this journal, I found several loose pieces of paper. One, a handwritten letter from me dated January 29. I wrote it stating, "I just feel that, if I put words in front of your eyes, I may actually be heard." I begged her for understanding, for a fair chance, to respect my honesty, for the opportunity to make my own decisions. "I want you to care, but sometimes I feel that you are overly concerned, and that seems to push me away. I don't want to run away from you, but I think you need to let go a little and realize that I have a life of my own, and I will be OK."

January 30, 1990. Too numb to cry. Too numb to write. It's so hard to write; words don't come. It is so hard to continue to love a daughter when there is so much pain.

Also tucked between the pages was a photocopy of a handwritten letter to me. It was undated, but I assumed it fell into this period of challenging days. I later found the original in my shoebox of extremely personal keepsakes. It had been mailed to my post office box at school.

There was a third, similar yet slightly different computer-printed version that was less personal, more polished and poetic, signed by its author instead of "Mom." She was proud of what she had written, and it was now among her literary works. I'll share the one that was directed at me.

To Heidi

Once, so connected, we now come face-to-face with the need to separate. As you are compelled to grow and change, so am I. As the last umbilical threads are waiting to be severed, I groan with one last breath and let you go.

There you stand, a daughter marked by beauty; alas, inside the turmoil rages on. Who am I? What am I? What's important to me? What do I believe and who do I want to become? These restless questions grip and gnaw, bringing you face-to-face with "Who, really, am I?" I watch you walk solemnly, yet inside the raging continues. This is a necessary time, for if you are to grow, to become, you must pass through this turbulence. As your mother, it's hard to view the turbulence and not rush to shield you from potential dangers.

No, I do not understand your magnetic fascination with Tyler. No, I've not seen the times where he's "been there" for you. Those are times you've sealed in secrecy, as if to shield me from hurt and pain. Perhaps I do understand why you quickly go to him. He comforts and supports your behavior—because it is also his behavior. But does he confront you, challenge you, or question your behavior? Likely not, for to do so would cause him to confront his own. Friends come in many styles. Some will pat your back and condone your behavior. Others will dare to risk a relationship by confronting and challenging your actions. Which is the lasting friend? Ah, my daughter, 'tis the one who boldly, yet painfully, cares enough to confront.

No, I do not understand your passion to drink. Perhaps, it is to flirt with the forbidden. To gulp an adult behavior with childlike ignorance. Perhaps, it is to ignore the call to travel inward, to delay growth or blanket the pain. Mothers were not made to accept all the choices presented to them by their daughters. Your choices are now fully your own. You are free to do, to choose those things that are important for you to promote growth and happiness. Likewise, the consequences are now fully yours, for I no longer hold responsibility for you. Even though I view some of your choices as potentially unhealthy and destructive, they are yours. They belong solely to you. Please claim them as your own, for I cannot compromise my values and beliefs.

Even though I do not support some of your choices, I continue to love you as my daughter. I've nurtured you and given you roots, one root being the freedom to make choices. Now, I give you wings to take flight, to feel and live your own choices, whatever they be. And as you soar into independence, may peace and fulfillment be your beacon. As you change, so do I. Change can be wrought with loneliness and tears, as well as pleasure and ecstasy. We both have been prompted to seek growth and accept change. Perhaps it is a gift we have given each other, wrapped in love and respect for each one's journey.

I'll love you forever,
Mom

What a letter! I simply cannot fathom receiving and reading this as a nineteen-year-old. But this was what I had asked for—space and freedom and the ability to live my life, make my decisions, and grow in my own direction. And she did what she needed to do for herself. She was not releasing me as her daughter but releasing herself from the pressure, guilt, and consequences of my decisions. She was giving me ownership of my life. I see it clearly now, as I have gone through a similar "letting go" process with my own daughter. Perspective is a beautiful thing but does not come quickly or easily. This marked a profound change in our relationship. Going forward, we began to appreciate each other as adults, and something new evolved.

February 20, 1990. What do I, your mother, mean to you now? Only a short time ago, we seemed to be enemies. We have changed, both of us and, in doing so, found a link that binds us. Even though difficult, I've learned the virtue and wisdom of struggling through meaningful relationships. I knew you were worth struggling with the distance, and I'm glad we eventually became harmonious again. Through change, wrought by pain and acceptance, we've learned more of what it means to be women in the mother-daughter relationship.

March 27, 1990. We spent wonderful moments together today. At times I marvel at our similarities, and yet, our apparent differences. We seem to be developing a deep respect for each other—as women, as mother and daughter. We've moved through a time of deep pain and distanced ourselves, yet we have come together again but on a different level. That's the way relationships move and find life in their own being. People move in and out of moments in life, never to be the same after a movement is completed. Like a musical score, divided into movements, each tells its own story yet remains connected to the entirety of the score. At the same time, each movement builds on that which has preceded it and gives strength and meaning to that which is to come. As we move and live and know our being, we grow and develop in depth. In each phase, we learn more of who we are and who we are becoming. We also gain perspective on others as we gain perspective on ourselves. It's such a joy to know you and be close to you at this time in your life. I cherish the moments we share in strengthening the mother-daughter relationship. I'm so happy to be your mother.

September 1990. I am filled with your excitement of the school year—new friends, new classes, schoolwork going well. You seem different—calmer, more at peace, more at ease with yourself. And, shall I say, wiser in your decisions. You are beautiful. It's a joy to see you at this point in life— one achieved because of some honest hardship—a time worthy of its challenges. It's good to watch a daughter struggle with issues and emerge with fresh, clever thinking. In doing so, you exhibit strength.

But in the end, at this point in each of our lives, our desires and needs for our relationship remained incongruent. I was nineteen; entering my sophomore year in college; and, very understandably, self-absorbed. As we began to navigate an adult state of connectedness, I wanted that bond of friendship instead of parent and child. But being her friend came saddled with an expectation I was not ready for. I continued to disappoint her. She so desperately wanted me to know her on an intimate level, to comprehend her pain, to want to share in this journey by her side. I needed to be young, carefree, and unburdened with her story. During this stage of my life, I needed it to *not* be my story.

October 28, 1990. Reflections on my daughter choosing not to go to the lecture with me—I felt the pain return, and I turned and walked away. The tears welled up in my eyes and then journeyed down my cheeks. I let them fall, for they silently spoke of my disappointment, yes, my hurt. Our interests clash again—my need to have you want to understand me pitted against your need to be involved with your peer group, to show with pride your home, your hall, your friends.

I struggled and cried with the reality that young adults live in the present, the now, and friends and school life are of utmost importance. I momentarily forgot how young you are, still driven by life in the present. I was divided in my thinking, feeling sure that you could sense my need and respond accordingly. I was sure you could sense my fragile sense of being and know that it was important for you to be with me. I know you could read my disappointment and observe the wet eyes. I thought you could grasp the meaning of this event—for both you and me ... I wanted you to enter the door of understanding my pain and sorrow, the story that has robbed me of the pure taste of life you knew as a child. I wanted you to enter it with an open heart, a readiness and willingness to enter my story. There's so much of me I want you to know. I thought you were ready.

I made a plea for you to come with me. You agreed. Then, in the last moment, you declined. I went on, saddened by your decision. Knowing I was not chosen brought pain, felt deeply—as when a child long ago. Your decision was honored. I left you alone with your own thinking and being, for I am a parent who honors choices of others, even though they bring pain. I am left with the question of when? Will there ever be a time when you will choose to journey with me, to hear my story and willingly want to understand me? Like many other events in your life, I will remind myself of the nature of patience and the necessity to surrender to the timing, the right timing, for precious moments to be shared. I remind myself to honor your independence and choices and to especially honor your own sense of timing. I trust you to sense your own readiness to enter my journey.

She had invited me to go to a lecture with her. I had agreed but then, under the influence of school and friends, backed out at the last moment. It crushed her, and I knew it. But she was asking too much of me. She desperately wanted me to be ready and felt like I was but clearly could not see that I had been plundered as well. I had very little left to give. She asked when. When would I be ready to enter her journey? Over the next ten years, life happened. I did not extend a hand to join her, and neither did she extend one to me. Perhaps she was afraid of being rejected once again. Sadly, her death and these unread passages lured me in. The journey was now mine to experience alone, and I am deep in the trenches.

CHAPTER SIXTEEN

Living with Pain

The next few journals, the majority of 1990 and into 1991, were plagued with physical pain. Her emotional pain was declaring itself with a bold, outward expression. Entry after entry, as close to daily as one can get, she described the manifestation of bearable but very present pain. She began a process called "creative journaling," in which she illustrated her pain in pictures. This journal, a three-ring binder, was filled with drawing paper and colorful hand-drawn pictures of her body and where her pain continued to take up residence. Her pain was always drawn in red with dense squiggly lines, most often in her neck and lower abdominal area but frequently visiting her arms and legs, giving her moments of inability and paralysis.

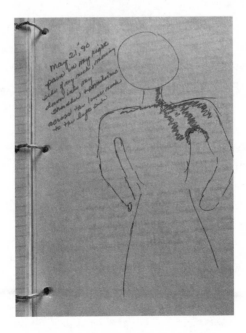

She acknowledged her pain and spoke directly to it in her writing. She recognized it for what it was—years of internal, emotional pain with no expression now waiting for a prompting, for permission to be exposed.

> *April 1, 1990.* Woke with pain and drew the picture on the opposite page. I acknowledge the pain as a message to me. I am listening to it. I feel it intently—as I move into the pain, I own it and speak directly to it:
>
> Pain, oh pain—open yourself to me. Like an unfolding flower struggling with the cool late March days, you seem ready to open, to let yourself be seen, yet outside circumstances dampen your ability to come to full flower. Like you, I need an outside force to enable the opening— likened unto warmth, that which provides the catalyst to open, to lay bare the inside, only to expose for a brief time and then to wither and die in that stage, knowing what was needed to be done and accomplished. I am ready to open up this pain. I am patiently waiting for the moment to open—to then examine that which is inside, waiting for exposure.
>
> I will let myself feel the pain—its movement. I will not medicate it. I feel it may be connected to my dreams of late and the message is an important one. I will move into my pain and invite it into my day. I will be present with it. I choose to let it inhabit my conscious, and I will not run from it. The pain is a significant part of me. It is wanting me to know of it. So, I take it in, not knowing how long its visit is this time. No matter, for I welcome it; it is me. I am not afraid of it or its message. Together we will come to a new understanding, of the purpose and meaning of its message. Like a kindly visitor, I take it in, willing to spend time during this unplanned visit. Times and events for growth are never planned.

My mother always had an unusual relationship with pain and illness. Pain became the messenger of something greater. And illness, although an unwelcome visitor, was never fought like an enemy but invited in to coexist peacefully. She did not like the idea of an internal battle, and I rarely heard her use the words that she was "fighting" something. She always seemed more comfortable with the concept of living with, embracing, and learning from that which invaded her body. I sometimes wonder if she made a huge mental mistake by choosing not to fight.

By May, her pain began to manifest itself in fatigue as well. She wrote frequently about simply being very tired; staying home; napping; and needing time to rest, meditate, and be alone. In June, she wrote about her fear of going for a physical but also about understanding the importance of finding out what kind of state her body was in. She never wrote of the results of that physical. On July 17, however, seemingly out of nowhere, nestled between quotes about legacy, opportunities, and generosity, I found this statement by Henri Nouwen from his book *Out of Solitude*:

About cancer (page 206)

That a cancer, being a kind of growth gone wild, lives something of the life that is unlived by those with repressed, constricted personalities. It is almost as if the absence of growth and excitement externally leads to its internal expression. All that energy that is kept inside seems to fuel the cancer, for it has no place to go.

Was she somehow foreshadowing what was destined to come? Cancer would not rear its ugly head for many years. Yet, for some reason, this stood out to her. I wonder if she read this and recognized herself and her circumstances. Did she, from this moment on, feel the events of her life had possibly predisposed her to the inevitable inhabitation of cancer?

October 28, 1990. I awake with a heavy feeling—cold-like symptoms throughout my body. I reflect on the meaning of a cold—the way the body reacts to pressure and stress. I knew it was time to seriously reflect on all I've put my body through recently. OK, body, so I've overdone it again, and you get to be angry with me. You know how to make me listen. I have the power to join with the creative and healing spirit to create my own circumstances. I have the power to choose to feel better. The heaviness and achiness inside are a result of choosing to carry some unnecessary strife. I can choose to let go, to give up harboring some thoughts and issues. I desire to be energetic and full of vitality. To do so, I must choose to relinquish that which creates heaviness. When I let go of the stress, the disease will let go of its grip. The body is a miracle—so wise and all-knowing. It speaks with such truth. Listen and respond.

Roses were among my mother's favorite things. In the house I grew up in, she had a rose garden that expanded every year. She designed, planted, and tended to this garden faithfully as a component of her healing process. She was meticulous in her care as she fertilized in the spring, trimmed the deadheads throughout the summer, pruned the bushes in the fall, and covered them with warmth and protection so they could withstand the elements of our Indiana winters. The uncovering in the spring was like a rebirth every year that brought her new hope and joy. When my parents sold this house in April 1991, the new owners were under strict orders *never* to remove the rose garden. To this day, they have listened and respected her wish.

As I have read and reread her journals over the past twenty years, she has spoken to me differently depending on my frame of mind and the perspective from which I was reading. Occasionally, words will creep off the page and touch me with a purpose and meaning like never before. Today, for the first time, I recognize the symbolism of the rose and understand her deep affinity for this delicate flower and its depiction of yet another aspect of her pain. As she wrote to her Healing Spirit, she cried desperately to be set free, to be able to discover herself, to move deep within her core and unlock her true potential—the rosebud.

> *November 4, 1990.* I know that deep within me is a rosebud—so perfectly shaped and so much beauty stored

inside. I want to open, petal by petal, and experience the gentleness and fullness of life. I want all of me to feel life. I cry to unlock the part of me deep inside—the part that stores secrets and pain and associates fear with pleasure. Deep inside I cry ... bundled up like the rosebud, full of unexpressed passion and beauty. Like the rosebud I cut late this fall, I fail to open. Do I refuse to open out of fear? Grant me courage, kind and gentle healing spirit, to let go of fear. Grant me courage to go deep and open up. Grant me courage to flower.

The rosebud, a representation of beauty and life, has an even more specific significance. It is the image of her sexual being that lived, locked deep within her core. The rosebud is red, beautiful, and perfectly shaped but can only open once it is lifted and freed from its past. It lies, tightly formed, awaiting exposure to the elements of permission, encouragement, and trust. I don't want to dwell on this aspect of my parents' relationship, but I would be remiss to ignore the physical and mental anguish that accompanies the intimate life of a sexual trauma survivor. For years, she wrote about wanting and trying to uncover the sensual side of her being that possibly never existed because of the early trauma. Even the slightest touch could be triggering, bringing forth tears and flashbacks of a perpetrator. In spite of her desire, decades of fear had left her with cerebral roadblocks and tangible numbness.

And so, she waited, as the rosebud, for the key that would release the flower and awaken her senses, for the invitation to fulfillment. Some days there was absolute rage at my father for the received message that she did not meet his needs—he was unfulfilled; *she* was simply not enough. And others, there was admiration for a man, who, despite his own desires and the longings of his broken wife, lived many years in a patient, selfless shadow responding to and tolerating the fear that punctuated that time.

March 4, 1991. Drained, emotionally drained. I went to the Celebrate Diversity workshop yesterday and never dreamed I'd share my story with a hundred people, mostly colleagues and students. It was a powerful experience for

101

me. I was moved to share—and I felt it was appropriate to do so. I'm glad I did. Today, my body feels tired for the energy spent. But it will soon recuperate. Stories need to be told and shared. Pain needs to be named and owned.

For nearly five years, her truth had been present and her healing in process. But some days, life was still unbearable. Hurt was overpowering, and energy to combat pain and negativity was nonexistent. She was uncaring, tired of fighting, and hurting. She was an incredible student of self-therapy. But even in the middle of a season of positive affirmation, she had moments of utter weakness. Although difficult to witness, even in writing, her words created an image of despair as they were painted on this tragic canvas:

> *March 29, 1991.* I just hurt. I'm on vacation, and here I am crying, probably a needed cry. I'm scared. When I get overwhelmed with feelings bigger than me, I get scared I will break someday. Just break—and can't do anything ... I cry and no one knows I cry. I can't say I hurt anymore.

And then her perspective changed along with her landscape. After twenty years in the same house, a house with a full spectrum of memories, it was time for a change. Her children had been raised in this home, but they were gone and not likely to come back. For all the good that took place in this home, its walls held an extreme amount of pain. There were visions of violence and voices of two men, other than my father, who invited themselves inside these confines with perverse intentions and scarring actions. How she stayed and healed as much as she did in this place is beyond me. But now there was excitement of a new, romantic beginning, something to look forward to. Dreams and possibilities flooded her mind and interrupted her sleep in a good way. She was ready to say goodbye and start anew!

> *April 30, 1991.* The reality is coming—this house will soon be passed on to someone else. I pause to think about the meaning of this house—what I've learned about

myself here in this place. I think about the tears shed in this house and the struggle to live. This house has been a shelter from the storm and a place where I struggled within the storm. I'm ready to leave this house and the story within it—behind.

December 31, 1991. As I look over the past year, it appears as if the move to our new home was a major move toward healing. In retrospect, I didn't realize how powerful the leaving of one place could be. I shed many memories that hurt and left them there. They did not follow me to this new house. I feel unleashed, ready to begin a new phase.

CHAPTER SEVENTEEN

Lumps and Blood Tests

The new year was marked by hope. More and more frequently, she began her entries with the words, "I feel good!" There was an air of excitement as she sensed she was becoming who she was created to be. She was exercising regularly, reading, taking piano lessons for the first time in thirty years, and baking bread weekly. She described it as "sitting on the peak of something." And that something was life, like she'd never experienced it before—a life of openness, surrender, possibilities, challenges, and loving. She was full, bubbling on the inside, and spilling over with joy. Joy, however, was usually short-lived for my mother.

> *March 9, 1992.* A very difficult morning—even my handwriting is poor. So much has happened in the last few days, and it's all piled up and seems to be closing in on me. I woke up feeling overwhelmed. My body feels tight and tense with all the weight. The result is depression— so heavy that I am nearly paralyzed. I feel like I can't function—and don't want to.

She listed four things that were weighing heavily on her mind and heart. The first three were work related. And then:

> #4. Finding a lump in my right breast—the worry, fear

As only my mother would, she formulated a written agenda in response to each item on her list. She would call her doctor on Monday for an appointment:

I do have choices and things to do to make changes. And hopefully, my life will improve. In the meantime, I acknowledge what I feel—and I know I don't feel good.

A few years prior and this news might have been received very differently. Her reaction was tame and composed as she patiently awaited answers and next steps. She allowed her mind to wander without commanding it to stop, an activity that manifested itself in both constructive and destructive escapades. She had worked diligently over the last few years not to be afraid of the unknown and was intelligently able to consider the what-ifs. How would her life change if she had cancer? Had recent changes been made out of necessity or coincidence?

> *March 15, 1992.* I feel extremely relieved this morning in spite of all that I face this coming week. Tomorrow, I find out what lies ahead—surgery, the time, concern, questions, and realities. I'm surprised at my calmness today. I'm eager to move to the next point, know the uncertainties of what's ahead. I feel prepared to tackle what may be next—ready without fear. I've decided I can handle anything—and I've learned that calmness and absence of fear are the best antidotes to illness. I've decided not to make any decisions until I know the next move on the board game of Life. What is next, I will face boldly. I will then decide who and what will be important to journey with me.

It took twenty days from discovery to pathology, but the tumor was removed and found to be benign. A flood of tears accompanied a multitude of feelings. They flooded and then drained, leaving her to ponder the direction of her life.

The next few months were ones of peaceful healing but peppered with days of tiredness and discomfort. The sore throat, heaviness in her chest, and pain on her left side were worrisome as she prepared for a bicycle trip in Vermont and pondered how much her body would be able to handle.

The trip was a success, a challenging but rewarding week of beauty and much-needed escape. Vacation has a way of allowing the body to sidestep pain and exhaustion for a period of time, but it almost always returns. The so-so-so tired entries returned, and she examined her much-needed break from school, a throat ailment that continually dragged her down, and looming menopause—all of which could be responsible for her fatigue. A doctor's appointment was necessary, but meditation, yoga, and exercise were all things she could do herself if she could only find the discipline and motivation.

I lost my first grandparent to esophageal cancer in July, and my brother was married six days later. My paternal grandfather had a lust for life. But following the removal of his esophagus and losing the ability to eat by mouth, he abandoned his will to live. His physical healing was no longer possible. His eternal peace came quickly, and our emotions shifted from one meaningful family experience to another:

> *July 26, 1992.* It's strange to think about a death and a wedding in the same week. When one relationship ends, a new one begins.

Again, a chilling passage I had never read until now. How ironic that she would put these words on paper, as nine years from now I would be married just four days following her own death.

> *August 5, 1992.* Matthew's wedding, I just thoroughly enjoyed myself—had fun, fun, fun! The entire weekend felt so good and right ... And then, as tired as can be, we left for Michigan. I had not been feeling well—have been battling a viral infection for some time. So, I welcomed Michigan this year with open arms. I feel so tired; all I want to do is *sleep*. David brought his bike. I, sadly, left mine at home. I know deep inside I cannot bike, hike, or walk much this year. But I *must* put my feet in the water. I am aching to heal.

November 22, 1992. On October 22, I had a series of blood tests to determine if my tiredness was real or imagined or due to work overload. On October 26, I returned to the doctor and was notified that my CD4 helper cell count was quite low—as low as persons who have HIV. Alarm spread through my body on a very quick course. I immediately thought back to being raped—many times—and wondered if I could possibly have HIV or AIDS. With the urging of my physician and the convincing of my own self of the necessity to do the test—to find out for sure—I consented to be tested for HIV. The rubber gloves became apparent; I was viewed as potentially dangerous and threatening. Not comforting at all. Incidentally, my CD4 T cell count was 344. Normal is 600–1200. I was informed that most people carry a count around 800–900.

After several days of waiting, I learned I did not have HIV and cried with relief. But I was alarmed by what my low counts meant to me ... The result, I have an immune deficiency; I cannot fight off disease like some people can. My condition was also referred to as chronic fatigue syndrome. The only thing I can do to help myself is get lots of rest and perhaps an exercise program. Well, I am determined not to let this get me down ... I am a determined woman. I will give time to myself to get well again, in spite of being told there's not much to do for it and that I will always feel tired and "not well." I tend to take on the impossible. I do not take "no" lightly. My belief in a spirit greater than myself allows me to have hope in the impossible. I have too much to contribute to life to take "no" for an answer.

December 23, 1992. I found a meaningful scripture—one I want to memorize and repeat frequently.

But those who hope in the Lord will renew their strength. They will soar on wings like eagles; they will run and not grow weary; they will walk and not be faint (Isaiah 40:31).

∞

Christmas Day 1992. A day to celebrate! Heidi received a diamond from Chris yesterday. She is one happy woman! Now we look forward to expanding our family some more—it will be a joy learning to know Chris.

But six weeks later in her writing, she was already expressing some uneasiness about my fiancée and the wedding date we had set for September. She was not comfortable with the timeline, wishing for a longer engagement so we could get to know each other better. Trying to sort out her own feelings, she named her fear that our relationship wouldn't last. What had she seen between us that left her with hesitation and distaste? Did she not trust her own daughter in this big decision or was she simply not ready to let me go?

Why do we tiptoe on eggshells around the relationship choices of our children? We are so afraid that expressing our concerns will push our children away, and they will proceed in life without us. For the second time, I wish my mother would have had the courage to have this conversation with me. These journals hold so much foresight, and I wonder what she sensed in us, and him, that made her afraid. In the months and even days prior to the wedding, I had my own reservations but, like my mother, no courage to speak them.

Chris had come into my life different from anyone I had ever dated. He was older by three years and a transplant local instead of a student. He had a job and was able to court me with real dates, including restaurants and culture. He was large in stature, dwarfing my petiteness but offering a sense of security with his size and protective nature. I had dated my fair share of good young men, but marriage had always been a wrong time or material issue. We had already been living together, and there certainly was not the room or invitation for me to come home after graduation. In the early months of my senior year in college, it seemed that marriage was the next logical and somewhat necessary step.

March 7, 1993. I had my annual Pap / breast exam, as well as a checkup on my blood counts. I wasn't prepared for the finding of another lump, and I wasn't prepared for the blood count results. B lymphocytes 900 (1,000–4,800) and CD4 T cells 551 (600–1,200). He finally gave me a diagnosis—myelodysplasia of the bone marrow. The result is a very deficient immune system. I don't have much to fight with. In terms of my job—a cutback soon.

March 21, 1993. I am confronted with surgery in two weeks. Four lumps have been identified, three in my right breast and one in my left. But we have a dilemma: What is the best decision for me—to risk not removing the lumps and risk cancer or to risk surgery, remove the lumps, and run the possibility of infection? My physician strongly believes the lumps must come out … I am too young to risk cancer. So, on April 5, I will have the surgery.

There was fear in some moments and peace in others, trusting this decision was the right one. She examined stumbling blocks that might be in the way of her healing—the broken relationship with her parents, her own stubbornness, her decision regarding future employment, and the struggle with surrendering it all to God. She toyed again with thoughts and plans for her memorial service—the flannel nightgown, pink robe, and socks were steadfast, and her altar display continued to grow. Location, speakers, and pallbearers were listed, but many would change over the years.

April 8, 1993. Surgery is over, and I am waiting for the pathology report. Wait. Wait. It's painful to wait. In my devotions on this Maundy Thursday, I read about "Thy will be done" and how painful it was for Jesus to speak these words … Family, work, health—letting go and letting God take charge. Thy will and not mine. Like Jesus, I find these are painful words to say—and believe. "If it isn't possible to pass through this time without drinking from the cup of pain, then I commit myself to you, O Father, and trust *your* will be done."

This morning, before I began my writing, I transcribed my notes from a sermon four months ago into my journal. I enjoy taking notes during church, and then, as a form of devotions, I transform my scribbles into entries, adding practical nuances and spelling out verses for reference. Today's sermon focused on how God wants to work not only in us but also through us, taken from John 15—"The Vine and the Branches." I wrote that we must be connected to the vine to receive spiritual nourishment. In verse 5, Jesus says, "I am the vine; you are the branches. If you remain in me and I in you, you will bear much fruit; apart from me you can do nothing."

As I began reading the twelfth journal, and found her entry from Easter morning, April 11, 1993, I came across a hand-drawn picture of a vine with branches. Along the vine she had written "Jesus—the Vine." And on one of the leafy branches she wrote, "Karen." To the side of the picture, "John 15: 1–5." My dear mother, we might be more in sync now than we have ever been! On the next page, her prayer:

Dear Creator and Sustainer of all Life,

I look at the image on the front of this page—the vine (Jesus) and I, one of the branches. My prayer is that we are intertwined—He in me and I in Him. Jesus is the support—the giver of daily sustenance and care for my life. This image means, O God, that I am dependent on Him for nurturance and direction. He is by far the most strong and stable—from Him I derive my strength. In a very real sense, this image calls for me to surrender to a power greater than myself and become the one who is given strength and direction. Lord, I struggle with letting go …

I realize submission is not easy. I understand that, when
I abide in Him, His power becomes my power; therefore,
I do not face my problems and decisions alone … Amen.

Ironically, the following day's entry spoke of the essence of life's mystery and that we are reminded to watch and wait for "God incidents." I had certainly just seen one! My mother was a woman of great faith. In the absence of "church" and "religion," both of which had failed her, she read and worshiped on her own, building a rock-solid relationship with her Creator. Since her death, I feel my faith deeply and emotionally. Tears are typically a part of my worship. Perhaps I have had the two greatest teachers as I strive to be closer to each of them.

There was no specific entry regarding cancer or no cancer, but on June 6, she wrote of a sense of relief, rest, and health. The past several weeks had been overshadowed by my brother's separation from his wife of eight months. Mom was heartbroken for her sad, lonely, rejected son and was counting the days until he would be home.

> *May 2, 1993.* Now that he is an adult, we can freely talk
> about our hurts and pain. Earlier, when the children were
> small, I sheltered them from my own hurts. Now that our
> children are grown, we can be fully human with them.
> This is a good time for parenting—to be a real parent,
> fully present with Matt.

I don't harbor one ounce of bitterness. I just find it interesting that, a few years down the road, when I was looking a marital separation in the face, this was not the response I received. No one wanted to hear my side of the story, to be adults or fully human. I had been the one to reject my marriage, and I had to beg to be heard.

July brought another round of blood tests and both lymphocyte and helper cell counts were down 15 percent. Not good news. Shots of gamma globulin and B12 were prescribed. There was no cure, no treatment, but these might help her feel better. A trip to Indiana University Medical Center ruled out certain diseases but did not specifically indicate what she had or what had caused it. The key was to remain as healthy as possible and maintain her present levels in spite of their dangerously low numbers. It was their belief that these numbers could only move in one direction. She would begin a six-month cycle of blood tests and breast exams.

> *August 29, 1993.* In some ways, I resent the intrusion of another school year—one that fills my time with busyness. Since the onset of my illness, I've gradually adapted to an appreciation of Kairos time (Greek for "opportunity")— living in the moment and experiencing "what is." I've decided that my teaching may take a looser approach— freer and more spontaneous. There are distinct advantages in life when I know that life means not knowing the extent or length—as if anyone does. But my plans have changed—I know physically I have limitations, and one of them is life span. So, if I may have limited time left, I have a different feeling about living and teaching. Be all I can be. Give all I can give. And love every minute of it! This should open new vistas to discovering more of who I am and can be!

CHAPTER EIGHTEEN

Perspective

My upcoming nuptials seemed to give her hope. And as her reservations dissipated, she filled her heart with adoration and anticipation for my new role as a wife:

> *August 22, 1993.* I sat and watched our daughter as she posed for her [bridal portrait] pictures. She was beautiful! I saw flashes in my mind as she posed. I saw her as the beautiful five-pound infant in my hands; the impish little girl who could steal your heart with her grin. I saw the pretty high school teenager with long hair, and then the young woman, a college graduate, employed in a job she loves-and about to be a wife. The feelings were powerful— she is so beautiful ... I am so proud of her—I'm glad she is my daughter.

> *September 12, 1993.* Only six days until the wedding ... Heidi has always been very special to me, and I look forward to being mother to her in her new venture in life.

> *September 19, 1993.* Yesterday was beautiful, a beautiful sunny day—perfect in every way. Today I am so happy, so filled with joy and love. Yes, I am a mother filled with joy and thanksgiving for a wonderful daughter and her husband ... As I looked at Heidi yesterday, I was reminded

many times of her beauty and strength. And yes, I felt pride—pride in who she is, has become, and will be in life; in her growth from a tiny infant; and in her determination to excel and contribute. I thank God for the relationship I have with her and for the love we share as mother and daughter. I love her so much and look forward to loving her in her new role as wife.

As I write, the majority of my research lies in her handwritten pages. Journal after journal is read front to back, along with the miscellaneous pieces tucked inside. Full attention is being given to every word. Today, I am caught off guard by a short paragraph found in the middle of her recap of the past week's happenings. Once again, I found her insight into my life, my happiness, written but never spoken:

> *November 28, 1993.* My brief discontent with Chris (his attitude about raising children). I wonder—is he joking or serious? I rarely, if ever, see a serious side to Chris and wonder if there is enough depth to him to sustain a meaningful relationship with Heidi. I want so much for my daughter, and most of all, I want her to be happy in her marriage.

On New Year's Eve, she completed her ritual of rereading her journal and reflecting on the past year. She noted that 1993 had been a year mostly outlined by her health, or lack thereof. She wrote that one "benefit" of ill health had been a more realistic view of life—deciding what is important and doing it, rather than waiting on "someday." Her recap was followed by a list of books read on the inside cover, spanning genres from self-help to faith and authors from Mark Twain to Danielle Steele.

The first page of her new journal outlined her goals for the upcoming year. She embraced the idea of turning fifty (as did I) with specific goals of maintaining her weight and increasing the distance and frequency of her walking routine. Change is a goal that would encompass various areas of her personal development. A five-month sabbatical to write and then teach kindergarten filled her with anticipation, an exploration into Judaism, and menopause.

On January 15, my parents embarked on a trip to Shelbyville, Michigan, in subzero temperatures for a six-week retreat. Dad would be interning at Ebersole Environmental and Educational Center, while Mom read and would write an article for an educational journal. The reading portion she described as a luxury to bathe in. But even as a brilliant writer, she questioned her ability and desire to do the piece. She longed for her writing to come from a place of freedom and not requirement.

> *January 25, 1994.* Happy birthday, dear daughter, Heidi. Twenty-three years! She's come a long way from five pounds of a tiny being. She's as beautiful as ever though. How well I remember that day—the joy of knowing we had a daughter, a tiny, petite one—and then how the joy was shattered a few hours later when we were told she was fighting a hemoglobin/bilirubin battle in her blood, a result of being an RH baby. This led us into the drama of fighting for her life (in Nigeria)! What a time to remember. I thank God for her and her life.

Mom always loved telling the story of my birth, the tiny champion I had become, and the miracle of the first week of my life. I was the five-pound twelve-ounce infant, born in a remote Sudan Mission hospital in rural Nigeria as my parents were on a three-year endeavor teaching at Hillcrest School. She and I (or at least our blood types) fought even in the womb. The RH proteins in our blood were incompatible, leaving me weak and jaundiced, with an extremely high bilirubin count that continued to climb following an easy birth. A blood "exchange" would have been common but not unless absolutely necessary. A baby fighting with her own blood to overcome was always better.

I was placed in an incubator, naked with patches over my eyes, under the light of four phototherapy lamps, and my parents were told to pray. My bilirubin continued to climb in the wrong direction, and I was failing the clinical tests that I had once passed. The blood donor was called to the hospital and the doctor began to set up for the exchange. As the doctor prepared, I started to wiggle and squirm. My spirit had decided I was not done before I had even started. My mother was called in, and I latched on to her breast for the first time. So many prayers had been offered, and it seemed they had been answered. Even the doctor exclaimed, "This one is going to be a fighter!"

> *February 7, 1994.* I found myself crying much of the morning—over my tiredness, the job predicament, missing Heidi, yet feeling disappointed over her forgetting to send me some things. I felt like I didn't count or didn't matter much to my daughter. I let the hurt come forth, cried about it, and then felt better. I also realized that, in feeling hurt by my own daughter's "uncaring" response, I become aware of my neglect of my own mother. I'm sure she's felt hurt many times, and I've not responded. Suddenly, I realized how my own faults stare me in the face. As the quote by Vernon Law indicates, "Experience is a hard teacher as she gives the test first, the lesson afterward." Yes, hard indeed. I guess before I point my anger and disappointment at my own daughter, I need to take care of my own faults. No sense in displacing them on others. Wow, perspective is a real teacher too!

I have been in possession of these journals for over twenty years now and had read them incompletely and in spurts until 2018. Shortly after her death, I started at the beginning. But the magnitude of my grief, coupled with the horrific story recounted in the early pages proved to be too much. I was longing to know the intricacies of this woman, but I was dying inside over the loss of her in my life. I put them away temporarily. When I was ready to try again, I started with her last two journals. I needed to understand what it felt like to know you were dying. From the previous chapter, I think she always knew her life would be cut short to some extent, but how does one process the reality of months, possibly weeks to live? I read and journaled with the desire to write about navigating living and dying at the same time. Again, I was overwhelmed. The next attempt resulted in a thirteen-page document, much like this book, with key journal entries accompanied by perspective in my words. It was our story in a tiny nutshell, but I left off with two years of her life to go. The final reading before now took me four years from beginning to end. It began with the urging of a marriage counselor to delve into my own story, created and complicated by my mother's. I read from a completely different perspective this time, fully examining, and dissecting the mother-daughter relationship, how she and her trauma had directly and indirectly shaped me. I extracted forty-nine typed pages of what I felt were critical passages conceived in her soul and scripted by her hand.

As I read and digested this last time there were a few things I needed to hear. I was looking for closure. I clearly remember the tearful explanation to my father of what these were and how she had genuinely come through without having to read between the lines. The first came in the February 7 entry, where she looked back and took responsibility for some of the impediments and challenges in our relationship as well as the ones with her own mother. She had spent her entire life grieving the loss of that maternal bond and everything her mother was not. She had chosen to distance herself in order to protect her heart and, in turn, had projected her own willful intentions on me. I never intentionally hurt my mother, but her heart was so open with me and perhaps the bar was set a little too high. I was human, and I disappointed her regularly. Perspective is an eye-opener, especially when you're looking in the mirror. I would certainly disappoint her again, but at least this once, she was willing to share ownership.

Over the last twenty years, I have found more and more ways that my mother and I are alike. When I was younger, and we were living in the same town, I was often mistaken for her or simply just called by her name. I would kindly tell whoever had mistaken me my name and say, "She's my mother." Since her passing, visits home are always accompanied by comments of, "You look so much like your mother!" I take it as a compliment and feel blessed that I can look in the mirror every day and still see her in my reflection.

As I've grown and matured, I have adopted some of my mother's mannerisms, character traits, and favorite things. She willingly taught me to love the beaches and stones of Lake Michigan and the reciprocal joy of baking bread for others. But by her example, I learned my need for order and perfection. My love for writing was gained intuitively. She did not deliberately teach me to write, but she modeled a use of intentional words and a love for descriptive and creative language. Perhaps my affinity came from having a secret that I could only write about in private. I am grateful for six years of English teachers who helped me refine a skill that would someday become a passion. My original and favorite teacher, with whom I continued a relationship well into adulthood, lost her own battle with cancer a few years ago, and it saddens me greatly to know that she will not be around to read this book.

One problem my mother and I share is the need for our passion to be perfect. Writing for perfection sometimes causes the process to be lengthy, frustrating, and cumbersome. As my mother stated below, making the transition to becoming a true writer involves accepting imperfection on the first try. The important part is getting the idea "on paper." The perfect words and context will come with time; distance; and, in a lot of cases, sleep. I knew I was encroaching on writer status when significant Facebook posts would take a few days to write. I would formulate my messages in my head, write them elsewhere, and then rewrite them before posting. If they weren't perfect, they weren't worth sharing with anyone.

> *February 18, 1994.* I really gained more of a sense of a "writer" this week as I experienced one day as a failure. It was just one of those days where the words didn't seem to flow, or even come to mind. I found myself chewing on my pen; daydreaming by gazing across the lake; hoping that somehow the words would blow across the water and appear on my paper, without effort. I decided to put words down, anyway, as disconnected as they seem. I suddenly was aware I had made the transition into writer when I could put words down and *know* they_weren't the final words or the final draft. I put them down and then left them until the next day. When I returned to them the next day, the were disconnected. But with a fresh mind, I could easily change, rearrange, and make them say what I wanted to say. It worked! The second drafting was very comforting; I learned the freedom of working with my own words until I got them to work

for me! I need to experience letting go of finality on the first draft and rewriting with ease the next day. I needed that in order to train myself better as a writer. It was an exhilarating and teachable moment. It freed me to let go of perfectionism—and trust my own abilities—after some distance!

By the end of the month, my parents were nearing the closure of their time in Michigan. Mom wrote that her body could sense the sadness of leaving this meaningful place. No winter had even come close to rivaling that of 1978 until now. Feet of pristine snow and a quiet place of respite were certainly a gift from God himself. To have set apart time in this set apart place, a place that spoke to her and healed her soul—it was everything she could have asked for and more.

CHAPTER NINETEEN

CFS: A New Beginning

Despite her break from church, spirituality and God remained a part of my mother's life and evolution:

> *March 30, 1994.* I wonder how God answers prayers. In my mind and prayers, I have been asking for a signal for my next spiritual steps … Then, in today's mail, a letter from the church asking us (or one of us) to become a Stephen Minister. "Well God, is this your signal?" Perhaps something David and I can invest in together?

She had already begun to consider going back to church after a valuable seven-year break. My father had been attending alone during this time. After much thought, she was feeling that her resistance to church could be problematic, in the sense that resistance prevents healing. Was she fighting what she really needed and what would restore her completely? The Stephen Minister's position felt like an invitation to come to the well, to drink from the living water. It showed her that even after a lengthy period of absence, the church continued to have faith in her; she was still welcome and valued. My parents decided to accept. My mother was eager to change from the inward focus that had consumed her for many years to investing time and spiritual energy in others.

I wanted to make sure I fully understood the meaning and role of a Stephen Minister, and so I looked it up. Stephen Ministers are lay congregation members trained to provide one-to-one care to those experiencing a difficult time in life, such as grief, divorce, job loss, chronic or terminal illness, or relocation. These volunteers come from all walks of life, but they share a passion for bringing Christ's love and care to people during a time of need. She quite honestly could have requested her own Stephen Minister, but I love that she chose to be one instead. Her empathy could certainly be a gift to someone else.

> *April 11, 1994.* My physician has now labeled my symptoms as chronic fatigue syndrome based on two facts: I show no improvement in fatigue, and my throat and ears hurt most of the time. He wrote a letter for my employer indicating that I am incapable of performing my administrative duties and should be relieved of them by the end of the academic year. I struggle with this new development. I realize he's probably correct, that I need to step down from my department chair position and only teach. I will do that, but I have to process the change in my soul. I need to allow a part of my former self to die—a busy, driven self, one who accomplished a multitude of things. I need to relinquish that life with no guilt. What then lies ahead? An unknown path. All I can do now is trust God's direction.

> *April 18, 1994.* I prayed one of my most fervent prayers this morning—I am ready to give up all those things that keep me in the darkness and in "dis-ease." I prayed to God for a life transfusion. I want to reach out, to give to others, to forgive those who have hurt me. I am ready to enter a new time of living—a time that is God-centered. I am certain my continuing illness reflects those times of hurt, pain, deceit, and wrongdoing. Oh, how painful it is to confront myself. I am not a good person. It is time to give up my control on my life. "Into thy hands I commend my spirit, Oh God. Take my life—meld me, mold me, use me, fill me. I surrender my control. I'm ready to follow—lead me.

People have asked me about her decision to forgive—when and how she was able to take that step. Well, I believe this was the beginning. Forgiveness would not diminish or deny what had been done to her. It would not remove her pain, but it would allow her to move past it. It would give her an active role in her own healing. This was her first encounter with forgiveness. I believe she had come to the point in her healing process where she accepted that she could go no further without it. The darkness that remained would continue to be an obstacle to truly experiencing life. The timing of this was not random or insignificant either. When you know your time on earth is likely limited, you want your days to be lived out in the light. Many people make amends when they know they're dying; blessed are those who offer forgiveness before they reach that point.

> *April 22, 1994.* So I have chronic fatigue syndrome. What does that say about me? I've decided not to fight CFS so hard but, rather, to work and live with it—to accept it, befriend it, and recognize it as a vital part of me. I must walk with this disease; accept its mark on me; and, hand in hand, work with it—to understand it and to understand its implication for my life. Part of my healing requires loving myself—an act of taking responsibility for my new healing—in partnership with God. Being responsible means giving up this act of being busy and working so hard and so much of the time. I do not have to prove myself by dying at work! Being responsible—caring for and loving myself—calls for me to be wiser and smarter. I choose to walk with God on this journey—to invite His presence and guidance to be with me. I ask for His loving hands to caress the weak areas of my body—and let His loving, healing grace filter through my tired and damaged tissues. With God's love and grace, I will heal. I am open to the time it requires. God, be my shepherd and lead me.
> "There is no such thing as an incurable disease, only incurable people" (Bernie Siegel).

And so, over the next few months, she began to take steps toward physical and emotional healing and improving her quality of life. Being told that her general health would likely not improve I think came to her as a challenge. She adopted Siegel's theory that our minds can either heal us or kill us. This feisty little woman did not take kindly to being told she could not do something. She did resign her department chair position and took the summer off completely from any type of work. She read a book about recovering from chronic fatigue syndrome, contacted two organizations for CFS, and reached out to the Indiana chapter for support groups for people with CFS. She was not working but she was certainly doing her homework. She began an aggressive herbal regimen and started taking more naps and simply pacing her life better. She agreed to bake bread weekly for a family with quintuplets, and together, she and my father rejoined their small group that met outside of church.

On July 17, 1994, she wrote about a sense of uneasiness gnawing at her insides. A brief encounter with her mother at church left her with the feeling that "Mother wants things to be a certain way—happy, all right, and no trouble." Yet, she (my mother) was still focused on the unresolved issues, still dealing with anger and hostility. She was ready to be heard and to have this burden eased. Two weeks later, she was abruptly awakened in the middle of the night and knew immediately she was in the presence of God. In that moment, He did not tell her exactly what to do but enabled her to role-play in her mind, allowing her to lay out a plan of how to respond to her parents. For months, she had been praying fervently about how to repair this relationship. God was changing her approach and her desire to take control was clear.

> *August 4, 1994.* Mom called tonight and opened the door. I calmly said what I felt—she cried, was obviously hurt, and said she'd always hoped I'd be able to forgive. I told her it took much more that that … When I hung up, I walked through the house, breathing deeply—smiling. I had done and said what I needed to do and say for years. I felt good—relaxed, calm, at peace, and not guilty. I rejoiced in my newfound sense of control over my life. Thanks be to God for His insightful presence. I received the courage and strength to do this important and meaningful piece of healing.

Another round of blood work, another lump in her breast, another biopsy, more waiting:

August 21, 1994. How good it felt to go to church and be among friends—good friends. I can walk about freely, give hugs, and receive them as well—meaningful gestures that communicate love and concern. I realize that I walk among many friends, and most do not know that I sat there among them today and wondered, again, if I had cancer. I am doing well with my spirit, staying as positive as I can. I pray and I hope—hope for once that I could have a good report. Then I remind myself that it is His will, and not mine. Come Tuesday, I pray I will have the grace and humility to accept the news—whatever it may be.

There was no report following this entry. So once again, I'm assuming that no news was good news. Another school year began with early morning devotions and exercise, forty-five student advisees, and a return to the church bell choir and Stephen Ministry. In mid-September, concern about sleep and a meeting with upper administration was followed by a two-month hiatus from writing. November brought an exciting entry, followed by another lengthy break from writing. As with most of us, when we become busier than we want to be, we sometimes give up parts of our routine that are meaningful, even though we view them as valuable and necessary.

November 22, 1994. My heart is filled with joy, and my body reverberates with ecstasy. Last night Chris and Heidi informed us that we would become grandparents in July. I am so excited, and David is more excited than usual. The advent season takes on new meaning – the beauty of anticipation, of the wait, for a very special birth. Heidi looked absolutely radiant—the inner beauty that appears when a woman knows she is carrying a child. My hope and prayer is that she will have a healthy pregnancy and the baby will be born a healthy child. And I continue to pray for renewal of my own health and strength. I have a new goal now—to be healthy and well to be a most

wonderful grandma. This is exciting, and I want to take
care of me so I may be able to "grandmother." Thanks be
to God for this special news.

I clearly remember the day of telling. I was only five weeks pregnant,
but it was important for us to tell them early. I'm happy to know that I
appeared radiant because I know there was some uncertainty in my heart
as to whether or not I was ready to become a mother. The months leading
up to my positive test had been somewhat contentious. I was twenty-three
years old and out of school for a little over a year, and we had just celebrated
our first anniversary. We both had full-time jobs, but we were already in
debt and had no maternity insurance. I had hoped to go to graduate school
but had not planned well during my senior year because I was too caught
up in planning a wedding. My husband was three years older than me and
wanted to have children "while he was still young enough to enjoy them."
My mother-in-law had taken a seat in his boat and told me that, if I kept
making excuses for not having children, I would never have them! And
so, I gave in, discontinued my birth control, and expected the typical year
of letting my body cleanse itself in preparation for housing a child. In my
calculations, I got pregnant on the first try.

The pages preceding this might lend one to think I did not want to be
a mother. Sometimes when childhood is difficult and the mother-daughter
relationship is strained, women decide that parenthood is not for them, and
they choose not to accept the challenge. I knew I wanted children. I had
been babysitting since I was thirteen and had spent seven years with the
same three children. I loved them as if they were my own and affectionately
referred to them as "my kids." They had been a saving grace during some
of the most difficult years of my life. I often offered to take them when I
was not "on the clock" because they loved me, and I craved that feeling of
being needed. They were my creative and loving outlet. With them, I was
free to read and sing, draw, and laugh. I loved snuggling with them while
watching movies and even the contested bedtimes. I helped raise them and
shape them, and they are all amazing human beings today. They taught me
how to protect my flock and convinced me I was capable of motherhood.
Yes, I wanted to be a mother. In many ways I was determined to be better
than what I had experienced.

My daughter is fully aware of my reservations and has never once questioned whether she was wanted. Looking back, I see the timing was perfect because she was my mother's miracle. She was her opportunity to get it right. My mother was able to love from a place that was completely closed off when I was a child. This child gave her purpose and a will to live and thrive. They spent six short but critical years together. They were a constant for each other, and their deeply rooted connection exists hauntingly and beautifully today.

Writing in 1995 was extremely sporadic. My mother was busy teaching and advising and, for the most part, healthy. Filled with anticipation, she was focused on the positive gains she had made and kept pushing forward with a very specific purpose!

> *June 27, 1995.* I'm feeling good! I had a good doctor's report last week—the first good one in three years! No lumps, bumps, tumors, or masses, and my CD4 count was 855—up 331 points from last December! Wow! Praise the Lord! I've just accomplished something my doctor and the IU Medical School said I could not do—reverse and rebuild my CD4 count. And I did! I have consumed many herbs in the last two and a half years, and I really believe they are helpful. I have rested a lot, meditated, and eaten super nutritious food. But of most importance has been my trust in God—turning the care of my life over to Him and trusting His guidance. I want to continue to care for me. I've got grandmothering to do!!!

> *July 2, 1995.* I took both grandmothers and went to Heidi's baby shower! Oh, what a glorious time! I'm anticipating this baby with every ounce of me! I pray to God that her labor and delivery will be safe and that they will be parents of a healthy child. I long for a healthy grandchild. And I long for a happy childhood for her. Only eleven more days to due date. Will she come on time?

The morning of July 13, 1995, brought mild contractions, far enough apart that I sent Chris to work and called my mother. We were so close to the day we had all been waiting for, and I wanted her with me. It was ninety-five degrees outside, but we still went for several walks, trying to goose this baby along. Twelve hours later, Mom went home, and we headed to the hospital. My contractions were about five minutes apart but not painful, my water had not broken, and the hospital staff wanted to send me home.

Nope! I was there, it was my due date, and I was having a baby! An internal monitor led to the slow leakage of amniotic fluid, increasingly painful contractions, and an unplanned epidural at 2:00 a.m. Jordan Taylor arrived into her father's hands at 4:49 a.m. on July 14. Chris had been an EMT for several years. He had saved countless lives but had never brought one into this world. Our OBGYN agreed that, as long as there were no complications, he could deliver his child. As I pushed, the doctor stepped back and motioned for Chris to take his seat.

From this point on, my mother began a separate journal for Jordan. I knew this one existed, but I think my father gave it to her directly. For years it was in our home, on her bookshelf but I had never asked to read it until now. It is Jordan's sacred and prized possession, and I am honored that she allowed me to include it in this book. A few years ago, Jordan had a passage from "her journal" tattooed on her forearm in Grandma Karen's handwriting. It was my mother's powerful wish for my child.

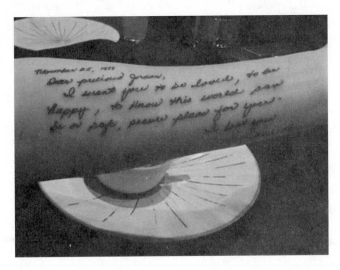

July 14, 1995 (Jordan's Journal). Jordan, what a beautiful gift! Grandpa and I went to see you in the hospital when you were ten hours old. Oh, what a beauty. You have so much beautiful dark hair, and your complexion is dark. You look like your daddy. I got to hold you, Jordan Taylor, and you slept so peacefully with your little hands right up by your face. I looked at you and marveled at the beauty and gift of creation and birth. How wondrous is God to believe in us and create us so wonderfully.

Eighteen years following this entry, I designed a tattoo for my daughter, an infinity cross with "Psalm 139" written along its base and the words "fearfully" and "wonderfully" respectively inside each arm. For years she had what seemed like an intimate connection with this Psalm. And now, reading this entry for the first time, I have chills wondering if that link was initiated on the day she was born. I share in her passion for this scriptural gift of poetry. "For you created my inmost being; you knit me together in my mother's womb. I praise you because I am fearfully and wonderfully made; your works are wonderful, I know that full well."

Jordan, I looked at you and marveled how we each create our own history. I am a grandmother—an honor to have. I realize part of me is continued in you ... I go on in another creation. What a powerful feeling!

CHAPTER TWENTY

Disappointment

I had already begun to struggle in my marriage, as my mother had feared I would. And the emotional roller coaster between mother and daughter continued alongside the disillusion of my marriage. I will be the first to admit that I was not an easy child, from becoming a teenager well into adulthood. For fifteen years, it was a constant cycle of disappointment and redemption. I was truly broken and trying to fill the void that neither of us realized she had created in me. It took me years of maturity and perspective to forgive her for something that had also been created in her. My biggest regret is that she left this earth before I found my well, the one that never runs dry. My days are not perfect, but I am whole. It took me forty-two years to find what I was looking for, and I know she would be rejoicing with me. But in this next entry, her feelings toward me were referred to as excess baggage:

> *February 21, 1996.* Ash Wednesday. This is a day of retreat and fasting. I'm using *The Ascent of the Mountain of God* as a Lenten devotional this year. The image is meaningful— today's reading begins at base camp, preparing for the journey. The question is, What do I need to get rid of to make my backpack more manageable for the forty-day journey? What is excess baggage and no longer necessary? I begin to think of these things:
>
> — *Anger*—at Heidi for being unhappy in her marriage and separation from Chris. Anger at her seeming lack of interest in motherhood. Angry, because I want her to be happy in a marriage and mothering. Angry at

her flippant flirtation with another man, especially when she says she needs to be alone. I want to shout and say, "Then give yourself the gift of being alone!"

- *Worry*—over the care of Jordan. I see her passed back and forth between parents, not sleeping every night in the same bed. I do admit I feel OK about Chris at the moment. Jordan is his prize, and he cares very deeply about her and her well-being.

- *Disappointment*—that our family isn't a "family in wholeness" anymore. I admit my happy feeling of children being married, having children, and celebrating holidays and events as a "family." Now there is a hole again. Even though I know holes can be mended, I still feel the pain of the hole—*now*! I am disappointed in a daughter who doesn't seem to follow her values from home and childhood. Chasing another man is not giving up Chris because of his values. How deep are her values, and does she block them from coming through?

- *Confusion*—about my appropriate role at this moment. I'm not clear on what Heidi wants. She asks for support, but how can I support her when I have such a clash with her values at the moment? I want her to enter counseling, to think through who she is and what she wants. But these are things I want for her. The other side of me says to hold completely back—to let her go do her own thing, and she will eventually find herself and find peace. But what happens to Jordan in the process?

- *Struggle*—with my own feelings, remembering what it was like to be unhappy, thinking about leaving, and then realizing the unhappiness was stemming from other issues in my life; and it was easy to project those feelings on other people and things. A part of me says she needs to do what she needs to do—as painful as it is to watch her from a distance.

She decided to leave anger, worry, and disappointment behind at base camp, for they were of no value on her upward journey. She chose to add "trust" to her backpack and allow for God's divine judgment in the situation. Confusion would travel with her and perhaps be emptied out along the way. Hopefully, the journey would offer clarity and lightness.

She wrote to Jordan:

February 21, 1996 - Dear Precious Jordan,

How my heart aches for you today. Last Friday your mommy called and told us that your mommy and daddy had separated. I immediately felt pain for you, a seven-month-old child, a beautiful, happy child who seemed to have everything going for her in life, and then—*bang*—two adults make an ugly decision that can only affect you forever. Jordan, I know too much about child development and early childhood days to feel anything but uncomfortable for you. You're an infant, and you desperately need two intensely caring adults who "gift" you with a sense of trust in this world. I cried for you, Jordan; I wanted to come get you, fold you in my arms, and assure you that I will remain a constant for you in your life.

I found myself to be angry with your mommy—she honestly admitted her unhappiness. However, I'm not sure she is all that unhappy with your daddy, but perhaps, unhappy with herself. Only time will tell. Your daddy loves you deeply, and you are the most important thing in his life. I trust he will take good care of you. I really know your mommy loves you, but I think she needs to sort things out. I love you deeply, Jordan, and I hope she uses this time wisely.

In the meantime, I think of you. I want the best for you, Jordan. I'm not thinking of "things" but, rather, of those gifts of security, trust, and the love of adults who are responsible for preparing you for life. You are so precious, so needy; I pray that all of us who love you so deeply can meet your most important needs. I love you, my granddaughter, and want to be a trusted constant source of guidance for you. I pray for God's arms to enfold you and protect you from the harms of this world.

I am finding that often when she wrote *about* me in her regular journal, she also wrote *to* Jordan in her special journal. When the feelings were fresh, she addressed us both. Occasionally, she expressed these words to me in person. But over and over again, her writing conveyed how I was ruining my daughter's life by choosing not to live under the same roof as her father and evoked the scars I would surely leave by not tucking her into bed each night. I distinctly remember the flood of anger when I digested these words for the first time. Perhaps this was what caused me to stop reading in 2001. She was dead, and I was so angry with her for pointing the finger at me and this choice that affected my daily involvement in the care of my child. Had she so easily forgotten the five years that she had chosen to be absent for ten weeks each summer? And how many more years had she been emotionally nonexistent? How had she installed security and trust in me as a young child? Where was her expertise then? Oh, I was furious with her, deeply hurt by her accusations; but unfortunately, I had had no recourse.

Later the same day (February 21, 1996) she reflected on her last ten years:

> On February 27, 1986, I wrote my first journal entry—the opening of myself to extreme pain and dis-ease. I was departing from holding on to fear and anger with no outlet. I chose to examine the unknown without knowing the extent of the unknown. I knew anything had to be better, and I risked opportunity to face the ghosts of my past. Ten years—a long time to struggle. But through that time I have come to journey through the streets of anger, fear, bitterness, abandonment, disbelief, courage, hope, illness, and now forgiveness. I was cautioned to begin the journey with the first small step and encouraged to

"trust the process." I listened to these wise people, and even though the hint of ten years' time to heal seemed formidable, I didn't abandon the journey, even though I considered forgetting the whole thing many times. My counselor had the audacity to, at one time, tell me I would be grateful for this experience and someday give thanks for it. How absurd at the time, and yes, he was correct. For now, I reflect on the struggle and gain wisdom from the pearls of struggle—those moments of pain and discomfort that, once examined and polished, connect and offer beauty to my life.

March 20, 1996. The first day of spring, and a blanket of snow covers the ground. The world beckons me to wonder anew at the simplicity and beauty of fresh snow. Snow is symbolic, representing cleanliness and freshness. I am reminded of Heidi and Chris's decision to reconcile and work on their marriage. There is a freshness about a relationship that embodies the wanting to make it work. I, again, am not surprised. I was not surprised at their separation, and I'm not surprised at their commitment to reconciliation. My prayer has been that God would enfold this young couple in his arms and guide them in their decision-making. I trusted God for direction in their lives. I'm grateful that he has enabled them to view their relationship from a distance, see who they are and the gifts they possess—as individuals and partners in a marriage and family.

The Lenten season had always been important. But this year, following her ten-year journey, was significant. For years, she had struggled internally with the idea of being anointed and the act of confession it would require. My mother had made great strides in her spiritual health and was working diligently toward forgiveness. What was it that remained in her way of asking to be anointed? This year, the struggle spoke to her, and what she heard was shocking to me.

My mother felt she had committed adultery! Through ten years of therapy, recognizing the violent abuses of power she had endured, she was still harboring a sense of responsibility. Sadly, her vision remained corrupted, as she viewed these unwanted sexual encounters as adulteress acts against my father. In my mind, it was absurd to consider this adultery or something that required confession and repentance. No one would agree with her, but I'm sure she told no one. She felt the lack of confession had been a barrier, not only in her relationship with God, but also in her wholeness and health. And so she confessed the sin of adultery, no matter the circumstances, and prayed for healing in all areas of her brokenness. I certainly hope she listened when her Creator told her her confession was unnecessary.

Following the anointing she wrote, "The burden, like Saul's scales, began to fall from my shoulders ... I was ready to experience the death and resurrection."

Life in 1996 was, for a lack of a better word, good. She was sometimes too busy with work, teaching, and newly directing the honors program. She was spending days playing with Jordan and had taken on a new endeavor of writing to a death row inmate. What could this woman *not* do? She had been able to maintain healthy blood counts, and her energy was rebounding to the point of being overzealous at times.

In June, she wrote an entry about her impatience, wanting something now, and the stress it caused. I love her honesty about needing control and wanting things now, but my favorite sentence reads, "I recall when I was sick, it was my goal to get well *now*." It brings tears to my eyes that she no longer considered herself to be sick. After years of physical illness, depression, and at times a daily weighing of the value and continuation of her life, she was finally seeing herself as well.

> *June 29, 1996.* I am filled with joy. Good news from my blood work this week—all tests in the normal ranges. I'm deeply grateful for what I've learned about myself—my abilities and limitations, my strengths and weaknesses, my fears and joy. God has taught me the meaning of patience,

of questioning, and of listening. And most of all, he taught me to confront myself, and surrender my truth and pain to him. In doing so, he taught me that grace is the soul of struggle. I have, indeed, been graced by his enduring love and patience. And because of that, he taught me that illness can be a friend, not an enemy. Illness is a powerful speaker, and I've learned to listen. Thank you, God, for this gift you have so freely given me. I am loved deeply, and in turn, I've learned to love more deeply ...

August 18, 1996. Heidi, Chris and Jordan came to visit. It was great to see Jordan walk and hear her talk! Her hair is getting longer—and curls! I felt good about Heidi and Chris. They've worked on a budget and have plans to be out of debt by the end of next year (1997). They've started a savings account. They're attending church—and are doing a number of positive, healthy things together. I hear more *we* as they talk—a good sign. They appear to give much attention to Jordan and seem to enjoy the parenting role. I sense they've learned many things this past year and have gained from their mistakes. I pray God will continue to grace them with love and understanding as they journey together in marriage.

August 21, 1996. I come to the end of another journal book, and I wonder, Have I written anything of value? Why am I drawn to write in the morning? From within, I am drawn to see my thinking and then ponder upon those thoughts. The journal is my close friend—probably the only one I've shared my most personal thoughts with.

This is one of my favorite entries. It was the end of her fourteenth journal, documenting more than ten years of her life. And yet, she questioned if she had written anything of value. Oh, Mother, if you only knew the insightful gift you have blessed me with and the lives that will change because of your words. I am eternally grateful that I, too, am drawn to see my thoughts on paper. Affectionately, she acknowledged the intimate relationship between herself and her journals, the friendship that had endured her innermost sentiments, which were later entrusted to me.

> *November 19, 1996.* A dreary sky mirrored the feelings inside my body. I was drawn to the piano and played several songs from my teenage piano lesson years. I was lifted by the sound and impressed with how easily the music was there, without touch or practice for the last few decades. For the last several mornings, I've gone to the piano for soothing my busy soul. When I leave the piano, I wonder why I never pursued it further— a regret that I didn't follow a talent. I now ponder the desire to take lessons again—to feel the spirit inside, the one that speaks to my tired, busy soul.

Toward the end of the year, she wrote repeatedly about her love for writing and playing the piano. Both were expressions of that which mattered deeply to her. In January she contacted one of the Fort Wayne newspapers and offered her interest in writing a guest column regarding children, parenting, and early childhood. Her offer was accepted, of course. She began to write and was published for the first time in March 1997.

> *January 13, 1997.* I ponder the possibility of acceptance. What all would this mean? Certainly, a new road to travel—reading, writing, self-discovery. I've realized, when I risk writing publicly, I become vulnerable to outside comments of all colors. Some moments, I shake with the thought of this; others, I bask in the joy of the challenge of learning, working with words, and releasing those words and thoughts hidden in the crevices of my soul.

February 3, 1997. Today I write. I've set aside my myriad of thoughts and organized them in five hundred words. This is a new venture. I wonder where it might lead, if anywhere. I have always wanted to write, and I wanted to be pushed and nurtured in this way. Beyond my own personal growth, this is an opportunity to give to others—others who I'll never see but may, in some small way, touch some parent or teacher's life. I have so much inside me. Can I organize my thoughts and give myself a voice? Something stirs deep within. I've touched and breathed life into a core of my being, a well full of words and ideas in need of being brought to the surface. I relish the opportunity to explore this newly opened door. I have no predictions. Perhaps self-satisfaction is sufficient.

These words are so familiar and could easily be my own. In so many ways my mother and I operate from the same essence. We are intrinsically the same person. For the past few years, I have been itching and overflowing with the desire to tell this story, but I kept putting it back on the shelf. I have been haunted by her request, preceded by the words that eventually came true. I always knew it would be my calling to honor her story in all of its ugliness and beauty. It's been twenty years since I first read her words, "If I should die, I want my story to be shared." But I don't think she's disappointed in my timeline. She knew I would need to work through my fears and hesitations, that I would have to be comfortable enough in my own skin to allow myself complete vulnerability. This story is as relevant today as it was then. I am her vessel, and the timing needed to be my own. I am now organizing my thoughts and giving *her* a voice.

CHAPTER TWENTY-ONE

Days of Grace

She wrote:

> *March 17, 1997.* "From what we get, we can make a living; what we give, however, makes a life" (Arthur Ashe).
>
> The virtue of forgiveness creeps into my mind lately—at first without invitation, and now with will … I'm haunted about my own trouble with forgiveness. I'm struck with the intense desire to be well. And for the first time, I have a deep desire to give attention to the need to let go of hatred toward my father, my abuser, and myself. I'm in a new place, and I know it and sense it.

With her continued desire for healing and wholeness came the reemergence of forgiveness. Two years after her initial entry on forgiveness, she circled back with a similar frame of mind but possibly a new perspective. She had achieved the unlikely; she'd reversed her blood counts and increased her energy. She was living her dream as a grandmother and wanted to feel complete. There was no action, but the desire for the act took up residency in her heart again.

Spring 1997 brought a multitude of significant newness. Growing her hair long had been on her annual goal list for the last several years. The hair at that time represented the rebirth of her inner child. Unfortunately, it was also present during her dark struggle with CFS. Cutting it felt symbolic of an uncovering, the anticipation that the end of the darkness was approaching. She felt light, pretty, young and was bursting with urgency and determination to show the world the new Karen, released following a long dormant period.

My father retired in May after thirty years of teaching. She wrote the following words in his honor. I don't recall, but what a crime if these were not spoken aloud at his retirement party.

> *May 28, 1997.* David has such a reverence for life—one that reflects his spiritual nature, one that exudes harmony with all living plants, animals, including humans. David lives what he teaches and teaches what he lives. He is genuine and sincere. This man is as he is. No cover-up. What he believes, he believes deeply. What he is, he is to the core of his being.

On June 5, 1997, my niece, Madeline Grace, entered the world with healthy lungs. Another grandchild for my mother. She wrote about her valuable and precious time bonding with my brother and his new family, and then came a weekend with Jordan. These words strike with a punch and then linger with fragments of jealousy. My brother and I missed out on her "presence" in our childhood, but she brought it in full force for our children.

> *June 14, 1997.* I grandmothered—read, played, sang, rocked—all those wonderful things I've always wanted to do. Life (and work) comes to a stop when grandchildren arrive. It's far more important to *do* and *be with* and *build* relationships with grandchildren than to do housework! That can always wait! Growing up in love with grandchildren requires every available minute of our "presence" with each other.

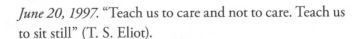

> *June 20, 1997.* "Teach us to care and not to care. Teach us to sit still" (T. S. Eliot).

In reference to this quote, she wrote about a friend from church who had recently been diagnosed with breast and spinal cancer, her life expectancy reduced. She would need to learn to "sit still" as she faced the reality of her illness, let go, and then let go some more. Mom's opportunity to "sit still" arrived just shy of a month later. As usual, just when she felt like true healing was in reach, the bottom fell out.

July 16, 1997. Started my day with a visit to the doctor to review all my blood test results. What a surprise. My expectations were high because I feel so much better—more energy, stamina, riding my bike and walking, even "forgetting" to take a nap on a couple occasions. All my blood tests were in the normal range, except CD4 and CD8s. My CD4s dropped in the past year from 575 to 491—84 points! And my CD8s, which we've never measured before, were 278, low for the normal range of 150–1,000. In the past years with my CD4 count above 500, the doctor had phrased his comments like, "You may be one of those people with a lower CD4 count"—meaning normal for me. This time was different. His words were framed in phrases like, "When your counts reach 200, you'll start with two meds. Then at 100, you add three more. Then at 50, you'll add three more." I noted the somberness in his voice and the change in his word choice ... The "when you" was prominent. The words pierced my soul like a serrated knife.

It was a busy day, and the feelings went below the surface. I'll deal with them later.

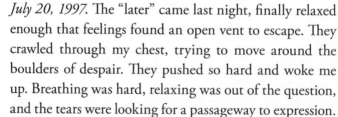

July 20, 1997. The "later" came last night, finally relaxed enough that feelings found an open vent to escape. They crawled through my chest, trying to move around the boulders of despair. They pushed so hard and woke me up. Breathing was hard, relaxing was out of the question, and the tears were looking for a passageway to expression. After failed attempts at reconciling the parts of my body, I yielded to tears—full of worry, despair, and grief. I felt like I couldn't find a way out of this despair.

Something was different this time. She had been able to reverse her blood counts before, but now that task seemed unachievable. Her cells had rebounded a year ago, and even though she looked good and felt good, they were now headed in the wrong direction. She described it as her immune system continuing to self-destruct. The tone and the phrasing had become negative, somehow terminal, and the focus was no longer on improving her counts but, rather, on maintaining her health while they continued to drop. Healing would not be hers after all.

In August 1997, Mom wrote Matt and I a six-page letter spelling out her current health status to make sure we understood her medical diagnosis and what she could do to protect her body, as well as her well-being. In a disappointed tone, she wrote that her spirit of feeling better had been deceiving and went on to map out her blood counts and how they compared to the normal ranges. Ingrained in my mind will always be the day she told me that she had counts similar to a person with AIDS but without the disease. She had no illness, no disease, just an abnormal immune system. In the letter, she described changes she would make to strengthen her defenses and precautions she could take to limit her exposure to unwanted germs. She would not set up walls where they weren't needed but would heighten her awareness, especially around students and the grandchildren. Shining through was always her determination and hope.

> *August 11, 1997.* I have no clue to the probable length of my life (do any of us??) but I know that those people who take charge of their lives in an effort to live long actually do live longer lives than those who give up. There is no giving up here! And of course, I plan to live out my childhood dream of living to be as old as my great-great uncle, who lived to be 104. Dad says I'm stubborn and determined enough that I will probably make it! Hey, I set my life goals high!

In November, she attended a women's retreat and allowed herself to be led into the radiance of sisterhood. As the group joined and began to interact, she sensed the invitation to share. It was her time, and she ventured forth, taking the lid off the tiny box that had stored her secret for so long. Her story was no longer one of sexual abuse, fear, and depression but, rather, the lonely truth about her health—the secret that, for over five years, she had been slowly dying of an AIDS-like condition. In her journal, she listed the names of her twelve new sisters. A few of them were very dear, influential people to me as well. She wrote:

> I spoke with ease and calm, knowing and trusting the wisdom of my sisters as I was guided through the story. I was drenched with relief, as if new energy was released throughout my being. My story gained support ... I have attained a new level of wealth.

Reading about this particular time in her life consumed me with emotion. As a family, we were aware of the CFS diagnosis, the low blood counts, and the need for extra rest. But when she referred to it as her secret, she painted a different picture. Once again, she had chosen to remain quiet and internalize her story. Revealing her chronic tiredness might have appeared as a sign of weakness. In today's world, to be immunocompromised is not unusual. But in the 1990s, the lack of warrior blood cells carried a negative connotation. It was a lonely, incurable disease with an unclear therapeutic regimen. It was barely understood in the medical field, and from the outside it may have been perceived as something she had brought on herself by her choices to overextend. Until I read the sentence that, for over five years, she had been quietly dying of an AIDS-like condition, I didn't absorb the gravity of her illness and what it had done to her spirit. My mother knew fear, and it came in all shapes and sizes. But for five years, she had lived alone with the real fear that a common cold could possibly take the life she had worked so diligently to save.

December brought the semiannual blood work, and the news was not good. The CD4 count dropped by 75, and the CD8s had lost half their army. She was dangerously low in both areas. More extensive tests were ordered, as was another consult with Indiana University Medical Center for Infectious Disease and Immunology. More waiting. She described it as "numb with glimpses of grief ... moving forward, knowing each day is precious in the midst of the unknown."

New Year's Eve brought the annual declaration of goals. This year, she qualified them as physical, social/emotional, mental, and spiritual and then probed into what might be on the horizon for this unusual year:

> *December 31, 1997.* I wonder what is ahead of me regarding physical health. Low CD4s and CD8s—what will that bring? And a lump in my breast—any need to be alarmed? I realize my goals are nothing spectacular, barely anything beyond the usual. What does this say about me? I feel rather unexcited, kind of blah, unmoving. I am aware of the feeling or, maybe better stated, lack of feeling! I wonder what my body is telling me, and I wonder what to do to recharge myself. It's not common for me to be so unconcerned by a lack of luster in my life. Perhaps the lack of spiritual discipline has taken its toll. Or is there a subconscious knowing of something to come? I'm perplexed but not discouraged. I just sense a difference—a lack—this year. I generally have a sense of my body's signals—and I wonder ...
>
> Wonder is not a bad thing. I continue to wonder, question, and ponder what the new year will bring. In all my questioning, answers and new direction will come, for I believe that the dullness of today will yield to a luster of tomorrows.
>
> People often questioned Arthur Ashe if he asked, "Why me? Why did I get AIDS?" His beautiful response: "If I were to say, 'God, why me?' about the bad things, then I should have said, 'God, why me?' about the good things that happened in my life."

CHAPTER TWENTY-TWO

Breast Cancer

I have read these journals multiple times, often attempting to consume their contents from a different perspective. As I read now and set the scene chronologically in my mind, I recognize that the next twelve months were filled to the brim with loss and affliction. She ended the last journal questioning the presence of another lump in her breast and the role it would play in the upcoming year. And the first page of the new journal stated, "I presently feel that my cup is almost empty."

Before the biopsy even took place came this devastating entry:

> *January 7, 1998.* My heart aches; the tears flow—in grief for our church that burned this morning. I am stunned to think the building is no longer there. My mind recalls memories—Sunday School as a child, my baptism when I was thirteen, our wedding on such a miserably hot day, our children's dedication, their youth activities, the play *Joseph,* being commissioned for Nigeria, Stephen Ministry, teaching the college Sunday school classes, bells—many hours of ringing. And just last Sunday, I was a Communion server. And now the place for them is gone, stored only in my mind forever. What a treasure! In a day of sorrow, memories and my faith live on.
>
> What is God teaching me? To trust the teaching of life, to hold fast to my faith, and to look creatively at the future. Fire can destroy a building but fuels the growth of my faith.

I remember the phone call from her and the heartbreak on my end. It was the only church I had ever known. I drove home a few days later to walk the perimeter block and bask in my own memories of this sacred place. Who knows if this would be allowed to happen today, but once the fire was determined to be accidental (an electrical short in the water heater), small groups were organized to tour the rubble. My mother was chosen to be a guide, and she was honored to lead her brothers and sisters through the charred skeleton of the building. The cloudless sky was now the roof, but the cross remained seemingly untouched. As she looked out over the sanctuary, she was unable to find our second-row pew; those familiar places and spaces were gone. Nothing was familiar; only the presence of God remained.

A week later, I accompanied her to the hospital for her biopsy. Due to her deficient immune system, her surgeon had opted for a needle biopsy, only to conclude that she was too thin! The threat of puncturing her chest cavity was apparently more severe than that of infection with an incision. They would have to reschedule. And again, we would wait. Fibrocystic breast disease had plagued her for years. Lump after lump had been removed, along with surrounding tissue—to the point where there was virtually nothing left. So far, there had been no sign of cancer, and we were hopeful for the same result.

My father was in Florida for a seminar, and she had chosen *me* to be with her today, so we were not about to waste it. A two-hour lunch and shopping—it was a rare, magical mother-daughter day!

On January 16, we were back at the hospital, but there was no magic in this day. We arrived early, waited nearly two hours to go into surgery, and then waited again to go home. She was happy to be home. But by bedtime, the first of our fears had come true; she had developed a fever. Her warm body was already attempting to fight an infection.

> *January 22, 1998.* A day that will change my life forever. I learned that I have breast cancer. The news hit hard, with a thud. I was home alone. I cried and then called my friend Susan. I had to talk to someone—now! David came home, and we cried together.

The afternoon consisted of trips to the surgeon and doctor. Both were encouraging about the prognosis but emphasized that her first task was to recover from the respiratory infection she was still battling. Her body did not have the ability to fight more than one thing at a time. Another surgery was scheduled to remove the malignancy and would be followed by six weeks of radiation. She was told under no circumstances was she to teach spring term. The teacher in her seemed to have a more difficult time swallowing this news than the fact that she had cancer.

Next came the telling. She had quietly worn the robe of chronic fatigue syndrome for years. It was a disease she had been able to almost secretly navigate without involving much of the outside world. Cancer was different. She needed to not be alone in this. As she told others about the diagnosis, her blessings multiplied, and her community began to grow.

> *Later on January 22.* Without application, today I joined a very privileged group of women - sisters with breast cancer. It's a group I would not choose to join, but now that I'm inducted, I will walk with and learn from those who have journeyed ahead of me on this path.

> *February 10, 1998.* Cancer—I realize I don't think about it very much, and I wonder why? Am I in denial yet to really believe it? Or am I in acceptance and tend to respond, "OK, I have cancer. What do I do next?" I really don't want cancer to become the focus of my life. Rather, I prefer to view my life as back to the drafting stage—drawing, or redrawing, the plans for my life. Here's a new chance to select the colors and design of my future years. I remain optimistic—here's a time to carve and create anew. Why should I be afraid? But every now and then, I just wonder if I'm fighting a losing battle.

> *February 18, 1998.* My life is a traipsing from one doctor to another right now. I hate this. Tears fall from my eyes so easily, so uncontrolled … I feel unable to control my life

or my feelings. Today at the hospital, I felt cornered and unable to get out. I couldn't handle any decision making. I'm not used to being or feeling distraught! Gosh, my only reaction was to cry and cry some more, and then I placed myself in the arms of God.

⊗

March 14, 1998. "Record my misery; list my tears on your scroll" (Psalm 56:8).

Radiation began. Questions abounded, with very few answers. She was wrestling with the feelings of emptiness and solitude, versus the conceptual beauty that both allow. That she'd thought the cup empty at the beginning of the year now seemed humorous. She hadn't known what empty was at that point! I still love the imagery of the amber goblet and am reminded that emptiness provides us the opportunity to be filled at our own will, with the "wine" of our choosing. Solitude, on the other hand, sets aside time for us to be quiet and to listen to the still, small voice of God.

I struggle with looking back to this time and feeling like I did not participate fully in this portion of her journey. I wish I could have been in a place to minister to her as I would now; however, regret is not a part of my master plan. I wish I had been in a position to play a bigger role, but I could only function within my limits. I know she had an entire community willing to be by her side. I was twenty-seven, living an hour away with an almost three-year-old, a failing marriage, and a fifty-hour-a-week job. I just wish my world could have stopped and given me the opportunity to simply be present with her. I wish I could have driven her to treatment, held her hand when she was scared, and prayed with her for God's healing hands to caress her spirit and mend her broken body. I want to think I did what I could as I maintained my own selfish survival mode. It was a difficult time to do more.

Grandchildren are often the best medicine, and I did take Jordan to visit as much as possible. I love how my mother speaks to Jordan in her journal as she recounted their days together. There was no "emptiness" in their time.

March 15, 1998 (Jordan's Journal). You came to visit Grandpa and me today—joining us for lunch and play. This was a special visit today. You came with your mommy and daddy to spend some time with me. You see, Jordan, I have breast cancer and am currently receiving radiation treatment. I'm not feeling too well, yet I'm well enough that I wanted to spend time with you. You and I sat in the big blue rocking chair, and I, or should I say *you* read stories to me. Your favorites—*Brown Bear, Brown Bear, Goodnight Moon,* and others. You slid your finger along the words as you read them. You are well on your way to reading!

As you sat on my lap, your head kept resting on my chest—and I kept moving it to a more comfortable position for me—but you would immediately slide it back. I finally gave up and just hurt! Later, you asked for a drink. I sat you on the counter amid your pleas of, "I do it," and you poured the remainder of the orange juice into a cup. You then looked in the empty carton and said, "Grandma, we need to buy you some more orange juice." I was impressed by your maturity of thinking beyond "all gone!"

When I started writing this book, my writing coach said, "Show, don't tell. Instead of telling me about something, paint me a picture." My mother was an expert at painting the picture. Sometimes it was the literal description, and I could visibly see her. At other times, it was the metaphor causing me to tangibly feel what she was going through. In both senses, this gift of her writing has enabled me to journey alongside her more than twenty years later.

March 26, 1998. This morning was a time of pain at treatment. I have a bad cold, one that leaves me with a stuffed cotton head feeling. Miserable! When I lay down on the table for my treatment, I couldn't breathe through my nose. I was so uncomfortable—and alone. The tears ran uncontrollably down my hairline and into my ears.

Breathing became more labored, and I just cried. The technician noticed my distress and halted the treatment until I calmed myself. She indicated I had to calm myself because my heavy breathing altered the line-up of my body for the radiation. She didn't rush me, and she acknowledged my behavior as OK, but I needed more at the moment. I needed an expression of care! Afterward, I retreated to the dressing room, pulled the curtain, and cried quietly ...

My body is battling so much at the moment—a difficult cold, cancer, and radiation. I feel so spent, like soggy coffee grounds once the water has run through and yielded an aromatic cup. I have so little to give right now; my needs are great. Today, it is not difficult to believe I have cancer.

Good or bad, this is an image that resonates with me daily as I empty my saturated coffee grounds into the trash. Since my first reading, this has remained one of my favorite passages, not for the painful image it conveys but for the beauty of her words in the shadow of her discomfort.

The eagle also became a significant image in her treatment process. Early in her diagnosis, she described her cancer cells as old wounds. As her body—marked with different colored circles and squares—lay on the cold, hard table, she would visualize an eagle swooping down to gather the cells and carry them away in its clutches. When the machine turned on, the eagle would make multiple trips taking off from the cliff, soaring through the light of the radiation beam, landing gently on her chest, clutching the cancer cells, and flying away to the sand dune bluff to bury them in a hole. Not only was the eagle disposing of the cancer, it was also extracting the old wounds from her being, giving her the capacity to heal. This process happened automatically, without forced thought, claiming her illness and giving potential for transformation.

CHAPTER TWENTY-THREE

Irene and the Organ

Dear God, I need to serve you within the womb of my faith again

—J.S. Bach

My mother continued to dream:

April 3, 1998. I dream about my capabilities as a pianist and, yes, organist. I pray for courage to follow my soul and let my dream carry me. I feel potential in the womb, a stirring, and I want to explore and use my gifts as an expression of creativity and thoughtfulness to God.

Sometimes we invite people into our lives with no idea what they will bring or the impact they might have. For the past several years, playing the piano had been on my mother's annual list of goals for the new year. She had practiced and played on her own and even taken a few lessons, but nothing had led her close to who she dreamed she could be.

April 6, 1998. I did it! I called Irene to talk with her about piano lessons ... Gosh, what have I done? What have I gotten myself into? Is this an opening of the door in my wilderness? Oh, I'm excited and scared! I hope this is a beneficial adventure for me. Maybe this experience and relationship will be a blessing for me.

My parents had met Irene and her husband while volunteering during a telethon for a local radio station. As they conversed and got to know each other, Mom learned that Irene was the organist for her church and also gave lessons. Irene didn't play just any organ; hers was a magnificent pipe organ, played for a sizable congregation, in addition to her position with the local philharmonic orchestra. She was a professional, but my mother was not intimidated by her; she felt an emotional connection as well. As she neared the end of her radiation, it was time to reach for something new and positive, and Irene brought both of these to the table.

> *April 7, 1998.* I think I met my soulmate—Irene. I met her this morning at her church. She immediately put me at ease. We walked to a small café around the corner and had coffee. We talked about my dreams and desires regarding music and cancer. It was an authentic hour—a right-to-the-heart kind of talk. We discussed composers and types of music—serious talk. We walked back to the church, and then she invited me to play the pipe organ. She showed me how to get started and then left me alone in the sanctuary—alone with this instrument and God! I thought I was in heaven today—playing hymns for an hour in a church, on a pipe organ. What a dream come true. And I will learn to play this instrument! A smile adorned my face all the way home, and I knew I had pursued this dream for a reason.

Three more days of radiation treatment to go, and she was feeling genuinely renewed. The smile had not left her face from her day with Irene, and she was overflowing with anticipation—dreaming of the expression and creativity this relationship would bring. If there was one thing my mother was not, it was complacent. It's not that she was never content, but she had an innate desire to do more. She had her moments of stillness and quiet, usually due to poor health. But as soon as she was on the rebound, she was ready to push forward, learn something new, or pursue a challenge. Abuse throughout her life had left her with a deeply rooted need to continually prove her worth. Early abuse had taught her that her worth was limited to the desires of others and that being a "good girl" was measured in remaining quiet. Through her abuse as an adult, her voice was still stifled, but she counteracted her objectivity with education, establishing her worth in other areas. Being a student of anything gave her forward vision, and mastering a new skill gave her confidence. Good health was on the horizon; her passion for music and admiration of Irene had created the perfect storm.

> *April 10, 1998.* A Good Friday unlike any other—a special one I'll never forget. My radiation treatments are complete … I have crossed another hurdle. Emotion welled up in me today—many tears and deep sighs. I believe, unknowingly, I steeled myself up for this six-week experience—I knew I had to do it. I had to persevere. I could not let it overcome me. Rather, I had to accept it; work with it; live with it; and, yes, even love it. Treatments became a part of me. I felt and wore the effects—green and purple lines, tapes, X's, the whole bit. And I knew I could do it, not because I wanted or chose to, but because I had to. I wanted to survive, and I put forth so much energy—to face it and learn from it. Like the disease itself, treatment is lonely, save for the loving staff at the center. But in my own loneliness, I had the desire to survive. It's a journey only another cancer, or breast cancer person can understand.

> *April 12, 1998.* Easter Sunday, "When Resurrection becomes Personal." This is the first year I've sensed the meaning of resurrection. Easter has always been difficult for me to grasp—nothing tangible and always leaving me with a sense of emptiness. And I approach this year with total emptiness—a compilation of lessons in the last few weeks and a sense of where God is in all of this. God seemed so distant. Through imaging with the eagle during radiation I was surprised at what came to my consciousness—the voice, calling me to let go of these thoughts, behaviors, feelings that have imprisoned me.

And in so doing, I have been able to experience new life—a life where I know more intimately the forgiveness that has been difficult for me. Through the letting go of the past, I experienced forgiveness and the door opened. I could feel hope, light, and promise for new life, renewed energy, and strength. "And He will lift you up on eagle's wings, bear you on the breath of dawn, make you shine like the sun and hold you in the palm of His hand."

For over ten years, she had been praying for a resurrection, although I wonder at what point she felt like she had "died." Had her childhood self died as a toddler in the predawn hours of darkness? Had this death made her vulnerable to a second death in a dingy hotel room in Florida? How many times can you metaphorically meet your demise and still continue to live, let alone regain your worth and excel? My mother was the ultimate overcomer, by far the most remarkable person I have ever known. She never liked battle terms in regard to illness, but she was the quintessential warrior. Instead of fighting *against* chronic fatigue syndrome and cancer, she journeyed with them. She did, however, fight with her will and her faith—*for* her life.

> *June 16, 1998.* My last two piano lessons have ended with the urge to cry. Why? Irene pushes me into expression—interpretation of the music I'm playing—pushing me to think what the composer meant by writing something in a certain way. What did he intend? Good grief, I don't know! I feel so dumb! So illiterate when it comes to music. I don't like to not know. And when I don't know, then I'm at a loss as to how to express the what! I play music without much expression because I myself am empty of expression. Empty. Stiff. Expressionless. Devoid of feeling. And then Irene referred to me as Robot-Karen. And that hurt—deep inside. Her words touched a tender point—a part of me that recognizes a truth about myself.
>
> I am indeed cold, stiff, robot-like. I know from previous encounters in counseling that I am bland when

it comes to matters of heartfelt expression. I am made of steel armor. I know I became that way as a child to survive incest and, later, to survive rape and the threat of continued rapes—and the threat of what would happen if I told anyone.

That's in my past and lends explanation, but doesn't help me today ... I am reminded that, perhaps, I don't let go enough. The resistance to let go—as if it protects me—remains with me. So, do I need it for a sense of safety? To protect myself from becoming vulnerable? To protect myself from feeling the hurt and pain? I realize that, in my stiffness, I avoid *all* kinds of feeling—not to the extent I used to. But still the lack of feeling is apparent in my life, and now it haunts me in my piano and organ lessons. I come face-to-face with more "growing work" to do. And I want to be done, to be over it.

Easter may have been a resurrection of sorts, the birth of a new creation, but she quickly realized her healing was not complete. She admitted she could give up working on herself and still survive fairly well but then asked, "Why survive fairly well?" There is a wealth of possibilities within and beyond the tomb. There is an unfinishedness to our lives when we seek all that it has to offer. Words that I choose to live by—"Jesus meets us right where we are, but he loves us too much to leave us there." We are all "works in progress," and with all the work she had done in her life, there was still more to do. Her need to resist feeling was part of her armor. But it was her unfinished business, the piece in her mind, that was not done yet. The piano and organ would be her keys to expression. This door would not unlock easily; but commitment, discipline, and desire would lead her in her quest for wholeness and her eventual surrender to emotion.

June 22, 1998. The feelings at the piano—I'm trying to make sense of them—tears; urges to cry; and last night my rising from bed and kneeling at the piano bench, sobbing! I had prayed to open myself, to let go the bonds of fear— of whatever it is that keeps me paralyzed in expression.

God has given me the desire to play and the gift of Irene to teach me. It is my challenge to let go of the resistance— to become what I dream of being at the piano, a pianist who can play with heartfelt expression, a self with no restrictions or limitations. It is my ambition to allow my soul to take me where I dream of going.

August 14, 1998. Scared ... anxious ... gut-aching raw ... these are feelings I know today, as I have my first three-month check up with my oncologist. I want ... and need ... to have a good report.

And I got the good report!

CHAPTER TWENTY-FOUR

Dear Karen

But those who hope in the Lord will renew their strength.
They will soar on wings like eagles; they will run and not
grow weary, they will walk and not be faint.

—Isaiah 40:31

The eagle remained a feature in her quest for healing:

> *August 16, 1998.* Someday I will mount on wings as eagles
> do, I'll run and not grow weary, I'll walk and not faint.
> I will be strong because I choose to walk through rather
> than around difficult things.
>
> David and I are reading *Forgiveness: How to Make*
> *Peace with Your Past and Get on with Your Life.* The author
> suggests writing a letter to myself from the person(s) who
> hurt me. Write what I want to hear—and deserve to
> hear. Well, I have more than one letter to write, and I
> realize I am postponing the writing. But here I am—a
> retreat day—confronted with the reality that, if I don't do
> this today, it will hang on me as a leaded weight. And I
> cannot afford that. I need to let go of that which keeps me
> chained, tied up, and tired. I know there is relief beyond;
> it's just getting to the beyond.

She had written undelivered letters before, but this was different. It
is often cathartic to write what you need to say even though the words
will never be read by the intended recipient. It's the process of getting
something "off your chest" that needs to be verbalized, released, and then

discarded. These letters were delivered as she wrote and she received what she had needed to hear for years. She, as the author, would be required to have a bit of unconventional acceptance, knowing the people who hurt her would never compose these letters. But as she wrote, she heard the perfect apologies and received healing word by word. As usual, she wrote with purpose, chose her words carefully, and then reread the letters to herself—as if they had arrived in the mailbox. She allowed herself time to digest them; to soak their messages into her soul; and to release the pains that had been harbored and compounded, one on top of another, nearly all her life.

Dear Karen,

This letter is long overdue to you. I've thought about writing many different times but lacked the courage to put my thoughts in writing.

I'm writing to apologize for what I did to you when you were a young child. You were only four when I started coming into your bedroom and molesting you. I know I must have scared you—I was so big, and you were so little. You were a pretty little girl with long pigtails, and I just wanted to love you. I now realize that what I did to you, and what I made you do, was inappropriate. I hurt you—I hurt you very badly. I know that my actions affected you as you were growing up and have affected your attitudes and feelings about sex as a married woman. I realize you have gone through painful counseling to deal with this that cost you a great deal of money.

I apologize to you, for the pain, suffering, and trauma I've caused you. I was wrong, absolutely wrong! I made a grave mistake and did bad things to you. I've never told anyone until now—in this letter. I wanted to be a good parent, and I didn't know that what I did to you was hurting you—then—and still does. I know in that respect, I was not a good father to you. I apologize for my wrong actions. I wish I could go back and redo my fatherly

157

role with you and for you. Unfortunately, I can't. But I want you to know I acknowledge my wrong behavior and the pain I've caused in your life.

Love,
Dad

Dear Kari,

I didn't realize that, when you told me things when you were four, you were really crying out to me for help. I remember when you sat on my lap and asked, "What does it mean when a man sticks his 'thing' in your mouth?" I thought you were a curious child. And yes, I remember I told you that men and women do things like that when they love each other—particularly when they want to make babies! Gosh, I'm sure my words scared you far more than they helped. Plus, I never thought about why you would ask me that question. I thought you were too young to know—let alone to have that happening to you by your own father. It never occurred to me you were trying to tell me something terrible in your limited four-year-old way. You needed me to be there for you—to listen to you and respond to your needs. And I didn't do any of that for you. I really let you down and failed you at a critical time.

Moreover, I closed a door in communication. You never felt free to come back to tell me or ask me anymore. Instead, you endured your dad's behavior in silence—without having a mom who could have listened to you and acted on your behalf to make your life safer. I apologize—I'm truly sorry—for letting you down and failing to respond to you. I thought I was being a good mom for you, and I really missed caring for you when you were hurting.

I now understand why you seemed to pull away from me and become a quiet child who never cried. I abandoned you when you needed me most. I'm sorry I didn't reach out to you and question you. I wish I could undo all the pain you endured because I failed to listen to you—when you were four and when, as an adult, you told me again ... and I didn't listen.

Love,
Mom

Dear Karen,

This letter is long overdue to you. I want to write and apologize for what I did to you while you worked with the Child Care Disaster Program. I always thought you wanted the relationship and didn't realize you reacted the way you did out of fear.

I apologize for taking advantage of you that night in Pensacola, Florida. I know you stayed in the bathroom a very long time. I didn't realize you were trying to figure out how to escape—and couldn't—from a second-floor room with no window. I didn't know how scared you were. I just thought you weren't good at sex! I didn't know you were awake all night—numb with fear. I really mistreated you the next day when I took you to the airport and said, "Thanks, kid."

I had many expectations of you from that night on. I fantasized and organized times we could be together so I could sleep with you again. I saw the entire relationship from my viewpoint only—never thinking you were so scared you were afraid to get out of the relationship. I now understand fear that results from being overpowered. I overpowered you in numerous ways. I used sexual power to keep you "in line" when you seemed to get so much attention from the media and Red Cross for your helpful program for children. I couldn't stand it that you got attention when I didn't. I wanted the attention and was angry when you got it. Instead of supporting you and respecting you, I devalued you by raping you repeatedly.

Now I realize that each time I subjected you to sex, I was stealing and destroying your sense of self-worth, your sexual self, and your ability to cope. When you were nonresponsive, I criticized you for being cold and distant—not once realizing I was the culprit, that I was destroying you. I apologize for my stupidity, my lack of respect for you as a woman and colleague, my out-of-control ego, and my poor judgment. Furthermore, I apologize for the hurt, pain, and sense of self-destruction I caused you. I know you've been ill—that you have cancer and have paid a very high personal price for all the trauma I have caused. I also understand you paid a great deal of money for counseling and that some of the effects remain.

I only thought of myself and my own desires. And you were the "handy person" available. When I surprised you and overpowered you, you "obeyed" me out of fear. I have taken much away from you—not only from your personal self, but from you physically, emotionally, spiritually, and sexually. My behavior toward you and other women has been very degrading, devaluing, and destructive. You have paid far too great a price for my misbehavior, poor judgment, and lack of sensitivity.

I have hurt you deeply, and I acknowledge my poor judgment and behavior. You've suffered many losses, and the church lost your dynamic contribution to young children and the world. I apologize for what I did to you and the long-term pain it has caused. I wish I could push the rewind button and do this work all over—correctly and respectfully. Alas, that is not possible.

Sincerely,
XXXX

These letters reveal the determination of a woman who wanted to be well. To write one letter would be a challenge for most of us, but to write three was a commitment to her healing. For so long, she had been controlled by her past, and now she was taking back the reigns. She would be in charge of becoming whole and healthy. Sometimes knowing what you need to hear is a gray area and formulating the right words, words that would somehow ease a lifetime of pain, would seem next to impossible. I imagine this could not have taken place earlier in her process. Being able to put words on paper from the mind of someone else and knowing exactly what they need to be takes time and growth. This was one of her final therapeutic steps. After rereading each of these letters, I noticed that her mother was the only one to say, "I'm sorry." I feel that she desperately needed those two words from her. But unfortunately, they were far too intimate for the men who had hurt her. There is a difference, and the apologies would have to suffice.

But she was not done yet. Her dedication to this process, so much of it being self-directed at this point, was remarkable. A week later she wrote a letter addressed to a specific part of herself.

Dear Self-Blaming Part of Me,

I apologize for not realizing how afraid I was and acting on that fear. I could have told someone and kept telling until I was certain I was heard. I apologize for keeping silent for six years—and more, for blaming myself all these years for thinking I caused the incest and rapes to happen. I've been so hard on me—calling myself stupid, dumb, careless, worthless, insignificant, incapable—all those horrible things! No wonder I don't think much of me. I have hurt enough. And I've caused much of the pain by not seeing myself accurately—as a victim. I've blamed myself and felt so responsible. *But I have punished myself enough!*

I have spent enough time calling myself names. I've spent enough time belittling myself—not seeing myself as worthy or important. I've spent enough time believing

I could never do or accomplish great things. I've spent enough time protecting others and keeping feelings deep inside. I've spent enough time denying myself some of the riches of life. I've cheated myself way too much—and missed out on fun, adventure, intimacy, and deep feeling. I've spent enough time holding back, doubting, fearing, refusing to believe life can be good for me. I've spent enough time seeing myself as a person with limits. I've spent enough time believing "I can't" and I don't deserve good feeling or a good life.

I used to believe that I deserved to be hurt, but now I know that I did not deserve it. I used to believe that I made the hurt happen, but now I know that it was not entirely my fault, that some or most of what happened to me I was not responsible for at all.

I used to believe that I had to carry this load of guilt and shame for the rest of my life, but now I know that I have punished myself long enough, and now I can leave the self-blaming stage.

I am a worthwhile, intelligent, talented person. I want to experience my gifts and not hold anything back. I am choosing to move forward into a life of meaning yet unknown to me because I can let go of the past.

I love you,
Karen

This final letter had to have come with a flood of emotion. To put this specific ink to paper must have been overwhelming at first and then profoundly freeing. I continue to struggle with the third paragraph. The words "entirely," "some," and "most" still leave the door open for a portion of personal responsibility. I wish that she felt complete confidence in her journey away from self-blame—that she knew she had done *nothing* to deserve what happened to her over and over again.

CHAPTER TWENTY-FIVE

My Role as a Mother

When my marriage ended, she wrote in her own journal and in Jordan's:

November 25, 1998. The phone rang after supper and Heidi announced her moving out—separating from Chris and likely divorcing. I was stunned beyond words of response. My thoughts surrounded Jordan—her need for a mommy *and* daddy in the same house, her need for some consistency, for abundant love and not needing to be jerked around between two adults who can't live together in a satisfying, productive manner. I cried and cried for Jordan—for the emptiness in her life, for the hurt and misunderstanding, for her needs that will go unmet. I feel so much pain—and helplessness is so much of my pain. There is nothing I can do in this situation to make it better. I can pray to God to fold little Jordan into his arms and protect her—to give her strength through this very difficult time. Oh God, I don't want this to be real.

November 25, 1998 (Jordan's Journal). Your mommy called tonight and shared the sad news that she and your daddy were separating. My immense thoughts were for you. I feel so sad for you, my beautiful granddaughter. I want your world to be a happy one, surrounded by the love of two parents who care so deeply for you.

I feel so angry at your parents for interrupting your life with their own incompatible issues. I'm angry at them for upsetting you, jerking you around between two homes, two schedules.

I feel afraid for you, Jordan, for having to experience this turmoil and unsettling time and space in your life. No three-year-old should have to endure the craziness of two homes and shared parenting. I am afraid that your feelings may go unnoticed and not be responded to appropriately. I worry for you—your understanding and misunderstanding, for times you may be neglected. I'm worried that your parents may buy your love or substitute it with gifts rather than themselves.

I want so much for you, Jordan. I want you to continue with your bright, curious outlook on life. You are so verbal and aware of your world. I want you to have parents who stimulate you to your full potential.

You have a gift for music, and I wish for you to have parents who recognize that gift and give you opportunity to learn and grow in music.

I want you to be loved, to be happy, to know the world can be a safe, secure place for you. I cry for you tonight—I ache for your sadness and loss. I pray that God will hold you in His grandmotherly lap and put His arms of love and security around you. May you know that, when your world seems to fall apart, God and Grandma love you dearly. Goodnight, precious one. I love you with all my heart and tears.

December 10, 1998. "Call to Me and I will answer you and tell you great and unsearchable things you do not know." (Jeremiah 33:3).

This verse was printed on the bottom of her journal page. She thought it was appropriate in regard to her feelings about me. There was so much she did not understand, but just like before, she was willing to let me go, let me find my own way instead of digging in with me to the root of my unhappiness. She prayed to God to enfold me but never came to me with an open heart asking what was hard and hidden in my life, what she did not know.

This was by far my most difficult struggle with her, and some days I can still feel the raised skin of my scars. Her disappointment in me was brutal. For someone who had questioned the potential for depth in my marriage before it had even taken place, she made a disturbingly quick shift—from concern for me to anger at my self-induced failure. She chose her side, and for what felt like forever, that side was not mine. She sympathized with my husband as he filed for divorce—he had understandably had enough. She was completely blinded to my side—to the part of me that did not have enough and desperately needed more. I needed a family.

She was so fixated on this new role that she had not chosen and what my divorce meant for *her*. She had a daughter who was behaving in ways she found unacceptable, but she would not be embarrassed by me. Instead, she decided she would be sad and discouraged by who she felt I was not—primarily a wife and mother. She told herself she would reluctantly come to terms with this and accept me—but not my behavior. She would remain true to herself and not rescue me, for I was certainly old enough to be held accountable for my actions and decisions. The knife cut deeply, knowing that she thought so little of me. Out of twenty journals filled with devastating information over the course of fifteen years, the most shocking and crippling sentence I ever came across was on this day:

> I am baffled how any mother can walk away from a precious child.

Pot, please meet kettle. I have no words.

> *December 18, 1998 (Jordan's Journal).* You are coming for Christmas—and you'll stay with Grandpa and me for three days. I can hardly wait … I want to be a very special grandma to you—a very special little girl. Right

now, you need a strong "mother" person in your life since your mommy left. Your daddy is doing a terrific job—getting you on a regular schedule and putting some routine in your life. He cares so much for you, and I respect him so much. I don't understand your mommy, Jordan. I don't understand her behavior and why she could choose to leave you. I hope and pray that someday she will figure out who she is and find peace with herself and harmony in her life. In the meantime, we have to be patient and trust and pray that she will take care of herself and come to understand herself. I love you, Jordan, and in your mommy's absence I will be here for you. I love you and will count the days until you come to stay with us.

I am extremely grateful that this journal sat on Jordan's bookshelf, unread until she was in high school. I can't imagine the effect it might have had on her and our relationship if she had read some of these entries at a younger age. My mother had clearly given up on me for the present time. There was hope for me to pull my life together. But in the meantime, there was a stellar father, and she was ready to fill my very small shoes as a mother. What she failed to see were things that were either quite obvious or aspects of my life that had not been questioned. Jordan's father and I agreed to separate, cried together about our loss, and slept in the same bed for the next week. We had each hurt the other in various ways, and there were no apologies. On my end, anger gobbled up any guilt I might have experienced. It was no way to live. Our decision to divorce was mutual, and I "chose" to move out because it was the best option for Jordan. I was working six days a week in the restaurant business, frequently late at night, while he had a four-on-two-off second shift schedule, which was much more conducive to finding childcare. I did not "leave" my child because I didn't want to be a mother. I was trying to make ends meet and lessen our debt since my savings account had been drained during our five-year marriage. I wanted to do better, but I needed a partner in life, not just a husband at home.

December 19, 1998. My prayer today is for Heidi:

Loving God, I raise my daughter to you; take her in your open arms, cradle her like a wanting babe—so deep in hunger and thirst for meaning in her life, but not knowing where the well of life is or how to find it. I'm not sure she knows there is a well of life—one that she can draw from so deeply.

Lord, I ache for her. She is in unknowing pain— blanketed by men, alcohol and busyness. Does she not feel her own pain? I want to meaningfully be present with her, and I struggle with how to be present. Lord, give me the direction to be the mother my daughter needs now. Guide me in ways to help her on her difficult journey. I pray that she will choose life and struggle to claim life. She is weak—and needs you in her life. Help her to refrain from total destruction. Oh, God, open my heart and mind so I may effectively reach out to her. Amen.

For Christmas that year, my mother gave me a simple gift—a journal. She had filled the first three pages with her hopes and prayers for me and left the rest with an invitation to journey inward, to explore my thoughts, feelings, and ambitions as I closed one door and opened another into the unknown. She asked me to grieve my broken promises, unfulfilled commitments, and the loss of a two-parent home for my daughter. She asked me to examine my pain, to trust the process, to discover my hidden closets, to know myself. Her hope was for me to find peace of mind in charting my own way and building my own nest, where I could return and regenerate each day. Her prayer for me:

I pray for deep soul searching—time to sort out who you are, what you want, and who you want in your life. Breathe deeply inside and pull forth your values, and then live by them.

I pray that you will discover the mother love of God— the one who can gather you in Her lap and smother you with a rich love you have not known. I pray that you ask

God each morning to walk with you and guide you in
all your decision making. Ask—and be patient for the
answer.

She prayed for healing and understanding in my motherly role to a
bright, curious child of potential who deserved so much. She begged me to
examine why my relationship with her was difficult. She called it a painful
exploration but one I must do because I owed it to myself and my child.
Mother, do you not ingest your own words? Was I not a bright, curious
child who deserved the same duty of introspection? Had I not been worth
this self-examination and painful exploration?

She asked me to ponder my wish for Jordan and how I wanted her
to remember her only mother and her images of "mommy." What roots
I could I offer her and what security could she depend on as the mother
who would "be there" for her in her time of need?

Decades later, there is so much to unpack in these three pages, and the
irony drips from a place that she, herself could not see. I am captivated by
her desire for me to interact with God as a mother, for the comfort and
companionship I should seek and the confession of a rich love I had never
known. Was this an unconscious apology buried carefully beneath her
words for something she had been unable to provide? She concluded her
consistent blue script with her own obvious pain and her need for strength
to reconcile these issues within herself. Her gift to me was genuine but still
gravitated around her own needs.

The rest of the journal is yours—to reflect and ponder
and come to a knowledge of yourself that will undergird
your future.

Love always,
Mom

The remaining pages are still empty, almost sacred in a sense. It's funny
how I could never bring myself to follow her words with my own script.

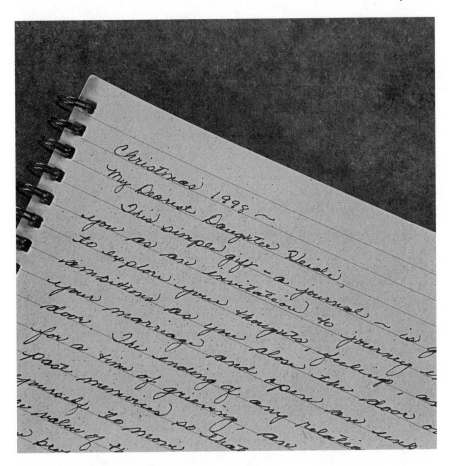

I stated in chapter 18 that there were a few things I needed to "hear" in her writing as I gained closure through the reading process. The first was her willingness to take some responsibility in our difficult relationship and the unfairness of projecting her own daughterly needs onto me. As I found what I needed to hear chronologically, I discovered they also grew in importance and meaning. My second bit of closure came in early 1999. There had been a snowstorm, and upon calling me, she learned from my roommate that I had been snowed in with a friend. (This "friend" has now been my husband for over twenty years.) Struggling with my absence and making assumptions about my "friend" and what this might mean for Jordan prompted the following entry:

January 3, 1999. Tonight is one of those nights I ponder my role as a mother to a young woman—my daughter. I don't know *how* and *who* to be. I mostly ponder my role as grandmother to Jordan, and amusingly, I ponder the mother-daughter relationship—me and Heidi, Heidi and Jordan. I feel full of grief—at broken and unhealthy relationships. As I observe Heidi and her relationship with Jordan, I cry—and I first examine my relationship with my daughter over the past twenty-eight years. Is it fair to myself to ask, "Where did I go wrong?" I was a working mom and achieved a doctorate. This meant I was gone from home at times; during grad school I was gone for ten weeks at a time, although I was home on the weekends. Was it my absence that has affected Heidi in her relationship and understanding of mothering? Did I "miss her" at critical times in her development? Did she view my absences as rejection of her? I wonder how she did view these times. Did she feel I didn't care about her? Is she "paying me back" for those moments and days of absent mothering? Am I, as mother and grandmother, now dealing with guilt for my past manner of being?

What was I feeling during my absences from her? Relief from some childcare? Need for stimulation other than mothering? Escape—brief respite so I could return home and mother again? I wonder if Heidi feels all of these things but to a more intense degree! She admits she wasn't ready for motherhood. One difference is I never left her; I always returned home and tucked her in bed. And Heidi left—abandoned Jordan to attend to her own personal needs. Left her—walked away from her, and that hurts me so deeply. And why does it hurt so much? Do I indirectly feel responsible for this weak mothering of hers?

The proverbial double-edged sword is defined as something that can have favorable and unfavorable consequences. As I unpacked these two paragraphs, some of her choice words pushed the sword deeper into my flesh, while others sliced through the ropes of bondage and set me free. For both sides of the weapon, I have cried more tears writing this chapter than any other so far. Most of us would likely admit that the intimate thoughts of our parents are better left in the dark. As brutal as her words were, I needed to hear them so I could sort out my rebuttal in my mind. She had written about me in the past, some of it unfavorable as well, but her attack on me as a mother deserved a postmortem response. Had she not written her side of the story in silence? Was her disappointment in me so great she felt she could not approach me in person? At that point in my life, it was probably best that she remained quiet in her jaded opinion. My response would have been a defensive and ugly retaliation. An argument with limited perspective could have drastically changed our relationship for the last two years of her life. Again, in 1999, I didn't know what I didn't know.

She saw the two of us through completely different lenses. Where I had abandoned my child, she was simply just gone and then returned ... to tuck me in bed. In her mind, she had justified her absence with her education, but didn't she also "attend to her personal needs"? She had clearly confessed to using graduate school as an escape from being a wife and mother, a way to separate her two worlds. By the time I was eight, she had already been sexually assaulted by two different men. She made a choice out of self-preservation and betterment, the aforementioned ripple effect of trauma. Were my father, brother, and I scarred by this choice, this means of survival by being alone? Absolutely. Ten weeks each summer over the course of five years equates to nearly a year. That's a long time to be "gone" without having a significant effect on your family. It took me two months from the day I left my marriage until the day I established a new home and was able to tuck Jordan into a new bed of her own. My leaving was not selfish. I knew deep down I was not existing within my potential. I was unhappy and unfulfilled and on a narrow road to self-destruction, but I could envision a different horizon. I couldn't see it clearly yet, but I had a deep desire for a household with parents who modeled a healthy partnership in marriage.

Closure looks different for different people. The questions she posed to herself, for the first time, told me that the scales were beginning to fall from her eyes. As she examined her choices over the years, she acknowledged her role, or lack thereof, in shaping me. Her question, "Where did I go wrong?" painfully implied that I had become a failure, probably as a person but most definitely as a mother. That was a hard pill to swallow but also an impossible question to answer because we all "go wrong" at some point in parenting. It's what we choose to do following our mistakes that makes all the difference. As adults, it's our responsibility to take ownership of our shortcomings and learn from them.

If I rephrase her question into, "What did I not teach her or model for her?" it comes across with a more productive tone. These questions are also answerable. As she continued to question herself, I believe her own words began to evoke her reality—she *did* miss critical times; she *did* create in me the assumption of being unloved and feelings of rejection and, yes, even abandonment. There was no intentional payback for absent mothering by absent mothering.

As we travel through parenthood, we can either emulate what we had or choose to take a different course. Her absence taught me to be present with my children and propelled me to want to be better. There is no personal satisfaction for me in her guilt. I cannot take responsibility for that. All I ever needed was ownership. It arrived twenty years late, still mixed with insults and disappointment, but it was there.

CHAPTER TWENTY-SIX

Mothers and Daughters

Why is the mother-daughter dynamic so complicated? Prior to writing this book, and even now, I struggle when asked if my mother and I were close. I loved her more than anything, but our relationship was strange. We were normal in some ways, but in so many ways, we were far from normal. We had a variety of hurdles to cross, separately and together, and I feel like we ran out of time before we reached the finish line. I told someone once that we were just learning to be friends when I lost her forever.

She so desperately wanted the relationship that she had missed out on with her own mother. But because of the constant turmoil between us over the years, I didn't know what I wanted or even needed from her. The traumatizing days of depression and the things asked of me during her healing process had forced me to pull away. Emotionally, I could not afford to need her. At nineteen, I had chosen to live my own life instead of the journey through hers, and she pulled away, refusing to let me hurt her again. The next ten years were filled with peaks and valleys in our relationship. I loved being in her good graces. I just wasn't very good at staying there.

Continuing from January 3, she wrote:

> I suddenly realize the fragility of my own mother-daughter relationship. I think I respond to Heidi more out of my needs than hers. I am deeply aware I don't want to repeat the strained relationship pattern I have with my own mother. Unlike my own mother, who doesn't ask questions or invite me into her life or invest herself in me in any way, I want to ask questions, invite Heidi into my life, and invest in her. She may be almost twenty-eight

and I, almost fifty-five, but I still need to be her mother. Yet, I wonder if I try so hard to be the "right" kind of mother to her because I want a certain kind of mother-daughter relationship—one I never had and have longed for. Am I searching for something I've looked and am still grasping for? Am I afraid of losing it and never having a "neat" meaningful relationship in the mother-daughter paradigm? Am I searching to have my own needs met—and maybe my needs superimpose hers?

But what is the "right" kind of mother? My mother was an educator and a student of life. When she didn't know how to do something, she read books and studied how to master her task. So, of course, she read books on the mother-daughter relationship, studied how to love me *through* our differences and how to let me go, to be my own person and not who she needed me to be. Luckily, she also turned to me and asked what kind of mother I needed and wanted her to be.

On January 25, 1999, she wrote in my twenty-eighth birthday card:

Dear Heidi,

I think of you so much now, wondering how you *really* are doing. You certainly are in a transition stage on your twenty-eighth birthday—different living arrangements, new job, change in finances, the whole works! I gave you the *Simple Abundance* book and a journal, with the hope that you would find strength and courage to move on in your life as you read and write about it. I remembered you liked to write when you were home, and I thought maybe you'd find it useful again.

I'm not at all sure what kind of mother you want me to be for you right now. I need you to tell me what you want from me. Do you want me to be distant—not asking questions about your life or how you feel, or do you want more attention from me? What kind of attention do you want? Nurturing support, invitations to come home, questions asked, freedom to call when you're feeling up or down?

I know that much of what I'm asking is a reflection of my *own* needs of mothering that were never met by my own mother. I missed so much from her and wish for that to be different with our mother-daughter relationship. Yet, I cannot ask to be something you don't want to be or do something that doesn't meet your need. I'm also smart enough to know that mothers have to let daughters carve their own life course, and I need to let you be who you want to be and choose your own values.

I know it's your birthday, but I need a small gift of clarifying communication from you. I want to give you the kind of mothering you need now. I'm convinced we never outgrow our need for mothering, no matter our age. So, think about it and let me know.

In all you are experiencing, please be assured that Dad and I love you and will never abandon you. We obviously have differences of feelings but our love for you as our daughter is constant. Love for children mounts above differences and carries us through difficult times. Deep love for you means openness for honesty and ownership of feelings, listening to needs, wants and hurts—and still loving you with that deep love that flooded us with the joy of your arrival twenty-eight years ago.

Love you bunches,
Mom

I wish I could specifically remember receiving this card and what my reaction had been. I wish I could say with certainty that I sobbed until I was a puddle on the floor. I know that my chains were not instantly loosed, but I do know that I desperately needed her. For a multitude of reasons and, perhaps, simply a learned behavior, she had been a distant mother all my life. In the past two months, I had left my home and my husband and lost my job with the company that had employed me for twelve years. I was living in an upstairs bedroom of a friend's house and working a new job fifty hours a week. I was exhausted and lonely; maybe I had let her get close enough to sense my vulnerability. I had been lost for so many years and I was tired of wandering. I needed her to find me. Cancer had changed her; it had given her the gift of new life. And I believe she wanted this "new life" to be different, especially with me. I, too, was embarking on a "new life" full of uncharted territory, and for the first time I wanted her to journey with me. Our lives had always seemed mutually exclusive, they had never coincided until now. This moment would prove to be a new beginning for each of us—but most importantly for us together.

> *January 31, 1999.* In the last couple of weeks, I've realized that part of my difficulty in letting go of Heidi is connected to separating from my own mother. Not that my relationship was or is close, but rather "difficult and distant" with my own mother. I've hung on too long— wishing for the kind of mother I always wanted. And now, with Heidi, I superimpose some of my longings into our relationship, and I don't think she wants, or maybe doesn't even need what I want to give her. As I've realized my differentness from my own mom, so I need to realize the differences in needs from Heidi. When I can deeply sense the differences in values, and appreciate them, I can let go. I feel I've come a long way in the last months— sorting this relationship issue out in my head and finding peace in my heart and mind.

> *March 1, 1999.* A beautiful birthday card from Heidi (two weeks late, but at least I got it!) and a letter. She's found a new man in her life—Jarrod—and she was ready to share some info with us. And then a precious phone call to Jordan, who, when asked what she was doing, said, "I'm standing here talking to you, and then I'll take a shower and wait for my prince to come!" She has discovered fairy tales—*especially* Cinderella. So precious!

Maybe I wasn't such a horrible mother after all! We had, indeed, begun a new chapter.

My mother kept a little bit of everything; things of meaning were treasured and saved. In almost every journal, there were papers of different sizes tucked in between the pages. From cards and poems to scraps of paper with quotes, lists of books read, and daily tear-off calendars. Things were always falling out. In addition to the journals, my father gave me photos and cards she'd kept along the way. When I first started looking for this letter, it seemed to be missing from the shoebox with all the others. Surely, she had kept this one. And then, just recently, I found it in the cedar chest with my wedding dress. I was looking for something else and saw a white box. Inside it were the especially sacred items—her baby bracelet, 4H pins, high school graduation tassel, pictures from their twenty-fifth anniversary vow renewal, and four cards. The cards were all from me—two Mother's Day, one Valentine's Day to both parents, and this special birthday card. I knew this was the one as soon as I saw it. The front of the card spoke of the transition from walking hand in hand to side by side, sharing our troubles, and lifting each other's spirits. Inside it was a beautifully handwritten three-page letter.

The letter wished her a happy belated birthday and described the strange feeling of having time to sit and write. I told her about my new job, the comfort and confidence I was rapidly gaining. I was loving my new home too—my own clean and organized space and my newfound independence. I really wanted her to come see it! Jordan was adjusting well, and she and I were building a new relationship on our own.

Half of my letter introduced her to the new man in my life. I told her how Jarrod and I had met and how supportive he had been through the trials of the last few months. He was a teacher (which I thought would give him brownie points), financially secure, and planning to attend graduate school in the fall. "He has goals and dreams, and they are consistent with mine," I wrote. His family had taken us in without hesitation and Jordan adored all of them. "He is somehow the person I think I have always looked for." I promised her that we would not run off and get married, that we were just building a relationship that felt right. "I hope you're not shocked. I want you to be happy for me. Thanks for listening. I love you!"

CHAPTER TWENTY-SEVEN

The Joy of Music

On Easter Sunday, April 4, 1999, a close friend from church died of breast cancer. She wrote:

> How glorious to die on Easter Sunday—what a meaningful way to pass from death to new life. I'm sad, but happy for her and her family—"the strife is over, the battle won." I need to cry, but the tears don't come.

April 10, 1999. Today has meaning only by reflecting on this week. I thought of my friend frequently yet could not cry or mourn her death. I "put it off" and paid the price of accumulated tiredness, until Friday night—I was so tired I thought I was dying. My unexpressed feelings were expanding and occupying all my spaces of energy. I felt so spent and empty.

In her death, I am reminded of my own precariousness of life—the knowledge that breast cancer has invaded my body and soul and wondering if it will make itself known again. Wonder. Fear. And if it does—how will I approach death and dying? Was my resistance (to grief) out of fear or feeling too close to the situation and having a deep sense of reality? The tears, which finally came from the deep, were cleansing and refreshing. Tears, like rain, made life seem brighter, casting newness and clarity.

Just recently, I shared the details of my story and feelings about this process with an old friend from high school. Throughout hours of intimate conversation, Cheree asked questions, and we dug deeper into my journey. We spoke of the misconceptions we had of friends growing up and how truly deceived we were by outward appearances and the inner turmoil that was never seen. We shared gratitude for a friendship that had been rekindled by the unfortunate, undeniable bond of losing a parent to cancer. She was curious about the genre of this book, who I thought it would serve and directly asked how this journey had affected my faith. I loved being challenged by her and was never uncomfortable. We parted with her saying, in a not-trite way, "I'm really proud of you!"

In 1996, my mother referred to her journal as a close friend—the only one she had shared her most personal thoughts with. In this transaction with my friend of nearly forty years, we questioned whether my mother had ever had a really close friend. She had many friends, colleagues, professional relationships, and women's ministry groups, but she poured her innermost thoughts onto paper. Did she ever verbalize those entries or confide in a girlfriend? I'm not even sure how much she opened herself up to my father. Did she discuss with him her disappointment in me, her unmet mother-daughter needs, or her constant fear that her life would likely be cut short? Writing was a wonderful outlet and a healthy release, but I wonder, deep down, if her life would have been different in some way if she'd had a best friend. How would the week proceeding April 10 have been different if she had picked up the phone and invited a girlfriend over for coffee or a glass of wine? Would her ability to release emotion have been different if she had her "person" who allowed her to fearlessly crumble?

There is a difference between telling your story and opening yourself intimately to a single person. It saddens me to think that maybe she simply didn't know how. Her past had left her with scars and each hurt had added another brick to the wall. She had told her story to some, let a few into her life bit by bit, but ultimately, she lived a guarded life, and trust would never come easily for her. She purposely surrounded herself with strong, educated women. She had no one in her life with whom she trusted her weakness. Opening her soul to anyone meant allowing herself to be completely vulnerable.

April 19, 1999. This is a special day—a day I've longed for for a lifetime. Tonight is my first organ recital—I've completed one year of organ and piano lessons … I'm ready to do this. This is a dream come true—to play in front of a group, to perform, to have people watch me. I recall the childhood dream of wanting to be a performer—a dream never realized, never pursued or nurtured. And tonight at fifty-five years of age, my dream will become real. It's been a long wait! I'm ready. This is the moment—the moment I've been waiting for.

Ah, let go, Karen, of the past and walk through the door to a new vision of yourself—the musician you've always wanted to be. Not only a musician but the speaking of the spirit when one dares to let the soul be its truest self. Music is a form of communication, and for me, it is my way of communicating that which is so deep within. Now is my moment to let my inner self be known. What a joy! Discovery of the inner self is an unfolding worth doing! This is life at its best and most rewarding. I will celebrate this day—recognizing my hidden dreams and talents, coming from the burial ground to resurrection!

What a glorious experience for her—a dream come full circle and lived out with absolute joy! I found a timeline of significant life events recorded in 1989. The second milestone on her list following starting first grade in 1950 was beginning piano lessons in 1952. She would have been eight years old. I love that this was so clear for her, so important that it made her timeline. My brother and I both took lessons, and my experience was never one I would have documented as a life event. We grew up knowing that our piano had been a gift from her parents when she was sixteen and was easily her most treasured possession. Some of my favorite memories took place around that instrument; it was where she would always shine the brightest. That very piano remained in our family for fifty-four years, resided in five homes, and eventually was donated to a foster family who could not afford one. It was a gift we knew would make Mom happy.

A love for music was fostered by our mother from a very early age.

Knowing and appreciating all types of music was right up there with education. We learned several instruments, we learned to sing, and we learned to purely listen. I could sit for hours in front of the record player just listening to song after song, memorizing the words of my favorites and letting the sound soak in and soothe my soul. I was never meant to be a musician—that was my brother's legacy to continue—but music would change my life. When I was a teenager, it would become an escape where I could close my bedroom door and drown out the rest of the world. In my adult life, it became a means of therapy, a method of worship, and an emotional expression of my faith. I feel music from deep within, and this ability was born and nurtured by my mother.

Instinctively, she knew that Jordan would love music as well. Mom introduced her to musical theater, and Jordan introduced Grandma Karen to Raffi. Jarrod and I continued "music appreciation" with the Beatles, Bob Marley, and Tom Petty. Her performance of "Yellow Submarine" at four years old was unbeatable. Possibly the most expensive but intentional gift ever purchased for a grandchild was the Yamaha electronic keyboard given to Jordan on her sixth birthday, exactly one month before Mom's death. She needed to make sure Jordan's love for music would flourish without her. And flourish it did. I'm sure my mother watched proudly from above as her precious Jordan performed in show choir and high school theater, led worship at church, graduated college with an arts management degree, and then worked a vital role in the opening years of a state-of-the-art music venue. Yes, Grandma had passed her passion on to her favorite person.

At the end of May, she began an entry with the announcement of another school year complete—and the need to slow down. Much had happened, and she coveted rest but saw her summer already filling up. When she was healthy on the surface, she really didn't know how to slow down. She enjoyed reversing roles and becoming the student for a few months. There was an educators' conference in Cincinnati, a leadership conference in Columbus, an opportunity to reenter the childcare field for two weeks at Fort Dix with Kosovo refugees. There was a strong desire to reclaim her space in this field, but careful consideration acknowledged her limitations with high stress, long days, heat, and no naps. She wrote about coming face-to-face with herself, her heart to serve these children, her need to complete something she's started many years ago; but the reality of her physical strength, abilities, and inabilities continued to be a roadblock.

She prayed that God would slow her down so she could move deep within herself and examine her motives. She chose not to go—knowing she would have given her all but accepting that she could not keep up the strenuous pace. Perhaps she did not want to fail and acted on behalf of her limitations.

She did soak up her and Dad's thirteenth annual respite in northern Michigan, a continuous dialogue with nature that deserves its own chapter later on, and a church musician workshop with Irene. The result of this workshop far outweighed the time and energy it required.

As her second public performance approached, she wrote about her mentors, the people she had watched in church and studied at the organ over the last twenty-five years, and how she was about to be like them.

> *July 6, 1999.* I've watched them all—carefully noted their expression, their movement, and listened, with joy, to the sound of their music. And secretly as I watched, I wished for their talent ... wishing I could be the one making the music. My fingers moved, my toes felt the beat, and my soul sighed with a young child's wish for Christmas morning. But my mind remained in control—telling myself I could never do that. And I listened and obeyed my rationale.
>
> Then cancer pushed me to the brink of abandonment. I saw closed, even locked doors, and pried them open with all my courage and newly found self-permission. I entered the door of music, piano, and organ music, with lots of practice but no questions about my ability. It is there—I need to uncover it, and slowly I am. This coming Sunday I will be at the organ console, playing for our church body—living the dream of the last twenty-five years. My body, soul and spirit are alive with joy!

July 11, 1999. And it was pure joy. I played every piece with confidence. This was my moment, and I thrilled in every moment of it, soaring to heights unknown prior to this. I was relaxed, calm, and primed to do my best. On this day, I cut a new door for myself—opening myself to many possibilities to come. I wonder what all is beyond this open door.

So many people thanked me for the classical music and the tempo of the hymns. And many persons spoke of their surprise to see me and hear me at the organ. I love surprising people in a healthy way. Oh, what joy! Where do I go next? Well, my own self tells me to continue the discipline and to purchase more music to expand my repertoire. I am committed to developing this talent—for my own soul and for sharing the beauty of music with my church family and for the glory of God.

August 10, 1999. I am feeling called to church musicianship. I want to sing, play, create, accompany—I want it all. I want to learn the literature and liturgy. I feel so moved by my music. It speaks to me where nothing else can touch. It calls forth from me the silent voices and movements, aged yet vibrant. I am unfolding and discovering the creative me, the lost self. My stone heart is opening, and joy, love, and possibility are flowing in. And my soul is so hungry for expression. I feel as if a noose has been loosed from my neck. I'm on my way to spiritual freedom and joy.

Her stone heart was opening; love and possibility were indeed flowing. I love the imagery of the hardened heart softening and possibility flowing like blood.

Unfortunately, there are times where we become more permeable and then something happens, or words are spoken that calcify our interior again. My father, the man of few words, would occasionally utter the wrong ones, maybe not unintentionally but unaware of their dagger effect. In a blazing entry directed at him and then shifting to all men in general, she described his audacity for criticizing the amount of time she was spending practicing music. He had attacked the very thing that had injected new life into her dead soul. He had silenced her with a single statement because her devotion to music was compromising her attention to him and their household. Oh boy, I will spare you the rawness of her voice, but she wrote many words that I have never heard come from her mouth.

Following this hateful entry, later the same day, is another, staggeringly intimate one, that I had never read before.

> *August 17, 1999.* Out of the dark night, I hear the child cry. Save me! Out of the dark night, I respond—I will not succumb. Out of the dark night, I gain my strength to rebuild my spirit, to reclaim the lost, and to start again on the path to personal freedom. Out of the dark night, I garner my strength, my courage, to wake on the morrow and walk tall once again—renewed and confident that I can weather this dramatic storm and emerge—unafraid, strengthened, committed to not be led by the blind, nor be blind myself, but to walk ahead and continue the journey of peeling away the barriers as I search for my "self."
>
> No one will steal the joy of music from me again. No one will steal the joy of unfolding. No one will claim me. I will rise with the sun in the morning, knowing that God has heard my cry and beckoned me onward. I will return to the organ—refreshed, renewed in determination to play, and play well. This I will do. Music exists to raise us above our everyday existence. I will follow it wherever it leads.

CHAPTER TWENTY-EIGHT

Opportunities and Challenges

As I have said before, when she felt good, my mother was unstoppable. She was one who was never content to just be. She had this innate drive to learn, to grow, to simply be more. When life seemed easy, she added something else to her plate; and when asked to join or contribute, she seldom said no.

September brought a new school year and a revised three-day teaching schedule that allowed for some extra adventure. She had been commissioned to freelance a monthly "*Voice for Children*" article for the Step Ahead organization, and she had decided to return to her roots with the Red Cross and train with their CAIR (Childcare in Aviation Incident Response) team. It was an opportunity to finish what she'd started and gain closure in the childcare field without the destructive memories and potential triggers of the natural disaster program.

September 22, 1999. On Monday, I leave for Philadelphia to be trained by the American Red Cross for CAIR— Childcare in Aviation Incident Response. I will be trained with people I don't know but who share a common love for the welfare of children. I'm excited—and scared. I'm definitely challenged—physically and mentally—and I pray to God for the courage and power to learn about and do this task to which I've been called. And I do feel called to this task. I have much invested in the childcare disaster program, and this seems a natural response for me. Yet it is also a call to wholeness—to take courage to answer the call to a cause I once started. It was a cause lost by choice to survive male inappropriate behavior and one I can now

healthily and vibrantly return to. This is what I spiritually
and psychologically need to do—and I'm ready.

Eleanor Roosevelt wrote, "You gain strength, courage
and confidence by every experience in which you really
stop to look fear in the face … You must do the thing you
cannot do."

I sometimes wonder if I'm physically "up" for this task,
but I also know that God doesn't call me to something he
thinks I couldn't do. He knows I can; therefore, I know
I can.

When you have endured the worst and survived, perhaps the thing you
cannot do doesn't exist. She had survived years of sexual trauma and even
more as she worked relentlessly to regain her self-worth. She was living with
an unexplainable immune deficiency disease and had been in remission
from breast cancer for seventeen months. She had been granted multiple
new leases on life and was filling her days will all things good. In her own
words, she was binging on life!

This new endeavor took her to Philadelphia for three days from
September 27 to 30. She journaled:

Three days in Philadelphia—what a joy to be back with
childcare teams again. This training is tough—issues of
mourning, grief, death, injury and of pain, anger, sadness.
I find myself questioning my role, motive, values, calling.
Even after the training, I still feel so called—so called to be
a member of this CAIR team. The training is stimulating,
yet I realize I hope I never have to use it—for to use it
means tragedy for others.

She had things in order in case she ever needed to use her training.
She had a backup list of people to teach her classes and had done some
advanced packing if the call came in and required her to leave in a hurry.
She was on standby for eight days after Egypt Air flight 990 plummeted
into the ocean off the coast of Nantucket Island on October 31, 1999, but
was never called to respond. She sat quietly and waited. She prayed and

asked God if she was "big enough" to do all that might be asked of her. Fortunately, that call never came while she was alive. It still gives me chills and, at the same time, warms my heart to think of the courageous role she would have undoubtedly played following September 11, 2001. She died less than a month before the ultimate aviation tragedy. Had she been able, she would have been in New York, Washington, D.C. or Pennsylvania in a heartbeat doing what she did best—comforting, teaching, and healing children in times of crisis and devastation. She would have been plenty big!

Later fall introduced a committee chair position at school and an invitation from the church to consider a ministry role. She laughed at that one but saw herself being led into ministries of music and childcare. She certainly knew her strengths and the direction of her heart. As a board member of the local day care center, three resignations in one day thrust her into another massive leadership role. My mother, the overachiever, saw this as an opportunity to enable the center to set forth in a new direction. What was God asking of her?

This busy time also allowed for some events of great healing. College homecoming brought a face-to-face reunion with her abuser. Her gut gripped as he publicly spoke to her, and she immediately felt unsafe on her own campus. Again, at church the next day, she was able to avoid him but felt his presence, her body keenly remembering his power. She left town for the afternoon but then questioned why she was still trying to escape after all these years. Was she ready to reconcile these deeply rooted feelings and fears?

October 9, 1999. Several events in the last two weeks have led me to examine myself once again. Who am I? What am I about? What do I stand for? And most importantly, where am I in movement toward forgiveness? Healing will not be complete until healing includes forgiveness—reaching down into the core of my spirit and touching the hurt and transforming it into holy power, unknown in its fury until I let it express itself. This takes courage and I'm feeling brave and confident. I won't know this sacred potential until I give permission for release. I can feel the excitement in my soul.

> *October 30, 1999.* A day of celebration—my parents sixty-fifth wedding anniversary … A day of joy and rich time together—a time I realized my healing. I could be present with my mom and dad, facilitate the celebration, and feel the joy.

And then, like a gunshot in the darkness, the phone rang at 4:15 in the morning on the Friday after Thanksgiving. My grandpa was experiencing heart problems and was on his way to the hospital. My parents were planning on fourteen people for lunch, so I went to help while they each made trips to the hospital with my grandma. She wrote about the chaos, the hospital transfer, the meal that survived without her, and the "different" Thanksgiving Day. At the end of the paragraph, she wrote, "That's what happened, but my feelings need to be explored." She had been catapulted into her day, had functioned out of shock and necessity; now it was time to stop and explore what the day had meant.

> *November 26, 1999.* I've often wondered what I would feel when my dad would be near death or have died. Today, I had a trial run with these thoughts and feelings. I was amazed how gripped I was in the thought of my dad dying—felt numbness but was surprised by the sadness. I am grateful for the healing that has taken place in my relationship with dad so I can be free to participate healthily and humanely in the last moments of his life. I believe his dance with a heart attack was a reminder to all of us that our parents are nearing a time of departing, and I need to think more realistically about this reality.

God must have given his blessing for her to take on the day care center because, by December, she was dreaming of possibilities and having trouble keeping her feet on the ground. She was fifty-five and considering retirement, and suddenly she found herself in the demanding and challenging role of establishing a high-quality center with supporting community networks. In all that she had accomplished in her professional life, she saw this as the cap experience of her career. This was what she had unknowingly prepared herself to do.

Do you know my mother by now? I feel like I might have tried to talk her out of taking on this challenging endeavor, but this was exactly the thing she was famous for. She had an insatiable desire to achieve and excel, to create and stretch herself, to apply her knowledge, and to make a difference for others. Her fears about fatigue and cancer seemed minuscule compared to this call to rediscovery and service. She was on the doorstep of realizing her new-found potential. This was, indeed, her call to a set-apart ministry. She had read that life after fifty was an opportunity to build upon the wise preparation of the first fifty years. I am positive my mother's first fifty years had prepared her to do anything. She was in a position to pursue her dream. And she, alone, would convince herself that she could do what she was about to do. She asked herself many questions, but the following one seemed most intriguing—as if she could ride on adrenaline for ten years: "Can I live the next decade of my life with an abundance of energy because I am passionately drawn to a cause I feel so intensely committed to—the care and education of young children?"

> *Christmas Day 1999.* A joyous Christmas morning—and in a different way this year. David and I had our own Christmas exchange here at home by ourselves—the first time in thirty years. The last time we exchanged gifts alone was the first Christmas in Nigeria, 1968, one month before Matthew was born. I am overjoyed with the simplicity of having our own Christmas—alone once more. Today, we savored each gift, unwrapping it slowly and enjoying the beauty of the gift and the joy of the giver and recipient. The room, filled with Christmas music, was otherwise quiet with our own voices.

Mom and Dad had decided to come to our home for Christmas that year. After their beautiful, quiet Christmas Day alone they joined the three of us in our apartment on the twenty-sixth. Her entry following that visit was the third and most important thing I needed to "hear" from her to have complete closure. As I write this today, it is the week of Christmas twenty-two years later, and I am sobbing. These three pages, written in blue ink, are by far the best Christmas present I have ever received. I'm not sure when I first read them, as they are toward the end of the journals. But these specific words, after all we had been through, have brought me comfort over the years and the necessary peace to move forward without her:

December 28, 1999. Sunday, the twenty-sixth, we went to Heidi, Jarrod, and Jordan's house. What a treat to spend leisurely time with them. Heidi had made gingerbread men for her tree and then painted them and attached buttons— all hung with plaid ribbons; how neat. She said earlier when making them, "You'd be proud of me, Mom." And yes, proud I am. How different a woman she is from a year ago. I began this journal with fears and anxieties about Heidi and her behavior. I worried for her physical and mental health, and I worried for Jordan. So many worries. She was living in a cold bedroom, no job—why wouldn't I worry?

I remember, when Heidi was born, Dr. Wilkinson said, "She's a fighter." Yes, a determined young woman whose ability to take charge and fight for herself has led her on an amazing journey this past year to where she is today. In one year's time, she has gained stability (mentally, physically, and economically) and found a new job, home, and man—all of which she loves. She's happy—it's obvious in her face and body. And Jordan has survived well too. An alert, bright, creative child, she has weathered the storm of the past year and has been strengthened by it—although she doesn't realize that yet.

I look at this young family and sense with, deep pride, the determination and commitment to a fuller, meaningful life. I'm pleased that Heidi made a personal decision for herself and grew through the darkness into the light of life … I am grateful to God for the strength and courage of this new, young family. I now see my daughter in the kind of work, home, and relationship I felt she was destined to enjoy.

I remember that day clearly as we examined the homemade ornaments; their painted bodies; and the feet that had been nibbled by our cat, Garcia. She was very comfortable in my presence and could see that Jordan was thriving with Jarrod and me. We were operating as a team around her. We were on the right path, one different than I had ever been on, and we were becoming a family. Ah, my final round of redemption. My decision to embark on a new life had not been a selfish mistake after all. I had not ruined my child; she would emerge stronger from the storm, and her life would be irrefutably different because of it. I had made a difficult decision, one I knew she would not support, but I had envisioned this ending from the beginning, and she had not. She had needed time to let the sun rise and burn off the fog.

Every daughter needs to hear these words from her mother. In a strange way, these words have meant more to me in the years following her death than they ever would have on that day. They say, "I see you. I see your potential and that you are truly capable of becoming who God created you to be." These words and others like them that were never spoken tell me time and time again that these journals were intended for me. I believe she understood her reality and knew that, someday, I would need to know her heart, and this was a way I could feel her presence. In the last twenty years, I have found myself many times wishing she could see me again, needing her to know I had stayed the course. The proverbial "she's watching you from above" is sometimes not enough. I desperately want her in my life, by my side, tasting the sweetness with me. There are, however, things I'm grateful she did not see, for I certainly would have disappointed her again. I have fallen hard on dry, barren ground plenty of times since her death; but I have gotten up, dusted myself off, and become better because of my scars. Perhaps it was her voice that called for me to get up.

CHAPTER TWENTY-NINE

Dreams and Nightmares

She continued to focus on the service she could provide:

> *January 1, 2000.* I know I can face each day with the trust that, by investing my life in such a meaningful cause, God will provide the energy.

> *January 16, 2000.* Two years cancer-free! ... I am so grateful to God for his continued guidance and grace for my return to health. I pray for a continued healthy life. I trust that will happen, as I have been called to the great task of serving children and families.

The potential power of this new calling would be twofold. My mother would save the day care center, and in turn, the fulfillment of her purpose would save her life. Because she was doing good—serving her community, leading the center in a new direction, providing quality instruction—because she was living her dream, she would have abundant energy and would remain healthy. But challenges are not supposed to be easy and are given that title for a reason. Doing good in the world and serving others does not ensure a life free of hardship.

> *March 19, 2000.* I've encountered stress that I didn't believe could be so in this new job ... What I'm doing needs to be done, but it is so hard. I've cried so much in the last seven weeks—tears that I'm glad I can shed, for they've been cleansing and healing. Some of my tears are

tears of stress—a need for relief—caught in the moment of do I stay with this job and make a difference, or do I follow my gut and run away to become an elephant girl with the circus?! Oh, how tempting at times … When I started this new job, I really didn't know what all was ahead of me. I knew it would be hard. I'm faced with many leaps—of faith, courageous acts, and what-the-hell moments. And frequently, I ask myself, Why am I doing this? Why am I tiring myself out so? Life could be easier, less stressful, and perhaps more enjoyable … I could give it all up. *But* I would lose so much opportunity to grow and become something or someone I didn't know I could be. Somehow, I feel and trust the rest of the pages of my life are still blank—just waiting for the words to appear, for the invisible to become visible. I chose to shed what's safe and predictable in an attempt to write the blank remaining pages. God didn't call me to a safe, predictable life. He called me to exercise what I know and discover what I don't know.

Throughout fourteen years of journals, I have learned to read her moods by the style and size of her handwriting. She always wrote in cursive with a consistent slant to the right. When things were good, her letters were small and uniform, easily legible, and tightly connected. When she was angry or upset, the letters became larger. They were written loosely with more loops and dashes than normal. You could feel her aggression just by looking at the page. Fury was denoted with printed capital letters and lots of exclamation points! Every once in a while, an entire entry would show up printed. These entries were written very clearly and consciously, as if to ensure that the message was precise and easy to comprehend.

Spring 2000 was documented with many large and loosely written entries. The words were put to paper with a vengeance, and her frustration saturated the air as I turned from page to page. She quickly realized she had bit off more than she could chew, and now it was gradually choking her and depriving her of breath. In all her years as a working professional, she'd never been in a position of managing people—people with a different work ethic, people with a different mindset, people who didn't share her vision. Perhaps her vision was unrealistic or just simply more than she could handle.

> *March 29, 2000.* - I want to cash in all of this job—every bit of it. I hate it—absolutely hate it! *Hate it*, I said—so time consuming, so energy zapping. It's seemingly endless work to do, and I feel so tired, tired, tired! I hate myself for thinking I could do this job. Who in the hell did I think I was—and could do? Who am I anyway? I feel so lost, so empty, so alone, so scared. And I'm wanting it all to work—to work so well.

Shortly after this last entry, my father lovingly confronted her about her mental state, and she rapidly reached out to her doctor for antidepressants. She had relapsed into a world of not sleeping, which she knew from experience would slowly destroy her physically as well. She was caught in a daily whirlwind of hope and regret and had no idea where she would land. After ten days of medication and corresponding sleep, she was filled with energy and ambition once again. She still sensed a mission to be completed.

But the roller coaster continued, and her car was plunging downward. Her mental anguish was taking its toll on her in more than just sleep deprivation. Signs of previous illnesses were concerning—earaches; sore throat; hunger but lack of appetite; and, most worrisome, the pain in her abdomen.

> *April 27, 2000.* Miserable. I hate it when I can't sleep. I'm so worried, so sick, so tired, so mad, so angry. I just ache physically and emotionally. I thought I could save the day care center and I feel like I can't. Tonight I am lost— so lost and alone. My mind is in a whirl; I can't stand this job any longer—it is eating me up. I don't feel like eating, yet I'm hungry. My body is so off balance—*so* off balance. I feel a deep loss—of self-confidence, of ability, of knowledge, a loss of trust in my own abilities. I'm scared. I'm scared cancer will return. I'm scared I'm going nuts!

Life is no longer fun, and it's all my fault. I chose to do this job, and I am slaughtering myself while doing it. I've failed the center, the college, the children and parents— the community. I need more children to keep this center going, and I don't know where to get them!

Memorial Day brought the sad realization that she would not have a teaching-free summer this year. She had used her past summers to recoup and revitalize herself, but this year would be different. She needed to learn how to function healthily in this new role. One thing that helped was the tentative retirement date of June 1, 2001. It gave her a finish line, something to look forward to. She had worked her entire life and knew nothing different. Her only opportunities to not work had been a result of being too ill to do so. Her dream was changing before her eyes, and the vision of staying home, cooking, gardening, and taking care of her husband seemed enchanting.

As usual, she also turned to her faith. She took her physically and emotionally drained body to the feet of Jesus and asked what He had in store for her. The balance of meaningful work and preservation of her health seemed far in the distance, if not impossible. But she excelled at placing her decisions in the hands of God and trusting his direction ahead of her own desires. She simply asked, "God, what do you think? Hold me in your arms and tell me I'll be OK. Whisper wisdom in my ear. I need help and direction in my lostness. I have faith in your knowledge of me—my abilities, talents, and needs—and I trust you will lead me in my decision making."

God seemed to answer her with a 5:00 a.m. phone call and a twelve-hour day without her lead teacher. Frazzled and convinced she could not do this work, she returned to her knees—begging for divine intervention. Clarity arrived in the quiet of the night. She awoke with a sense of direction; she would resign from the day care and return to full-time teaching. For the second time, she would walk away from something she truly believed in in an effort to regain her health and save her life. Her immune system was beginning to fail her once again. Gamma globulin shots had been ordered, and multiple rounds of antibiotics would eventually take their toll in their own way. It was clear she needed to weigh the cost and save herself.

June 9, 2000. I did it! I finally did it. The "it" being the courage to resign in the face of defeat, embarrassment, guilt—only six months on the job. I realize … I realize I'm too upset to talk or write about it.

❧

June 11, 2000. I feel that my present situation has thrown a curve to my inner pilgrimage. Oh, more than a curve, it's been a punch and a complete detour. I have messed myself up so much—experiencing days of unhappiness, crying, and depression and, in general, down in the dumps. What a detour—a nasty one where I'm lost, dismayed, alone and discouraged. Sometimes I feel like I don't know who I am. I've lost my spirit *and* soul—that inner part of me that keeps me ticking. The inner part of the odyssey is so blurred I find it hard to see the real me—like a dirt-spattered windshield smeared by wipers after a few drops of rain. I can't see through it to make any sense out of what's happening. All I know is I've lost myself, and I need to find her again.

Sometimes her best imagery comes out of the darkness. The muddied windshield is somehow perfect. As she lamented on her detour, she also began to examine the entire journey and what she'd learned along the way. With each swish of the wiper, her vision became clearer, and she could begin to see the road ahead.

June 17, 2000. All journeys are a search for something—a place, person, sense, feeling—something we desire that is lacking, something to fit together, bring closure, or perhaps insight, some small tidbit that will enable to find "it" whatever "it" is.

My job since February 1 was a journey—one where I was sure I would learn more of my spirit and self, my gifts and limitations. And in a short amount of time, I've learned new things about myself—some painful stuff, some things I really don't want to face. I've learned I'm not as agile as before. Nor do I tolerate noise very well. I prefer the quiet—the serene life of birds and breeze outside my window. I've learned that children have changed in drastic ways. I've learned I'm not as young as I once was, and I'm not as well as I once was. I know I become ill easily, as well as easily discouraged.

I've become more aware of my introvert nature—the necessity of pulling myself away and feeling myself, alone. I must have plenty of alone time; without it, I cannot survive. That is what I did not have in my life, and I yearned for it as a nourishment to feed my hungry soul. I am so hungry for that which sustains me—and my next journey is to search for that which creates and sustains wholeness.

When I made the decision to resign, I felt intense guilt—guilt to leave a job so soon. (I don't view myself as a quitter.) But more than that, how does one leave a job that God has called me to do? How could I let God down after responding to His call? I wanted to run away, hide, hide even from God—yet I know that God is everywhere, and there is no place that one escapes God. So, heavy with guilt, I spent my hours under a blanket of quiet shame.

With the help of her friend, Helen, who also had the special role of being my mother's "holder," she was able to come to terms with her guilt and view her calling in a different light. What exactly had God called her to do? He had called her to expose her gifts, to step into a time of need, and to use her talents. She had answered the call to provide aid to a cause in desperate need of change. She had not failed. She had arrived in chaos and slowly, bit by bit, changed each tiny piece for the better. The task loomed large and had consumed her many times. Her disappointment was not in the job itself but in finding the balance in giving aid to others without destroying herself. She had, in fact, served as an interim—one who goes into a broken place and slowly induces healing, so growth can once again occur. In that capacity, she had worked through the difficult to find harmony; she could now move forward.

CHAPTER THIRTY

A Time for Healing

The newly discovered peace of the last entry was crucial, as three days later, a routine appointment with her oncologist revealed another mass, lump number eight, in her right breast.

> *June 20, 2000.* Another day of pain and anxiety ... I was filled with worry and memories of having been through this before. My body remembers! One never forgets cancer—and the trauma of diagnosis and treatment. I wanted to scream or even to cry—but didn't. I relived all the questions: What if ... Could it be ... Does it mean ... What about working? All these images and questions were racing through my mind.
>
> My legs ached, my stomach cramped, and my back hurt. I was just miserable—and scared! Yes, scared that I'd go through all this again—and I'm emotionally at a weak point. Could I do it again? But then, the mammogram and the ultrasound, back to the oncologist—all emotionally laden events. And the result—don't worry now. See my surgeon and family doctor in the next two weeks and come back in October!
>
> I realize, once, again, the fragility of life and how quickly my perspective and grip on life can change. I am glad to be leaving the day care job and will more solemnly swear to really take care of me. This life is too precious, and I'm not ready to lose it. May I sleep in peace tonight— wrapped in the arms of David and God.

Healing is not something we consciously choose. It happens only when we are ready. Our bodies know and respond to a physical, internal change. Healing is, however, contingent on the deliberate act of forgiveness. By the end of my mother's life, it was apparent that she had forgiven her abuser. Those of us who knew her story marveled at this, not in disbelief but in wonder and maybe amazement of how she had been able to reach that point. This was not a decision she made on her deathbed to prepare herself for heaven; it came consciously and wholeheartedly before she knew she was dying. It happened naturally and was her final step in complete healing.

July 17, 2000. A day of celebration and healing. Kansas City, Missouri—the annual conference and the twentieth anniversary of the childcare disaster program. The luncheon was held today, and my abuser and his wife were the speakers. I feared isolation and avoidance, but "he" did well and gave me fair treatment. I let go—let go of the hatred and anger and let myself enjoy the remembrances with the rest of the group. I felt the ice melt, and I could once again see him as a coworker, concerned with young children.

Afterward, the three of us talked about our children and recalled other memories—of Nigeria and our shared hometown. We stood alone, the three of us, in the hallway of the KC Convention Center and there, amid the glass and steel of the building, felt the presence of God's healing love. We parted then, likely surprised at ourselves but surely bathed in God's grace. Twenty years is a long time to harbor anger and hate—a long time to let vicious feelings eat away my soul and spirit. Twenty years is a long time to wait for healing, but I know deep in my heart that healing blessed us at the time we both were ready for it. For now, I know the healing is real. I am physically and emotionally exhausted tonight. My body has been cleansed of hate and anger. The spaces long filled with poison have let go of their burden. Now, perhaps my body can heal in other ways as well.

For when I grow tired and weary, I am reminded of the scripture Isaiah 40:31. "But those who hope in the Lord shall renew their strength: they will soar on wings like eagles; they will run and not grow weary, they will walk and not be faint."

It was a sermon on forgiveness in 2012 that brought me back to her story after a long but necessary hiatus. It struck me like lightning, unexpectedly, and brought with it a flood of uncontrollable tears. My mother had been gone for eleven years, and I was still carrying a heavy load that was unresolved. How could I possibly forgive the man who had stolen so much from me. It wasn't just decades of my mother's earthly life; he had deprived me of her and her ability to mother while she was still alive. I would often daydream as I methodically drove the lawnmower back and forth in our yard about what I would to say to him, given the opportunity someday. I had not seen him in person since Mom's funeral, and I struggled to tolerate the sight of him on such a sacred day. Surely, he was the embodiment of Satan himself. It seemed to be no mistake that the rare memory I have of him as a child was when he caught fire from leaning back in his chair from our dining table into the candle that sat in the windowsill.

At that point in 2012 and even more so today, I have found that my anger has subsided and faded into sadness. I'm not sure if that qualifies as forgiveness. There will never be a way to quantify what I have lost because of him. As I sit here waiting for the words to come, I feel almost paralyzed—my arms stuck in my lap, my hands clasped tightly, my fingers not remembering how to type—because there are no words to describe my loss. I cannot begin to imagine how different my life could have been had she not spent over two decades hiding and healing from this man and his selfish destruction. Over fifteen years, my mother wrote in great detail about what she had lost by falling victim to him. I understand deeply and fully what she lost; perhaps I can comprehend her loss better than my own.

This man has now passed. He died several years ago without my knowledge. Would I have been brave enough to go see him had I known he was dying? I don't know. Do I feel that I have been deprived of closure because I never got to share my broken heart with him? No. My closure and my complete healing will come in the form of this book. Honoring her story in the way she wanted it to be told, describing the intricate, destructive nature of sexual abuse, detailing her journey to wholeness, and celebrating her healing will mend my broken heart. My heart will always have fissures simply because she is not here, but I am no longer broken because of her absence. Knowing her in every way possible, digesting page after page, holding her words in my heart and putting them on paper again has made me whole.

CHAPTER THIRTY-ONE

Warning Signs

In late summer, my mother took on yet another new venture:

August 8, 2000. In preparation for my first retreat. Thoughts? Feelings? I'm scared in a way. I'm traveling alone, staying alone—in the woods—and I wonder what will happen in this time. This is new. I knew I wanted to do this. Or was it that I *needed* to do this. I need to let go—let be—and listen to God. I need my spiritual and emotional battery recharged. I need quiet time—slowed down time. I need to do something I haven't done for myself. I'm hungry for nurturing and nourishing—in need of a huge amount of self-care. I'm ready, even if I'm scared. I trust God will be with me in this venture for healing.

She spent three days alone in the quiet of a hermitage in the forest. The silence of nature was welcome as she escaped her normal routine and busy world—awaiting the encounter with the Spirit. She hiked and watched the clouds, allowing the great fan of wind to blow through her hair on high speed. She explored the library and read about the natural sequence of growth—how parts of our body die daily to allow for something new to exist. On an emotional and spiritual basis, we often resist growth. We are stubborn and timid; therefore, out of fear, we prevent what is new from emerging, and we cease growing. She closed her eyes and meditated on the many layers she had continued to heap upon her soul. It was time to let those facets of disease die and allow for the budding of new growth to break through. Her retreat ended with a time of confession, a prayer of forgiveness, the burning of each individually named sin, and a burial of the ashes at the foot of the cross. Her burdens were lifted, her yoke no longer heavy. She had been renewed and cleansed by this time in such a holy place.

∾

Before she headed home, in between her gratitude for a time away and her last walk, she interjected this tidbit of concern into the next entry:

> *August 10, 2000.* I had hoped to get rid of the diarrhea I had before I came; even though it has lessened, I still am plagued by it. I wonder about its cause—drinking out of used water bottles where bacteria resides? Too many herbs? Cancer? Fresh fruit and vegetables? I will go home and throw away my old bottles, do some cleaning, and change my diet. I want to believe I can make changes that will improve that area of my health.

In her next entry, just three days later, she wrote about the birthday cake she made for her mother's eighty-fifth birthday and followed it with another health concern:

> *August 13, 2000.* This afternoon, when I came home, I had painful and bloody urination—suddenly. Scared me somewhat, but David much more. He was worried, and then I began to wonder about cancer or other infection. Then in the night and this morning, my urine returned to a clear color, and the pain was gone. Felt relieved and wonder if I had passed a kidney stone because of the sudden onset and sudden passage of symptoms. I will watch myself carefully and pray for God's guidance and direction through this.

I touched on this hypothesis in an earlier chapter, but I just found an entry where my mother made the realization that her life might have been different if she had had just one really close friend. She had been reading

Circle of Stones by Judith Duerk, and her daily passage had been titled, "A Sense of Her Need." It described how women overextend themselves and ignore the inner voice of their own need. In doing this, they continue to adhere to an unhealthy lifestyle, which denies growth and the unheard voice and then manifests in depression and illness. Her life validated this theory many times, as she revealed several times that the only thing that ever forced her to slow down and listen to her body was illness. She went further to question how different her life might have been if she'd had just one woman who offered open arms and a shoulder to cry on. She often struggled alone, painfully searching for a way out of her self-imposed despair. Often described as "one tough woman," perhaps her weakness was a lack of vulnerability. You cannot ask why no one stepped forward if you, yourself, did not invite or allow them in. Yes, one person surely would have made a difference. But for "one tough woman" that would have required admitting weakness, brokenness, possibly even failure and asking for help in finding herself again.

> *September 20, 2000.* I feel strange today—unsettled, unfocused, and even depressed. I question myself. What am I feeling? Why am I feeling this way? Is God sending me a message? Do I really care? Physically, I feel tired. There are things I'm not interested in doing; I've lost my motivation. What's going on, God? Am I worried about my next oncology visit—worried about cancer?

> *October 6, 2000.* Feeling low. I've not had a good week with organ practice. It seems as though I'm regressing, not making progress … Could cancer be spreading to my brain and affecting my motor control and coordination area? Am I subconsciously worried about cancer and my next appointment? I need to admit I am worried and scared.

For a body once invaded by cancer, it's return is always on the forefront of one's mind. Every random ache, every undertone of pain, everything that doesn't seem normal evokes the fear of an unwelcome homecoming. I wonder, though, if this fear is accompanied by the fear of the truth. With back-to-back incidents of diarrhea and blood, why would she wait two months for her next scheduled appointment to ask questions? Buried between her words, I feel a sense of not wanting to find out until she was forced to. As someone who has never had cancer, I find myself overly conscious when my body speaks to me. I choose not to live in fear of cancer, but I do live with the understanding that my risk is greater than most and I need to be proactive, to pay attention, and to listen when spoken to.

My mother spent the majority of her life tired. Because she endured sexual trauma, because she had at least two immunodeficiency diagnoses, because in spite of all this she was an overachiever, she always pushed herself to the brink. Tired was sometimes all she knew. So how would she know if something had invaded her body and was beginning to break it down? How would she know cancer had returned until the symptoms were severe and she could no longer write them off as something that would pass?

A follow-up visit with her oncologist on October 19 showed no change in the lump in her breast. She was pronounced "still safe" and given the green light to begin living fully again, without fear. I wonder if there was any mention of the diarrhea or bleeding in August or simply of the unsettled tiredness that had taken over in the last few months. Was she so focused on the unchanged breast that she forgot to consider the surrender of other parts of her body to the same affliction?

> *November 7, 2000.* Election night, and no president elected! History in the making *and* I'm in the hospital, bleeding and scared! Is this cancer again?? Oh, I'm scared, and too scared to cry!

> *November 8, 2000.* Going home with an anal fissure and several weeks of treatment. Low hemoglobin count—and I'm still scared.

November 19, 2000. Lots of bleeding—*still!* I feel miserable and scared. Went to church, and three people immediately asked me if I was OK. I was white, and I can no longer hide my lack of color. I am determined to call the doctor tomorrow and push this issue further. What is my hemoglobin count?? Why am I carrying a low fever? What is going on? I need to remind myself to pray to God for healing and keeping me safe.

I remember our conversations during this time. For nearly three weeks, she had been bleeding with no clear explanation and several that kept changing. First was the fissure, a tear in the lining of the anus that would heal on its own with proper diet and rest. Second came the possibility of diverticulitis. This option, because of its infectious nature would explain the fever and nausea as well. This, too, would heal itself with time, but the bleeding would not stop. She was dissatisfied with both assumptions and would push further for a different diagnosis, but her body beat her to the punch. She was severely weakened and eventually found herself motionless and barely alive on the bathroom floor.

Thanksgiving Day 2000. A day not to forget. A Thanksgiving Day of enemas, laxatives, vomiting, colonoscopy, and CT scans. A tumor in my colon, under my liver, is the culprit. A tumor the size of a tennis ball, seemingly well-contained (and hopefully it stays that way) has been growing for at least two years.

The phone call came from my father. With all the testing that needed to take place before having answers, my brother and I were told to stay with our families for the holiday and wait. I waited, quietly withdrawn from the chaos of Jarrod's large family, for the news that I somehow already knew. This holiday of gratitude would always wear the mark of the beginning of the end. She had cancer again, a tennis ball-sized tumor in her colon, and they were sending her to surgery to remove it immediately. This pain in her abdomen that she frequently referred to was real, not stress or tension, but cancer. It had been growing for years, tucked beneath her liver, showing its ugly face here and there but never enough to make anyone look for it.

With today's medical standards it would have been caught earlier, but the protocol was different then. There's no guarantee that it would have been caught in time, but even a clear colonoscopy at fifty would have likely prompted one at fifty-five. She was now nearing fifty-seven with a two-year-old tumor. They would end up removing eighteen inches of her colon, cancer intact, and once her body had recovered, they would begin chemotherapy.

> *December 3, 2000.* First Sunday of Advent. The anticipation of Christmas blended with the knowledge I have stage 3 cancer. All the joy and mystique of Christmas blanketed by this overwhelming awareness that my body is weak, tired, and sprinkled with microscopic cancers floating around! Not a recipe for joy.
>
> My first taste of cancer came during Lent of 1998. And now this one appears on Advent and Christmastide. What is the meaning in this?
>
> I look out my south living room window and view the contrast of the naked limbs of trees against the fullness of the lush evergreen sprinkled with light snow. Full life and death existing, simultaneously before me as evidence that all this is possible—to be living and dying at the same time. And that which looks dead, stark naked against the gray clouds, is in its rest time, preparing for its new growth in the spring. As I anticipate winter and the road of chemotherapy ahead, I find solace in dead-looking trees before me and the promise of new life to come.

We are all living and dying at the same time, embracing life, and contemplating death simultaneously. She found hope in each given day and even when she knew she was, I never heard her say the words, "I'm dying." She lived with the incessant prayer for healing, the hope of future Christmases with her grandchildren, the promise of an organ/piano duet with Irene, the commitment of eighteen friends willing to travel cancer journey number two with her, and the peace of knowing she and my father could endure and conquer difficult things together.

> *December 15, 2000.* Another big day in the life of a cancer patient—visiting my medical oncologist for the first time, to learn about chemotherapy! How grim!
>
> Eight months of treatment, once a week, cycles of six treatments—two off, six on, and so on—until mid-August. This is a long time! Can I do this? When I think about all the side effects—oh, I'm already tired of being sick—I can't imagine being sick for eight more months!
>
> Christmas Eve Candlelight Service: When we sang the last hymn, "Joy to the World," and lifted our candles higher on each verse, I cried and cried—thankful to once again be "home" at church and, more importantly, hopeful to return for many Christmas Eve candlelight services in the future. Oh, how I hope to live many more long years. Oh, please, God, I offer this simple request, that I may survive cancer and rejoice and celebrate life with family and church friends for many years to come. Amen.

She wrote, too, of Christmas 2000 in Jordan's journal:

> This was a special Christmas for me. Just five weeks earlier I had been diagnosed with colon cancer—had surgery and a long ten-day stay in the hospital. It was special that we were all together—laughing, sharing presents, and enjoying our time with each other.
>
> But in some respects, I wonder if I have many more Christmases with you, since I now live with two cancers. Jordan, I pray to God every day that I may live a long life, that I can survive cancer and spend many more Christmases with you, Zak, and Madeline.

The year 2000 ended with her typical read-through of what she had documented over its course. It had not stacked up to be a good year, if good was measured in terms of health and happiness. Tears welled up as she recounted the disappointments and losses suffered in the last twelve months. The year seemed, on the surface, a loss, but she sensed the only way out was up. But how do you hope for a better 2001 when eight months will be consumed by chemo? Overwhelmed with fear of the unknown, this was the first time in fifteen years that she laid no plans for the upcoming year. I suppose, when goals are meant to be realistic, measurable and obtainable, it's nearly impossible to project for a year when you don't know the reality of tomorrow.

> *December 31, 2000.* Usually on this night, I set goals for the next year—the new year—goals filled with hope. Tonight, I feel too empty, too distraught to plan ahead. Tonight, I need to feel the depth and intensity of my pain, fear, and loneliness. God, where are you in all this mess? And it seems a mess to me—no sense of timing, consideration of plans, or respect for goals. Nothing! Life just kind of stops, along with everything about it. Tonight, I let myself feel—deeply feel—the depth of my pain and fear.

CHAPTER THIRTY-TWO

The Chemo Journey

New year, new attitude. Have I mentioned that my mother is the most remarkable woman I have ever known? After a night of sleep and a morning devotion from Ecclesiastes 3, "A Time for Everything," she decided this was a time to move forward, to seek the newness of life, and to sever herself from the old.

> *January 1, 2001.* A new year—like a new baby, so full of hopes and dreams—wishes for a good, happy new year, and one full of surprises. What can an eight-month stint of chemo bring in the realm of surprises? What will I learn about myself? Others? What will I learn about giving? Receiving? Loving—fully and deeply—on the edge? What will this year bring? I feel full of questions, and empty on answers. But if I enter the year with questions and no answers, I allow myself to be vulnerable, open to take risks, to reflect, and to wait patiently for answers to come—in their own time. Yes, there is a time for everything—in its own season.

Somewhere during this short enlightenment period, she decided 2001 was worthy of goals as well. She mentioned "a few" goals. But in true Karen fashion, she listed five categories, each with at least two detailed goals. Her physical, social/emotional, and spiritual goals felt similar to those of the past, but her professional and family goals stood out to me. Exercise, daily spiritual devotion, and the organ would serve her in critical ways. But this would be a different year, and she knew from day one that these two areas of her life, her work, and her family would be affected the most. She needed to make them count.

Professional goal number one was to teach part-time while enduring chemo, to be open with her students about her health, and to grow in human sensitivity. She noted, "Not all learning comes from a textbook." Goal number two would be to consider her future in teaching. When would retirement seem appropriate? This may have been the single most important semester in all her thirty-five years in the classroom. Her honesty during this time gave her the freedom to teach like never before—like it could be her last opportunity to touch these young lives. She embraced her love for children and her passion for education, and she taught some of the best teachers in our schools today. I remember watching the many students at her viewing and tearfully grieving *their* loss as they huddled together and sobbed. It was an odd combination of pride and heartbreak to see the number of lives she had touched and carefully molded who were now left without a mentor. I could not help but hurt for them alongside my own pain.

Family goal number one was to splurge in the joy of being in Michigan with her most precious people—her children, their spouses, and her brother and sister-in-law. Goal number two was simply to enjoy time with family. These two seemed to go hand in hand. For fourteen years, my parents had vacationed in northern Michigan alone. It was my mother's favorite place in the entire world, but it had always been *their* sacred time away. Now, she was finally ready to share it with us. She wrote endlessly about the healing qualities of the sand, the waves, and the breeze. But I had no concept of the lifelong effect this place would have on me, the treasures I would bring home, and the way I would feel her presence with each return to the shoreline.

> *January 3, 2001.* My scripture for today says, "Forget the past—I have made a new thing." Since yesterday is behind me [a negative barium test in her small intestine], *I am* ready to put my worrisome past behind me and move forward with hope.
>
> I went to my office today—put things away, filed items, cleared sixty-two messages off my email. It felt

good to be back on the second floor of the Administration Building. Even my plant hadn't given up completely—I watered it and encouraged it to grow! I told it that we both had been through difficult times—a pruning of sorts—and we will flourish again!

∞

January 5, 2001. A day I've been anticipating for several weeks—my first day of chemotherapy. I don't really know what I'm in for—until I do it for the first time ...

There was apprehension, not only about the chemo but also regarding the doctor-patient relationship with her oncologist, Dr. A. She didn't have a sense of safety and trust with her. She entered her first dose questioning if her bedside manner would be different or if she would be forced to "clear the air" with her and be honest about her uneasiness. She needed this negative experience to at least be mitigated by a positive relationship. On that day, Dr. A must have passed the test because she remained until the end. She journaled before going:

> I have so many questions about chemo—what's it like? How will I feel? How will I react? Will I feel a difference? What will it be like to be still for two hours and let "poison" drip into me? In a few hours, the answers will begin to come, and then I will begin to know. The scripture for my devotions this morning is helpful as I stand on the doorstep of chemotherapy.
>
> > You will go out in joy and be led forth in peace; the mountain and hills will burst into song before you, and all the trees of the field will clap their hands. (Isaiah 55:12)

Chemo came with the expected sickly effects. She was nauseated by everything; food didn't look good or smell good. She felt tired and "blah," sleepy but restless, and completely unmotivated. A cousin and fellow cancer survivor assured her that these were temporary feelings, and tomorrow would be better. My father reminded her that, even though it didn't feel good, this process was making her well—and she was confident she would be. In subsequent weeks, they would combat her side effects by fine-tuning her medication, adjusting when she took it, and adding one to jump-start her bone marrow. All of this helped, and she progressively felt better, or as good as one can feel with poison running through her veins.

January 11, 2001. In the night last night, when sleep seemed to escape me ... I decided to sit quietly with my cancer anxiety and chemo side effects, rather than bemoaning the fact that I couldn't sleep. So, I said "hello" to my antsy feelings and thought of them in friendly ways. Soon, I was asleep again. It makes no sense to fight that which has taken up residence inside me. Instead, I will be friends with the feelings—to acknowledge and sit quietly with them.

January 24, 2001 (Jordan's Journal). You and your mom came to our house for supper. Tomorrow is your mama's birthday—she'll be thirty! Gosh, Jordan, I remember *so well* the morning your mama was born in a tiny Sudan Interior Mission hospital, in Jos, Nigeria. She was a tiny lady when she entered the world at five pounds twelve ounces—so special and so petite (seventeen and a half inches long). Little did we know of the hard week ahead of her—struggling so hard to overcome a dangerously high bilirubin count. It's a long, tender, and special story of how your mom fought so hard to live. She was a miracle and is now the proud mother of you! Sometime, ask her (or me!) to tell you the story of her birth and the first week of her life.

You are growing up so fast ... I love it when you come to my house. I hope we have many more times together. I say that only three weeks into chemotherapy and wondering how many years I will live. I *have* to beat this cancer because I need to watch you grow up.

Of all the stories my mother could tell, the one of my birth has always been my favorite. It was emotional but full of love and pride for her baby girl, who simply needed to survive. During the three years my parents were in Nigeria, my mother wrote a weekly letter home and mailed five copies to their parents and siblings. On most weeks, she just left the paper in the typewriter and would revisit her letter when she had time. My maternal grandmother had kept every letter in its postmarked envelope in a box that looked like a tiny suitcase with baby blue satin lining. The letter announcing my birth was written and mailed just hours after I had arrived, when all was thought to be well. The envelope of the next letter was labeled "Heidi's Illness" in my grandmother's handwriting. It began, "Heidi is a week old today and we are still in the hospital." She had borrowed a typewriter from the nurses so she could share her little miracle in a timely fashion. She described my unexpected decline in health and then my equally sudden intention to live. Mom wrote, "She seemed to hit rock bottom but had enough strength in her little body to be able to pull herself out of her condition." I have to imagine that, as I lay listless under the light, my mother whispered to me from a slightly different perspective, "I need to watch you grow up."

> *January 25, 2001.* I woke up late this morning—feeling very tired and realizing this is one of those days I'd like to stay in bed. But I got up, had some breakfast, and cried. I really dislike this cancer—it's such an interruption to my life. God, how will I make it through this time? I feel so beaten and weak—I can't imagine another six and a half months of this. Sometimes I want to scream, push the fast-forward button, and get to mid-August.

I gasped when I read this last sentence. This period in time was exhausting and frustrating, but unknowingly, this was the only time we would have. Thank God there was no fast-forward button, for we needed every day of those last few months!

> *February 4, 2001.* Lord, I feel so sick and lousy today; it's all I can do to put one foot in front of the other. I am

weak. I am weary. I am tired of pushing on. But I just read a book given to me by one of my students, *The Little Engine That Could*. I read it and cried—I know I can. I know I can! It is so difficult, Lord, but these students need me and want me—I must keep on the teaching track. The energy had to come from someone greater than me, so it's clear to me, Lord, I'm needing you and I'm counting on you—*now*! Please, God, together let's create the strength machine that gives me the energy to do today's preparation for tomorrow's work! Amen.

A week later, she turned fifty-seven years old. She wished herself a happy birthday and almost congratulated herself on making it this far. I know, without a doubt, there was a time (possibly many) where she didn't think she would make it another day. But today she was grateful to be alive, even if that meant living with a second cancer. Her new goal was to celebrate fifty-eight, not to live a long life but to take realistic baby steps and simply make it to her next birthday. As I get closer to my fifty-seventh birthday—and even my fifty-fourth (when she received her first cancer diagnosis)—a different reality sets in for me as well. There is sometimes a legitimate fear of outliving my mother and whether or not I will be blessed with the decades she was robbed of enjoying. I am living with several genetic risk factors, and as vigilant as I am about my health and all the necessary preventative testing, I know that my destiny is not wholly in my hands. Knowing what I know now, I know my mother did everything right to be healthy. It's what had been done to her that lowered her defenses and disabled her body's fight mode.

I'm not aware that my mother ever had a bucket list. If she did, it would not have included skydiving and traveling but, instead, intangible things such as forgiveness and wholeness, and she had already checked those off. The next thing on the list would have been playing an organ/piano duet with Irene. It had been her dream, and Irene had promised they would achieve it. It would be Irene's last Sunday playing for her church and Mom's last time playing for anyone other than her beloved teacher and friend. On the day before, she greeted her fear, acknowledged its presence, and used it to empower her for the day to come.

February 17, 2001. "Here I am, Lord" is our number—the postlude—and I want to do this so well. This is a gift of mine to Irene and to God. This morning, I recognize the uneasiness, the fear I have. I want to play this without mistakes—no "oops" is written in the score! So, hello fear. I feel you inside my tummy, my arms, and my legs. You are kind of all over me. I feel your presence throughout. You are a good friend, for you remind me of my awesome task, my gift of music to God, Irene, and others. You remind me of my talents, my sense of risk, and my ability to give. You also remind me of that part of me that feels fear and nervousness—my own questioning of, "Am I good enough?" I invite you to go with me tomorrow, to remind me of my humanness but also to remind me of my ability and power. I want you to be with me but not get in the way of my sincere expression of the love and healing power of music. Together we can do this and do it well to the glory of God.

On February 18, 2001, she fulfilled this dream with the utmost perfection on an organ with hundreds of pipes. The church bulletin stated, "This postlude concludes our worship, and we invite you to sit and listen. Those who must leave are asked to do so quietly. This lovely setting of Hymn No. 593 is shared by one of Irene's organ students. Karen is a local college professor, and her organ and piano study is part of her journey toward healing as she has fought breast cancer, and now colon cancer. We thank her for participating with Irene and providing her musical talents to our worship experience today."

The glow from this day donned her face and surrounded her being for weeks, or at least until the start of the second round of chemo.

CHAPTER THIRTY-THREE

Fear and Acceptance

Tiredness showed up again:

> *March 13, 2001.* Empty. Tired. Just want to sleep ...
> and cry. My cup of life feels empty when I don't have the
> energy to do the things I want to do. I am aware of my
> resistance to the tiredness that comes with chemo—that
> equates to a long trek of five months to go! I desire energy;
> however, I am tired. My cup is empty. I can't fill it up like
> I used to. But then ... when it is empty, I have more room
> to receive—God's gracious gift of life and loving ones
> around us. Be open, be open and vulnerable to receive.

About a year after her death, I became preoccupied with the idea of
living and dying simultaneously. I realize we are all doing this daily, but I felt
like it had to be different when you had an innate understanding that death
was moving closer and likely at a pace you didn't like. I pulled out the bag
of journals for the second time and read the final two beginning in January
2000. I studied them thoroughly and quietly, sometimes reading and taking
notes alone in the sanctuary of our little country church. I paid attention
to how her language changed with the second round of cancer, how her
desperation emerged when her hope seemed further in the distance, and how
she gently learned to relinquish control. I wish I'd had more conversations
with her during this time, but how do you ask someone to talk about dying
when they are still holding out hope? She had always appeared to be the
picture of determination, and to this point, she had always overcome. I'm
not sure I even believed she was dying until six days before she did.

March seemed to tear holes in the filter and allow for these thoughts to seep through. Her entries moved from her displeasure and discomfort with chemo to the painful reality that she had been trying to ignore.

> March 14, 2001. Restless! That's it! I've felt it all day yet couldn't name it. Restless, I am so restless. Where does the restlessness come from? My fear—the fear of cancer returning, the fear of cancer again, and no more time left. No more time. Is that my fear? No more time to do the earthly things I want to do? I am afraid, dear God, afraid—afraid of dying before I'm ready. I worry—and I know that I'm afraid. I want to live, God. Am I not allowed to live longer? Why do I worry so—and find it difficult to surrender my fear and worry to God? Can I just let go and let the surrender happen on its own? Am I forcing myself to surrender because I know that's what I should do? Let go—oh, Holy One, help me to let go of my fear and worry that zaps my energy and strength. Let go, Karen. Oh God, help me to let go—to empty myself, to prepare myself for the next leg of my journey, whatever that may be. I realize I want to maintain control, but I realize more deeply that I am not in control. Perhaps my restlessness is the tension between my desire for control and God's desire for me to empty myself—to let go of control …

∞

> *March 15, 2001.* Following my awareness last night, I realize my fear is facing the reality of living with two cancers—the possibility of my death at an early age, far earlier than I wish. I admit I want to avoid it at an early age, and to even think of the contrary challenges me too painfully. I cannot imagine dying so young. I know this could be a reality for me—and I'm pushing it away. Pushing it out of my thoughts helps me to "think and believe" it won't happen.

Was she practicing the common coping mechanism she had taught herself all those years ago? Was it the burial of a thought or an act that made it cease to exist? Could she prepare herself mentally to leave one set of circumstances and enter another? For years of her life, she had been successful at repressing the events she did not want to remember and things too painful to be a part of her reality. Unfortunately, this time, there was no alternate life, nowhere to hide; there was not a life without cancer.

March 28, 2001. Miserable—difficulty sleeping last night, pain in my legs, hours of wakefulness. I got up this morning to start my day with devotion, and my scripture and meditation was about the cup of suffering. I feel like I am fighting my pain and suffering. I lie in bed and cry— angry at cancer, chemo, and medication for the anguish, loneliness, sadness, and anxiety they have brought to my life. As usual, I analyze. Why? What am I not doing? What am I doing wrong? I didn't choose any of this; it just is ... But I can choose how I feel about these invasions of my personal life. I can choose to turn anger into love. I can choose to turn anguish into peace. I can choose to get up early in the morning for devotions—to spend time with God. I can choose to work with these visitors, rather than resist them.

April 16, 2001. I've thought a lot about death this past holy week. Maundy Thursday, Good Friday, a time of darkness—no lights except candles—and then waiting for Easter. My moments through these holy days have been special ones—worship services with new meaning, feet washing, the walking of the stations of the cross. I'm aware I'm recalling events and not feelings. Yet, I have a feeling that is present—that of sensing death, my own, yet resisting it. Didn't Jesus experience this too? Unlock my storage cabinets, oh God, and open my eyes, ears, mouth, and mind so I can "see and know" what will set me free. Will it be the acknowledgment that I "know" I am dying ... yet am fearful and uncomfortable saying it? I am struggling with the tension of holding onto hope and acknowledging the coming of death. Does it have to be an "either-or," or is there some way these two exist together?

Could there be a time when intuition tells us we're dying but no audible voice has confirmed? I imagine there has to be inner turmoil when the body says, "I'm fighting a losing battle," but the heart begs it to keep pressing on. After all she had been through, my mother, possibly more than anyone, was in tune with her body. Over the years, she had become well trained on how to listen.

"A Time for Everything" continued to speak. If there was truly a time to come to terms with your death, wouldn't you want to share that experience with Jesus? The season of Lent played perfectly into her hand, and the ability to identify with Jesus became a source of comfort. There was no irony in this part of the story; she was sharing something very special with Him, even if she wasn't yet ready to share it with us.

There were other congruences as well. A resurrection of sorts was on the horizon. She would not walk out of the grave in three days, but she would certainly be brought back to life by a canvas bag full of paper and ink. My mother was intentional about everything. She planned and orchestrated everything until the very end. The canvas bag sat in her closet, neatly packed with her life story in chronological order. She gave no orders to burn them. There were no private instructions on a sticky note inside the first book; nor did she whisper to me on her deathbed. Mom was a genius with words, but occasionally, she didn't need to use them. She trusted that my father would know what to do and that I, in turn, would pursue her unspoken wish. Her resurrection would take more than twenty years, but through the reading of her words, I have touched the pink robe she was buried in. She is very much alive in me.

May 25, 2001. Last page of this journal—and a long time of not writing. That's a symptom of the end of the school year. I made it with no missed days! And now I'm down to seven more chemo treatments and eleven weeks of my treatment plan—and then I'll be done!

June 6, 2001. A gray day. Rain ending this afternoon after days of rain. I feel like the out of doors—gray, heavy, soaked with a dull feeling. Nothing seems good today. I'm tired—tired of what? Rain? Gray days? Chemo? Cancer? All of them. Even Socks [her cat] doesn't satisfy me. I feel lonely and wonder about the rest of my life. Went to the dentist this morning and wondered if I'll be here this time next year to get my teeth cleaned. Seems like a dumb reason to want to live.

June 18, 2001. Pain! Pain! Pain! Since Friday night, I've had this abdominal pain on my right side. At any sign of pain, I panic, especially when the pain is in the area of the colon surgery. I guess my fear is strong, and I wonder why I suffer again. Enough is enough, God. I'm tired of pain and discomfort. Haven't I had enough?

June 19, 2001. A glorious morning—sitting on the deck reading *Praying Our Goodbyes*, thinking about saying the goodbyes in my life. I've already said some goodbyes, and yet, I realize with each goodbye, there is a hello. I've said goodbye to parts of my body, knowing they will never exist again. I've said hello to untapped talent—playing the organ and piano again. I never would have experienced that hello if there hadn't been a goodbye through cancer. And now, with colon cancer, another goodbye to a part of my body, but I'm not aware of a strong hello this time, and I wonder about that.

June 25, 2001. I sit on the deck—alone—and wonder about life. I love our back yard ... This is all mine—my sanctuary, my place of peace and reflection. Tomorrow is another chemo day—damn! I'm getting so tired of taking in poison. Thirty-two weeks is a long haul—and I'm getting weary. And the pain in my right side continues—quite modified but hurting, seemingly more than the last couple of days. And I worry, momentarily, about cancer—again.

I have found it impossible to interject anything between these last several entries. The physical pain and emotional anguish are very telling. I don't need to help you digest them. In a strange way, this is the part of the book I've looked most forward to writing. Pain is a different animal, and even though it's unpleasant, it has a way of branding things into our memory. Writing this is almost like reliving it, and the details are vivid, as if it were only yesterday. I can feel the apprehension in my own body as I read on and prepare how to convey it in the most honest sense.

Physical pain had always been a part of my mother's life. In addition to numerous illnesses and surgeries, her trauma, anxiety, and stress seemed to manifest in physical pain, typically housing themselves in her lower abdomen. It was a pain she had become used to, somehow comfortable with, and although she acknowledged it, even in her writing, it did not alarm her to the point of scheduling an unplanned doctor visit. And so, she waited until July 9, her next preplanned gamma globulin shot, and casually mentioned this "slight discomfort" on her right side. Her innocent visit took a detour and continued at the hospital with the intake of two bottles of "white stuff" and a CT scan. She was alone—and suddenly the memory of Thanksgiving Day flooded her conscious. She drove home in tears, stopped to tell my father how her day had transpired, and proceeded into town to buy a necklace and a shawl for my wedding.

Yes, in the middle of all of this there would be a wedding. Jarrod and I had gotten engaged in April 2000 and had set the date of August 18, 2001, for our backyard wedding at his parents' home on the lake. There was no big surprise proposal. We just decided one day to go buy a ring, knowing we wanted to spend the rest of our days together. We chose August in hopes of warm, dry weather. I chose the day because I like even numbers, and it seemed a perfect choice nestled nicely between my parents' anniversary on the fifteenth and Jarrod's parents on the twenty-fifth. Mom did not go with me this time to buy my dress. In fact, I believe I went alone. But I went with her to purchase hers, one that came up high enough in the front to cover her poison port. Mid-August would mark the end of chemo and the beginning of my new, married life.

July 10, 2001. David left early this morning to take his mom and aunt to a funeral in Michigan. The phone call came from my doctor, asking when *we* could meet with him that day. I knew then the news was bad. David— gone for the day. So, I called my Stephen Minister, Susan, and she went with me. The news of the CT scan was not good—one large tumor two and a half inches in diameter and six to seven other (smaller) tumors surrounding it in the liver. I must see my oncologist for next steps.

Susan and I cried and cried. My doctor held me while I cried, and then his nurse, Mary, held me even longer. Bless their hearts! Susan and I drove to the hospital to pick up my scans and then to the pharmacy and then home. We ate lunch on the deck, laughed, talked and cried. She drove me to my hair appointment and back home—stayed with me until about an hour before David came home. God bless her; what an angel!

And then the telling began. First came the trip out to see Mom and Dad and then the calls to Matthew and Heidi, my brother, pastors—all of which were so hard. It's hard telling bad news.

CHAPTER THIRTY-FOUR

Decisions

Hands down, the news of more cancer brought the most memorable day of my life. Dr. A was on vacation, but this could not wait. A family meeting was scheduled with one of her partners (who was wonderful). We would digest her prognosis and make a decision together. I know exactly what I wore—a white linen shift dress that fit me perfectly and contrasted well against my suntanned skin. My long hair was in a ponytail, and my sandals clicked as I walked the sterile hallway and approached my parents. My mother greeted me by saying, "Heidi, you look like an angel." I took her hand, wishing I could be the angel who would protect her from what was about to happen.

What a task for a doctor who had never met this patient. Professionally, yet very tenderly, he explained our current situation, along with two courses of action. The new tumors were aggressive and had grown quickly over the last six months. They were inoperable and incurable. A stronger, more frequent cocktail of chemotherapy would retard the rapid growth but would not change the end result. Her body, with all it had endured had earned the rare title of "chemo-resistant." There was no fluff that could have been added to that kind of news—nothing to soften the blow; it just was what it was. It was heartbreaking, but I don't think any of us were shocked, especially my mother.

Her immediate reaction was to choose quality of life over quantity. Yes, she was young, but she could not tolerate more. I remember her telling the doctor, "I feel pretty good, and I want to feel pretty good as long as I can." She would not spend the rest of her days miserable. The decision to cease treatment is always accompanied with the question of, "How long can I expect to live?" It's a question you want answered but don't really want to know. I believe the generous answer was three to six months ... possibly, but it's always a crapshoot.

Jim and Irene had offered their nearby home as a quiet place to unpack and process our news. We sat and talked over the pros and cons of each option yet came to the conclusion that no more chemo was the most suitable option. For my mother this was not an easy decision, but it was a clear one. She was tired of fighting, and she would surrender in her own way. Ultimately, it was her body, her life, her decision. We were there, not to convince her to live longer but, rather, to support her in the decision to die gracefully.

> *July 13, 2001.* The hardest day ... I don't want to put energy into fighting death—rather embracing death as a part of my living. I'm dying the way I want to—embracing the process of letting go. Hard as this is, I don't want to miss it. I want to learn from this—and grow in strength and spiritual knowledge.
>
> Oh, God, these are hard times—trying to find the balance of hanging on to hope, wishing for a miracle and simultaneously coping with the reality of dying soon.

This was the most difficult of all entries to read, even though I lived it by her side. Her perspective was uncanny, and her choice of words to describe the worst of days remained positive. My mother's willingness to embrace death rather than fight was consistent with her attitude all along of welcoming and coexisting with the illness that had taken residence in her body. She chose grace—to not give up but, rather, to give in to the process and learn from it. She had always been the model student of life. And now, she knew there would be important lessons in dying. She wanted to be present, not medicated and muddled, for the journey.

The memory of choosing death over misery was ingrained in my mind. However, I have no recollection of my drive home or what took place once I got there. I can't remember if I wiped away tears or if I held tightly to the wheel as if it, too, would slip away if I let go. Did I sit in my car, trying to compose myself before walking in the front door? Or did I forgo pretending and, instead, crumble on the doorstep? Was I even able to speak? Was Jordan at our house on the night before her sixth birthday? Did I hold her and sob, understanding the gravity of what this loss would also mean for her? I'm sure whatever happened for me, as well as to my mother, that night got tucked away the next morning, as our hearts refueled and the smiles were pasted on in celebration of turning six!

> *July 15, 2001 (Jordan's Journal).* You were six years old yesterday! I've watched you grow from a nineteen and three-quarter-inch little baby to a grown-up girl. You are so much fun—growing up, adapting gracefully to life's changes, and greeting life with enthusiasm and bounce! We came to your house late afternoon to celebrate with you. You opened your present from us with such curiosity—a big, big box. What could it be? Your glow of excitement when you saw it and exclaimed, "It's a keyboard!" What fun it was to give that gift to you. I wish this to be a beginning of a love for music for you—and remembering Grandma and Grandpa and our joy in helping you get started. Blessings on you, Jordan, as you learn to play. I know you will do it well. Happy sixth birthday! We love you.

These were the last words written in Jordan's journal. The following page had been jaggedly torn out ... She had written something and then decided it was not meant for the eyes and heart of her precious grandchild. Perhaps she had attempted to say goodbye but simply couldn't find the words.

> *July 18, 2001.* Started the task of cleaning out my office—ugh! Emotionally and physically, this is and will continue to be hard. On the other hand, I do have many things to give away, and there will be joy in giving objects of meaning to others.
>
> Dr. A called today to express her sadness at the progression of my cancer. I will meet with her on Friday—I'm not looking forward to rehashing all this again. I fear

she will push for chemo—and I've decided no more! I hope I don't have to fight her on this. After I hung up from talking to her, I reached that spot deep inside that felt the unfairness of all of this. I'm not angry at any particular person, but I'm angry with treatment failure that should not have happened. I cannot face returning to a center that has meant failure for me … emotionally, I cannot do it. I cry out of my sadness and the feeling of betrayal by modern medicine. I am sad and heavy.

I don't appreciate false hope, but maybe a glimmer was what she needed leading into a week of vacation with the family. Her dreaded oncology appointment took an unexpected turn. Dr. A's bedside manner may have been a little lacking, but her conviction in the medical process and finding an alternative was big. Mom's care team was not ready to give up. Between Dr. A, her colon surgeon, her breast cancer radiologist, and the specialist who had read her CT scan, it was determined there could be another solution. But it came with a handful of contingencies. If the liver cancer was only in the right lobe and a metastasis of the colon and not the breast, then barring a major artery issue, she could be a candidate for a liver resection surgery. Considering this would mean a chance for longer survival. Was God opening a window where he had closed a door?

Dr. A's advice was to go to Michigan, enjoy, and come home refreshed and ready to start with the new plan.

CHAPTER THIRTY-FIVE

The Annual Baptism

Ah, Michigan. I purposely waited through fourteen years of journals to paint this picture of my mother's heaven on earth. Every year, every trip represented a different time in her life, a different place in her healing. It was the well she drank from, and she would savor its sweetness from one taste until the next. There were four years that she did not write. I combed and retraced the pages but found no mention of this healing land. The years 1989 through 1991 were some of her darkest in terms of therapy, relationships, and anger. Perhaps Michigan had worked its magic during that pocket of time, and she soaked it all up without sharing it with anyone. Jordan came along in 1995, and I imagine she spent her week basking in newfound grandma glory, along with the sunshine. In that sense, she had already been healed before reaching the sand.

> *July 6, 1987.* From chaos to calm, from tension to release, from trials of life to breathing in the refreshing spirit. The water calms the wounding from today.

> *July 13, 1988.* Today I came alive. The child in me emerged. There is something mystical and magical about Point Betsie. I feel awakened there; my spirit and soul come alive. The western sun was warm on my face in the late afternoon, and the wind was fierce as it blew through my hair. The waves repeatedly sounded their voice—strong and determined. I slid out of my flip-flops and danced to the shoreline where the incoming waves

and receding waves joined in their show. I felt so at home and, somehow, so in touch with myself. I was in love with life. I felt baptized again and again. New power surged through me, and useless, tired feelings were drained out my feet and washed to sea. I began to dance and skip the distance between the two breakers—I was my child.

August 5, 1992. I welcomed Michigan with open arms. I *must* put my feet in the water. I am aching to heal ... I want to return to this place every year of my life. This is where I am renewed, refreshed, and invigorated for the rest of the year. This place is my emotional, physical, and spiritual retreat center.

July 26, 1993. Back in Michigan again! Yes, like returning home, this special spot in the world has become so familiar it seems as if we're returning home. As soon as our car crests the hill on M109 and straight ahead is the postcard view of Lake Michigan and South Manitou Island—I know I have arrived. This is the place I wish to return to for as long as I live. The sand and water combined with the wind and sun is the best medicine.

∞

July 8, 1994. The clouds parted, and the sun reminded us it was time to visit the beach. This was Point Betsie day … The breezes were quite cool as we trod through Betsie's beach, undaunted by gray clouds and threat of rain. We found our favorite driftwood log and parked ourselves. With our toes nestled in the sand, we reminisced our favorite memories—days of furor and madness in her waves, the ice formations of this past February, and a Sunday when devotions were experienced on her shores. As usual, she reminded us of her healing force and powers, how her behavior has spoken to us at critical points in our lives. Betsie, the annual pilgrimage to her shores, is a very necessary place and experience in our lives. She speaks, and we listen, though her message is provided without words. I bend to touch a few stones, examine a few in depth, and then pocket a small number. Betsie is like a spirit. She gives; I take. I take what I can in my memory of sound and sight. The rest I carry home in my pocket as a reminder of her beauty and strength richly given. A few special stones will extend my memory until I return next year.

∞

July 25, 1996. The beach was perfect yesterday in spite of the cold water. I walked in the water—my annual baptism of the soul. And now I know I am getting well! I am aware I am so lost in time up here. I am oblivious to time and days, not counting how many days we've been here or how many left. I am immersed in this time and place!

∞

July 23, 1997. Sitting on the beach reading and writing. Clouds cover the lake like a thin, gray canopy. Toward the horizon are snippets of blue—hope for tomorrow. This is wonderful. I am essentially alone, with my aloneness temporarily interrupted by people beachcombing in front of me. Alas—what more could I want.

July 30, 1998. Back again in Michigan! Another year of grace—to be given the privilege of coming here.

July 26, 1999. And today we drove to Glen Arbor for the thirteenth time—to reunite with the fresh water and beauty of "Up North."

August 1, 1999. Full of beautiful memories, we reserve our room for next year and head south—meandering on M109 and then M22, tears welling up in my eyes as my heart beats with sadness in our exit. I'm never ready to leave the grand Sleeping Bear. Fifty-one weeks, and I earn my return.

July 25, 2000. Back "home" again in Glen Arbor. This is my first retreat to begin the nurturing process of healing myself once again. (When will I ever learn that my body and spirit cannot be neglected, no matter how busy I am?!) Still finding it hard to slow down and embrace the quiet—to realize I don't have to do everything today and have faith there is a tomorrow.

July 28, 2000. A beautiful day yesterday at Point Betsie; the beach was so sandy and wonderful to walk. The sand greeted my soles like a longtime friend, and we spent two hours together, renewing my spirit in the gift of water-splashed waves on the pure sandy beach. Oh, so wonderful. I want more! It was my annual baptism of the soul. And I want more!! We were spared rain showers that moved on both sides of us, as we were sandwiched in with sunshine and dryness. Nature is so wonderful, and it is nature each year that draws out my hungry soul, bathes it in water and sand, and sends me forth for another year. I pray this coming year to be graced with wisdom and vision as I leave, more open than ever to listen to God.

July 29, 2000. The shoreline beckons me to walk and walk. I love this beach and will return here for years to come. I leave Glen Arbor for the fourteenth time, blessed by the healing spirit of this place on earth, knowing I am better for being here, and touched once more by the healing hands of God.

In 2001, we would all be better for being there. We had been given the gift of time; and no matter how short, there was no better place to spend her last good days. For the better part of a week, the eight of us took over the Sylvan Inn in Glen Arbor. The owners, Ralph and Rose, were honored to host us but equally heartbroken that this would be my mother's last stay. After fifteen years, they had become like family. She was like a child, excited to show us her favorite places. We ate at the local restaurants and shopped the bookstores and pottery shops. My Uncle Dewayne and Aunt Cindy bought us a wedding gift, and I bought Jordan a beautiful violet parasol covered with jungle animals of all colors. We snacked at the Cherry Republic and stocked up on salsa and coffee to take home.

We hiked the Sleeping Bear Dunes, and I danced on the shores of Point Betsie. I was equally captivated by this lighthouse with the sky-blue backdrop. I was a lover of the sun and the sand already, and my mother taught me a new appreciation for them. She taught me how to walk the beach slowly and look for the perfection of the water-washed stones.

Together we looked for color and stripes, stones that had been shaped by the furor of the crashing waves and then washed clean by the tide. The depiction of her annual baptism was real. I could feel the transformative power of these waters. We walked together, and when my pockets became heavy, she had a bucket in waiting. She knew me and knew that a few stones would not be enough to carry me through until my next visit. I took pictures of my parents sitting shoulder to shoulder in the sand, swapping hats and being silly, walking hand in hand in the tide, and stopping for a few kisses. I vividly remember falling apart at the drugstore a few weeks later when I opened the envelope to look at my photos. My pain was fresh and raw, but I had her face in my hands.

> *July 23–29, 2001.* What a glorious week in Glen Arbor with Dewayne and Cindy, Matt and Terri, Heidi and Jarrod, and us. All eight of us in the Sylvan Inn! We spent wonderful "bonding time," each of us grouping in different ways at different times to enjoy whatever pleasure was at hand—hiking, shopping, sitting on the porch; laughing, crying, recalling memories; and obviously and beautifully creating many new memories. We all got along so well; no one seemed dominant or receding from the group. It was just a joyous group.
>
> We spent time Wednesday evening talking about symbols of my life and objects from me that the children wanted and some form of memorial service arrangements—not easy stuff to talk about. But we all faced it with courage and openness—with hearts dealing with hope and reality. What a beautiful family to live with—and, someday, die in their loving presence.

I don't remember growing up with the overwhelming feeling that my mother had to be in control. Her method of discipline was quite the opposite. She was never afraid to voice her opinion, but she did not dictate what we could and could not do. Our decisions were always our own—we lived with the benefit and consequence of our actions. In our home, everything had its place, and you simply put things back where you found them. Things were not spotless, but there was always order. My children may say I have taken this need for order to another level, but I got it honestly.

Much like our home, Mom needed order in her life and also in her death. On this Wednesday, night we sat in our wicker rocking chairs on the open porch of the Sylvan Inn and discussed what her memorial service would look like. She had specific instructions as far as who would speak about the various aspects of her life, who would sing her favorite hymns, and what Bible verses were *not* to be read. She had written multiple times about the altar—the symbols of her life that she wanted to be displayed. But now she told us and very specifically. The altar would hold her doctoral hood and gown, piano music, early childhood textbooks, fresh bread, cross-stitch projects, Michigan stones, and roses. Her service needed to be on a Saturday so students and working friends were able to attend. She would wear her white flannel nightgown, her pink robe (the only robe I ever remember her wearing for thirty years), and socks on her feet. She wanted to be comfortable and warm in her final resting place. It was a difficult but beautiful conversation—one she had every intention of being a part of while she was still alive. Something this important would not be left to chance, or even to my father.

The next few days were perfect. We savored our time together in the sun and the sand, and we all prepared to go home. Friday evening at dinner,

Mom was nauseous and didn't eat much; the uneasiness had been creeping up on her quietly during the day. Back at the inn, I snuggled with her and tucked her in for the night, hoping she could rest and recover before the trip home. Morning came, and she had been vomiting throughout the night. Anything she ate or drank came right back up. She did not come down for breakfast, so we went to her bedroom to say our goodbyes. Tired and weak, she was still in bed. I hated to leave her in that condition, but they had purposely scheduled one more day alone before their departure. Leaving Michigan this time would be a death in its own sense. I shared in her sadness of seeing the M109 in the rearview mirror. Seven of us would earn our trip back the following year, but the one who loved this place the most would not be with us. Hopefully, what my mother had earned in her life would feel like Point Betsie every day.

I don't remember the five-hour drive home—I was too preoccupied with who I had left behind. As we entered our apartment, I was drawn to the flashing light of the answering machine. There, a long message from my father that cut off before he had finished. The vomiting and dehydration had continued ... Rose had taken them to the hospital in Traverse City ... There was a blockage in her colon, likely scar tissue from the surgery in November. What a helpless feeling, and I instantly regretted our decision to come home. A phone call to Dad reassured me there was nothing I could do. The blockage would require surgery, and they would stay in Traverse City until she was able to come home.

In a much different but still legible style, she printed her final journal entry. She progressively struggled with each paragraph, and in an eerie sense, the ink in her last two sentences began to fade.

> *July 29, 2001 (Sunday).* Oh God, what happened? Here I am—in the Munson General Hospital in Traverse City, Michigan. We were supposed to be going home. A beautiful week just wasn't supposed to end this way—with a blockage in my intestine, some pain, lots of dehydration, and a tube down my nose and throat. God bless Rose's heart; she drove us here and stayed with us for about an hour. It was a miserable night last night—almost 3:00 a.m. before getting out of the ER!

Today, it's been packing up our stuff at the Sylvan Inn (David did that). And I've lain here wondering what will happen next! I pray that somehow, God, your healing hand can break this stuff up in my intestine, and I can avoid surgery. I'm just not ready to face another one. And this throws off our schedule of going to the Cancer Treatment Center of America on Tuesday.

Well, I'm back to one day at a time—what's in store for tomorrow, God? Give me peace, grace, and courage to face this next step.

I closed her final journal to the picture of a beautiful angel in a green dress with long, dark brown hair. Her arms are folded behind her back; her eyes are closed; and her face is illuminated, tilted slightly upward. She is peaceful.

CHAPTER THIRTY-SIX

Coming Home

On Monday, a week later, she was escorted home by plane. The medical staff in Traverse City suggested she might not survive the car ride. They gently got her home and set up camp on the living room sofa bed. I can imagine her demanding that room. There was so much light, she could have visitors, and the mattress was better than most. She would not be tucked away in her bedroom on the back side of the house. She needed to be present.

Wednesday brought a painful visit with her doctor. Correspondence from the surgeon at Munson General indicated that her cancer was growing rapidly, and she and Dad were encouraged to "make arrangements." She was given a blood transfusion in hopes of giving her enough energy to make it through the wedding. I had arranged my work schedule so I could spend a long weekend at home as her recovery nurse. Little did I know I would soon add hospice to my résumé as well.

I entered the front door Thursday morning to find her in bed in the living room. I approached her and said, "Hi, Mommer," as I sometimes called her. Dad had not prepared me with the news of the day before, and I instantly knew things had shifted. For the first time, she looked like she had cancer, a completely different person than I had said goodbye to in Michigan. Her eyes were sunken into her face and rimmed with dark circles. She was gravely thin, other than a swollen abdomen that made her appear to be several months pregnant. I touched her tenderly, as you would an expectant mother, anticipating the swelling to be from her surgery. The cancer, she corrected, was taking over.

Overcome with a flood of emotion and a million questions, I went in search of my father. "What's happening?" I inquired between sobs.

He explained the details of the doctor's visit and was extremely honest about the limited time we had left. I was not here to help her heal; I was here to help her die. I couldn't breathe, and I could not let her witness my pain. I still needed to be strong for her. Outside, I let myself absorb this new reality and began making my own difficult phone calls. Work was first—she's not going to get better; I don't know how long; I cannot leave her side. Next were calls to Jarrod, Chris, and Sara (seven hours away but she was still my safe place). Before I went back inside, my boss called me, compassion dripping from his words. I did not have to return to work until after the wedding.

Oh, my God—the wedding. One month ago, the only issue was being able to hide her port. She had bought a new necklace and a shawl in case the evening air was chilly. We had progressed to questioning her physical ability, but we had a wheelchair that would transport her from the driveway to her front-row seat in the lakeside yard. Today, the conversation had turned to a video camera. She needed assistance to set each foot on the ground; attending our wedding in nine days was out of the question. Our photographer would set up a video camera, and we would watch it together later. She would be there in one way or another.

I cleansed my emotional palate and shifted back into caretaker mode. I needed to do something for her, with her; it didn't matter. I needed to be her person. She had no appetite, but watermelon sounded good. It would also give her some hydration, which was perhaps more important. I went to the store, cut the watermelon up in bite-sized pieces, and happily sat in bed feeding her. It was sweet and juicy, and she was smiling; that was all that mattered. Dad had called hospice that morning, and they showed up to assess their patient. The morphine prescription was filled and could be administered in small amounts as her pain, discomfort, and/or agitation increased.

By Friday morning, she was asking for some relief. When you're 105 pounds, we found, a little bit of morphine goes a long way. She slept all morning, while Dad and I sat in the dining room making arrangements with the funeral director. In the afternoon, my aunt and uncle came to visit. She was alert enough by this time to let the morphine crazies out! As I fed her more watermelon, she defiantly accused my uncle of not being my dad's brother. We talked and laughed with her even if she wasn't making sense. After a great deal of gibberish, she slipped back into a deep sleep and rested peacefully for the remainder of the night.

By Saturday morning, the fog had lifted, and she was with us again. I curled up with her, took her hand, and welcomed her back. She looked at me with a sense of relief and said, "So, I'm not going to die?"

How do you answer that question when you know the truth? "No, Mom, not today. You are not going to die today." I felt pretty confident in my answer, but ultimately, I didn't know.

One thing I did know—she was not going to die in a morphine-induced coma. When I told her she would not die today, she was relieved but was also emphatic that she be given nothing stronger than Tylenol—absolutely no more morphine. Once again, she needed to be as present in death, as she had been in life. And I needed her to not sleep her life away. As long as she was not in pain, I needed every minute and every word.

Hospice returned with some other ways to help. The sofa bed was folded up, and a hospital bed was placed in the living room along the row of windows. She could raise and lower the head and feet, and the mattress would be more comfortable for her sedentary body. A catheter would be inserted, as the trips to the bathroom were becoming dangerous. She could walk, holding both my arms as I walked backward, but she was dead weight; and if she fell, she was taking me or anyone else down with her. It was a medical convenience that simply made life, and death, a little bit easier. Tylenol was in good supply, but I'm not aware that she ever asked for any.

On Sunday, I decided to take a short break. I was hesitant to leave her but confident she would not die without me. My brother and Madeline were coming, and this would give them undivided attention without overwhelming our patient. I needed to lean on the other side of my family, wrap up a few wedding plans, and prepare my little girl for what was about to happen. It was a quick twenty-four hours, but there was a strong pull for me to return to her side.

There was a revolving door of visitors—students and friends seeking their final goodbyes. Matt was still there, but our conversation led him to leave. Jordan came with her daddy, and I was not prepared for what that encounter would do to me. I had explained the night before that Grandma Karen was going to die soon and that we should not be sad because she was going to live with God. I hugged her and warned her that Grandma might look a little scary with her dark eyes and swollen belly. Their relationship

239

was immortal, but this was the one goodbye I could not bear to witness. She took Grandpa's hand, and I collapsed into Chris's arms and sobbed. I hurt terribly for both of them—what they were losing and what each of them would miss. But children are stronger that we think, and my sweet daughter returned to comfort me. Grandma had not looked scary at all; she just looked like Grandma.

Mom had faded throughout the day, but it had been an exhausting one for all of us. As she rested, her body began to void itself of the things it no longer needed. Hospice had not prepared us that this was the beginning of the end; her organs were shutting down. Jarrod came for the evening to bid his farewell and to give me whatever it was that I needed. That night and for years to follow, I didn't know what that was.

Then came the serenade. A small but mighty group of women came from the church to sing over my mother. I sat on the bed beside her as they sang carefully selected hymns of grace and praise. Song like "In the Bulb There Is a Flower" and "Will You Let Me Be Your Servant" were especially meaningful and relevant. God was surely looking down and thinking, *Well done, my good and faithful servant.*

She was motionless and quiet until the very end, when she seemed to become agitated. She whispered, "Thank you." And then with a little more forcefulness, she pleaded, "Just leave me alone."

The tears came again as my body shook, and I gasped for air. She was done. I cleaned her up for bed, massaged her calves, and rubbed her stocking-covered feet. I simply needed to touch her. I snuggled up beside her and cradled her body with my own, closer and closer, as if by osmosis I could absorb all her discomfort. She drifted into a peaceful sleep, and when I was ready, I caressed her forehead, kissed her gently, and told her goodnight. My father decided to sleep on the sofa by her side. Down the hall in my room, I resigned myself to sleep. But before the weight of the day was lifted, I prayed the prayer I will never forget.

"Dear God, please take her quietly. Don't drag this out or make it painful. Let her go peacefully and gracefully, the way she wants to. She is ready."

At 3:00 a.m., I rose to get a drink of water. Hesitantly, I crept out to the living room and paused in the doorway to listen for her breath. In the silence of the night, I could hear the soft delivery of each in and out. Relieved, I returned to bed.

As gently as he could, my father ushered me out of a deep sleep the next morning. "Heidi, you need to get up."

"Are we close?" was my immediate response.

"No," said my father. "She's already gone."

God had answered my prayer. She had surrendered peacefully in the night with no one standing over her, no one holding her hand, and no one to witness her last breath. She had done it her way and spared us of that moment. Her body lay flat on the bed in front of the windows, and Dad had pulled the sheet over her face. We waited until Matt arrived to call the funeral home. He needed to see her. I chose to remember the feel of her warm skin and the touch of my lips to her forehead from the night before. I chose not to look under the sheet.

CHAPTER THIRTY-SEVEN

A Wedding

It was Tuesday morning. The logical timing for the funeral would have been Saturday, but that was to be my wedding day. In the days before cell phones and social media, contacting 150 people to postpone a wedding was next to impossible, but pushing a funeral out for eleven days was no easy feat either. My brother protested that he did not want to put his grief on hold and attempt to be happy in the middle, but I was convinced that Mom would want us to go through with the wedding. The funeral home was on board with the wait, so it was settled. I wasn't sure how we would do it, but there would be a wedding in four days.

Those four days went by in a blur. Luckily, we were highly organized and well prepared before the trip to Michigan. So there were very few last-minute details. My future in-laws took charge and didn't skip a beat. All I had to do was get my hair done and show up. Sara, my rock, had jumped in the car as soon as I told her Mom had died. She drove seven hours and came two days early to be with me and help me mentally prepare for what was supposed to be the happiest day of my life.

Originally, my father was going to marry us. We had done premarital counseling with him, but we had not counseled each other on what to do if Mom died before the wedding. We had not anticipated that minor emotional hiccup. A few days prior to her death, Dad admitted to me and, more importantly, to himself that he could not officiate the wedding. It was too much. He had needed to focus on what was before him, in his living room, and not how to make it through a wedding ceremony without falling apart. He was off the hook, and I had another plan. A college classmate of mine was now the associate pastor of my parents' church, and she threw together a remarkable service in a matter of days. Christen did not know us as a couple, but while visiting my mother in the last week, she had looked through a stack of photos from our recent trip to Michigan. They all documented beautiful memories, but one stood out to her. Someone had taken my camera and captured Jarrod twirling me around in the sand on the shores of Point Betsie. She framed the entire service around that "dance" on the beach. The majestic power of Betsie had healed us once again.

The sun rose on our wedding day, and I watched the scene unfold from an upstairs bedroom window. Our guests arrived and took their seats in the lawn as a storm brewed across the lake. Nosy boaters even parked themselves in the water to watch from a distance. My grandparents, amid the anguish of losing their daughter, had put their grief on hold as well in order to be present for me. Following my precious Jordan, I took my father's arm and walked down the grass aisle, pausing for a moment to gaze at the front row where she should have been seated. We climbed the steps to where my groom was waiting; I took his hand and a deep breath, just praying for the strength to survive.

The music stopped, and silence fell as Christen began to speak. She warmly welcomed friends and family and acknowledged the one person missing—the one whose physical presence we were mourning but whose spirit surrounded us, especially today. I heard a few muffled gasps from the lawn. Not everyone had heard the fateful news. Christen gently described the time of sitting with my mother during the past week and finding the picture. "The picture," she said, "of the two of you dancing as the waves licked your heels. Both of you have chosen to dance even in the face of sorrow. Each of you has chosen to dance when the pain was imminent. The dance of love will lead you on wild and exciting journeys."

God added his crescendo with a loud clap of thunder. We had each written our own vows but similarly pledged loyal hearts and lives, tender care and individual encouragement, and support in strength and weakness. Our road to today had not been easy, but together we vowed to build a past full of love, laughter, and adventure. Jarrod's parents and my father stood and endorsed their commitment, and Jordan importantly took her own vow to support us in our new life together.

Rings were exchanged and Christen added this charge: "Putting on these rings marks the beginning of a long journey together, filled with wonder, surprise, laughter, tears, grief, celebration, and joy. *Wear them with great expectation!*"

Punctuation was added once again by a flash of lightning. We could see the rain clouds patiently waiting across the lake, giving us just enough time to finish in prayer.

"God of all love, thank you for the gift of love that has brought us together today. Grant Heidi and Jarrod your grace that they may learn to grow into this love, that they may dance to the rhythm of the Holy Spirit, that they may be taught by your presence. Amen."

On that day, we had no idea how much grace that dance would require.

The rain came, tears from heaven as many of our guests exclaimed. We greeted our friends and family under the protection of the tent as congratulations went hand in hand with condolences. It was a mixed bag of tears and laughter. But all in all, it was good. My mother was somehow making her presence known as the sky let loose and then the clouds parted, inviting the shades of orange and yellow to rejoin our celebration. As the sun peaked through, everything began to glisten. The storm had been necessary to make our day unexpectedly beautiful.

And then we danced.

CHAPTER THIRTY-EIGHT

And a Funeral

Shifting gears, I tried to find some normalcy on Monday by going back to work, but normal no longer existed in my life. After a day in the office, I was asked if I needed more time, and I took it. I went home again. My father had already begun to clean out closets and wanted me to have first dibs on anything before he gave it away. I struggled with his almost frantic need to remove her presence, but I understand now that it's an important part of the grieving process for many. Looking into a closet full of her clothes every day was just too much. He wasn't trying to get rid of her; he just wanted to get dressed every morning without falling apart. I took a few clothes, some books, a couple of teddy bears, and I would take her wedding rings after the funeral. I also went home with a bag of journals.

There was a great deal of work to do in preparation for the funeral. As my mother's daughter, I found that even this work allowed me to busy my mind and protect my heart for a few more days. We took her clean nightgown, robe, and socks to the funeral home and ordered the casket flowers—as many roses as they could possibly fit. Nothing else, just roses. We collected all of the items she had requested, and someone baked fresh bread. Songs were chosen for the congregation, and soloists were invited to sing the hymns that were especially meaningful. We followed her instructions as if they were the letter of the law, even though some of her requests were more difficult than others. In her fifty-seven years, she had made an impact in so many areas of education and early childhood. She needed someone from each facet to speak effectively of her contributions.

On the day my mother died, we were all sitting in the family room, and Dad informed us that she wanted the man who had raped her to speak at her funeral. He was the only person, she felt, who could accurately describe her involvement and commitment to the Disaster Childcare Program. This was a huge portion of her legacy, and she needed it to be portrayed with precision. I'm not sure exactly what came out of my mouth, but then I fell silent. How could this be possible? How could we ask this man to be a part of such a hallowed day? In her soul, for her healing, she had reached that seemingly unattainable place of forgiveness. I'm not sure the rest of us were there yet, or ever would be, but we had not put in the work that she had. She had earned this position, this identity in peace, and we would honor it.

My poor husband (husband-to-be still) learned about this man for the first time on that day. In three years of dating, I had not told him the story that, in my mind, had inevitably led us to this moment. It was not something that easily came up in casual conversation. In the process of writing this book, I shared the story with two of my childhood friends for the first time. They had already loved me for forty-five years, and the telling was deeply affirming. But to share this with someone I wanted to love me meant going to a vulnerable space I was not yet prepared for. In my life, I had only told three people. The nuts and bolts were conveyed, and compassion resounded. Little did we know at that point how her story would impact the rest of our lives, most importantly our marriage.

In many respects, my mother knew the quantity of people she had impacted in her relatively short life, but I'm not sure she fully understood the sheer quality of her touch. I pray that she knew this. She did know the funeral home would be too small to accommodate her constant flow of visitors, and she knew she did not want people standing in line. She insisted guests be able to mingle and talk and absorb the various representations of her life. On that Friday, the church fellowship hall held her open casket, tables displaying precious pieces of her life, and more people than I could count. As a family, we had time alone with her prior to opening the floodgates.

She had waited ten days for me, and it hadn't mattered a bit. She looked beautiful in her nightgown and robe. She was exactly my mother. I didn't check, but I'm sure there were socks on her feet! "Hi Mama," I whispered as I stood beside her and gently touched her hand. My empathy was in overdrive as I watched person after person pause, wipe their eyes, and walk away. My grandparents just about brought me to my knees. As I stood with them, my grandpa painfully sobbed, "Oh, Kari." And Grandma shook her head, tears flowing freely, and cried, "It's not supposed to happen this way." Even in your eighties, you should not have to bury your child.

It was a long day, and my soul needed to rest before the next one took hold. According to her plan, in the morning, we followed the hearse to campus and stopped in front of the bell tower of the Administration Building. We rolled down our windows and sat silently, just listening as the familiar sound of the bells rang out over the street. From there, we drove outside of town to the most peaceful countryside cemetery. To this day, I love to go there and sit, surrounded by the trees and farmland. It's a place where I feel completely alone (in a good way) with my mother. In a small family service, we buried her privately in our own sanctuary of nature, each of us pulling a rose or two from the casket spray. We would return without her physical presence for the funeral service.

In all honesty, I remember very little about that day. I don't recall greeting anyone in particular; not a single face graces my memory. My emotional paralysis had taken over by that point. I was clearly in the final stages of holding myself together. I do, however, remember what I wore. I had bought two new dresses, similar in style, one in olive green, which I had worn the day before, and one in deep red. I chose red for the funeral, as I'm positive Mom would have wanted color and been disappointed had I worn black. Modern technology recently gave me the opportunity to watch this twenty-year-old event on DVD with open eyes, full awareness, and a multitude of perspective. I watched first with a friend and then again alone. As I sobbed through the second viewing, I fervently scribbled down five pages of notes.

Christen, the same Christen who had married us just a week before, opened the service with poem and prayer. And then Marlin stepped forward to lead the first hymn, "Great Is Thy Faithfulness." Marlin had been a part of the plan from the day she'd first envisioned her funeral in 1987. He had led nearly every hymn I had ever sung, and I loved to watch his arms rise and fall as he directed every note. He had been a staple in my childhood, and it warmed my heart to see him on the screen. Even Marlin found a few times that the emotion was too raw to offer his voice. It was incredibly humbling to see him not be able to sing.

Psalm 30:4–5 paved the way for the choir to move into "Joy in the Morning," which I initially thought was a strange song choice for a funeral.

When the second verse began, I understood the selection. The powerful lyrics sang out, "There'll be love and forgiveness everywhere, the way of the Lord will let them be restored." My mother had handpicked everything about that day with specific intent and purpose. In the days and weeks before her death, she had orchestrated every minute and left nothing to chance. There would be no open microphone for funny stories. Rather, one specific person from every facet of her life, asked in advance and given time to prepare a meaningful speech, would speak.

Andy, a favorite student gave the first of several eulogies. He began with a quote from Mark Twain. "Keep away from people who try to belittle your ambitions. Small people always do that, but the really great make you feel that you, too, can become great." My mother, he said, was the epitome of a great teacher, she made every student feel as if they, too, could become great. She did more than just disseminate information; she provided her students with meaningful learning experiences. His closing would have made her proud as he struggled with his own words. "Live fully, live well, and embrace the world with the understanding that it is as narrow or as wide as we will let it be."

Jo, Mom's dear friend and the president of the college, described my mother as an innovator; a powerful role model; and a gutsy, gusty woman. She was curious, adventurous, playful, and appreciative of the beauty around her. She took informed risks, and if something didn't work out, she would simply try again. She lived what she taught and certainly taught by her example. She taught us by her words and by her life to be better people, a teacher until the very end.

Janina, a colleague and friend, joked about how they were often mistaken for each other. They had seen each other through numerous life experiences and Janina had watched my mother take on one challenge after another. She described her as no mere visitor to this earth. She then quoted the expected eloquence of the one we were mourning and celebrating. "As I have begun to empty myself of fears and things, I have experienced the paradox of becoming full."

At about this point during the first screening, I began to feel a bit guilty, as if I had done my mother a disservice with this book. I stopped the video and, instinctively, my friend/editor looked at me and asked, "How does this make you feel?"

I paused and replied, "This is exactly who my mother was! She was loved and well respected by everyone."

Her response, "Do you feel cheated?"

Wow, that was a really big question, and it continued to dwell in my mind for several days. The people who spoke at her funeral had their own experiences with my mother; they were not mine. I loved her as much as, if not more than, anyone, but my love had grown out of the depths of our struggle. I knew, in her element, she was capable of being this person. But very seldom did I see her curious grin or the playful spirit or hear her laughter in the hallway. She chose to excel in the things she was good at, and once again, there were others who got the best of her.

Watching the man who had repeatedly raped my mother step to the podium was more than I could handle. He appeared uncomfortable, as he should have been, but my mother, the choreographer of the day, had wanted him there. He described the initial phone call and how, within four hours, Mom had called him back with a plan. She knew children, and he knew disaster; they would be a perfect team. He said, "For the first two years, she served as a consultant. The pay was only a token, but the rewards to the program were huge. It was a joy to work with her."

Hmmm … how do you possibly quantify the pay and reward on her end? Ultimately, she was paid in a currency that would rob her of decades of her life. Her reward would be the legacy she left behind—the thousands of volunteers who were trained under her program and the tens of thousands of children and parents who were aided and touched by her expertise.

He closed by saying, "As long as trained people are called to minister to children following disaster, Karen's presence will be with us."

I wonder if, in that moment, he felt a fraction of responsibility for what had led to the ultimate extinguishing of her presence.

My brother, Matt, had to follow, as if speaking on this day wasn't hard enough already. He eloquently painted the picture of our immediate family gathered around her casket the night before to say our final goodbyes to the most extraordinary woman we had ever known. He spoke of the unfair news just six weeks ago and her decision to, once again, be the teacher; as a family, we had been enrolled in Karen's final class—how to die with grace.

Matt was eloquent in describing his peace that centered around two

God-given gifts. The first gift was that we had an emotionally strong and healthy family. We didn't have years of issues to address or problems to fix. We didn't have last-minute amends to make; we could simply be at peace. He said, "We share an open and profound love for each other—a love that forgives pettiness, jealousy, ignorance, and forgetfulness. A love that is without bounds and without reason but, simply, love." It was the kind of love that allowed us to let her go when the time came.

The second gift was that God had given us time. Our mother had not been taken from us in an instant. We had been given the gift of a week together in her earthly heaven, and the smile that donned her face on those days had not been the smile of a woman who thought she was dying anytime soon. We had been given time to sit by her bedside during her final few days, as she continued to teach us the lessons of presence, humility, and selflessness.

He acknowledged our father as "the rock on which our mother stood" and how he had loved her well through exactly thirty-six years of marriage. He'd cared for her without complaint; it was simply part of the man whose existence was so intertwined with hers. He was truly a strong man, a devoted husband, and a gentle spirit.

He closed with this charge: Every one of us had been touched by her in some way. Yes, her absence would be difficult to get used to, but if we wanted to see Karen, all we had to do was turn to the person beside us and ask, "How has she touched your life?"

And then, in true Karen fashion, she would say, "Don't stop there. Take what you've just learned and share it with someone else."

My mother understood that worship is a critical part of grief. And so hymns like "My Life Flows On" and "On Eagle's Wings" were sung. And then came Pastor Susan, sharing with us the valuable lesson she had learned from her favorite teacher over the years. She set the scene in John, chapter 20 as Jesus had just risen from the tomb and appeared to his disciples. Verse 21 says, "Peace be with you! As the Father has sent me, I am sending you." And with that, he breathed on them and said, "Receive the Holy Spirit. If you forgive anyone's sins, their sins are forgiven; if you do not forgive them, they are not forgiven." Forgiveness is not your typical funeral sermon, but in my mother's life, there had been nothing more important.

The two men who had betrayed her body and crippled her soul were present in that sanctuary. Her words were directed at them but meant as a teaching moment for all of us. Whether these men had chosen to take any responsibility for her pain, my mother needed them to know that the act of forgiveness had rested solely in her hands, and *she* had done the work. She had courageously taken the hard and threatening path, and in her journey, she had been transformed. She had not chosen to forgive and forget. She chose to forgive ... remember it all ... and still forgive. She had accepted the call to forgive as she had been forgiven. She had chosen to stop swimming against the tide. She, herself, had embraced the grace of God. And in that act, the impossible had become possible. She had moved from wounded to teacher and from hurt to healer. "Forgiveness is the true gift of the Spirit," said Susan, and my mother had welcomed it. She was, indeed, uncommon and exceptional.

Isaiah 55:12 reads, "You will go out in joy and be led forth in peace; the mountains and hills will burst into song before you, and all the trees of the field will clap their hands." This is the song my mother had chosen to be her end cap, her punctuation. It was not a grim organ postlude but a spirited song with hand claps. The three hundred plus people sang with delight, "You shall go out with joy and be led forth in peace; the mountains and the hills will break forth before you. There'll be shouts of joy, and all the trees of the field will clap, will clap their hands."

And all God's people said, "Amen."

As we, her family, were escorted from our front-row seats out of the sanctuary, I felt it—the finality of the day, of her death, that I had not yet allowed myself to feel. It rose from my feet; numbed my legs; and was swirling inside my chest, trying to steal my breath. She was actually gone.

Knowing my mother's story in its raw, unfiltered entirety has awarded me more than I will ever comprehend, but her death would take responsibility for unlocking and opening wide the floodgates of my emotion. She taught me well, and I, too, had become hardened over the years. Somehow, her death brought me freedom of expression and permission to be vulnerable; I no longer had to be tough. It was finally acceptable for me to feel the pain so deeply rooted in the loss of the woman who had given me life.

CHAPTER THIRTY-NINE

Lost

It's astounding how quickly grief pounces when you no longer hold it at bay. I filled my days with work and various forms of busy. But when my head hit the pillow at night and my brain shut off, I allowed myself to go to a place of deep sorrow. I buried my face and sobbed, sometimes quietly and others so violently I had to get up and pace to catch my breath. My mother was gone, and she was never coming back. I didn't know who I was without her. There's never a good time to lose someone, but for me and my infant marriage, the timing could not have been worse. A year prior, Jarrod had decided to change careers and start his own insurance business from scratch. My husband does not do anything halfway; he just doesn't know how. He was working around the clock, meeting with clients in their homes in the evenings, and joining every professional organization around in order to establish himself in the local business community. By the time *his* head hit the pillow at night, he was sound asleep. As I sobbed, he slept.

Occasionally, he would gently ask if there was anything he could do. "No," I would cry, "there's nothing anyone can do." And so he would go back to sleep.

Isn't it ironic? When we tell our loved ones there's nothing they can do, it really means, "I need you to do something!"

My poor husband had no idea what to do with me. My behavior was far out of his comfort zone. He had come from a family that expressed little emotion. This was by no means a shortcoming or character flaw; it was merely a difference in expression. This entire family loves through acts of service. They were and still are doers of love. In the face of grief, there was always something to be done; life carried on.

Night after night, I cried, and he slept. I didn't know how to ask him to hold me, to make me feel safe. And so I simply became angry with him and with the world. I was living in a community where no one had known my mother. In my small professional and social circles, my trauma was quickly forgotten or purely unknown. I needed to talk about her, but I had no one to listen. On one occasion, someone told me I should be happy because she was no longer suffering. That just infuriated me. She was not here, gone forever; nothing about that gave me the slightest hint of happiness. My faith existed, but I was not mature enough to find comfort in it. And so, I regressed into darkness.

A six-page letter from my darling Sara on October 1, 2001, laid out her love for me and addressed everything I was going through. She offered support and advice with no judgment. She was astonished by my ability to function amid the range of emotions and wrote, "I'm sure you are discovering strength within yourself you didn't even know you had. I have no doubt when you get through all this, I will be even more amazed by you!" She wisely advised me to put the journals on a shelf for a while and to allow myself the time to fully come to terms with the present. "In a few months or even a year from now, you will be able to read your mother's words and be somewhat comforted by them … process your grief first, you are surely overloading."

As for my husband, she encouraged me to embrace our differences, grieve in my own way without a time limit, but to love him as I was willing and able during the process. Communicate. Don't shut him out. And reassure him that he is not the cause. "You can't expect him to change, and he can't fix you!"

Jarrod and I courted each other for three years with notes, letters, and cards. It was rare even then to communicate this way, but there was something very special and sacred between the two of us. We have kept every single one. As I was milling through a box of old letters and cards, I came upon the following two typed letters. They were both undated but written around the same time, November 2001. The first was written by me to no one, or anyone, just putting my broken heart on paper:

> When my mother died in August, something changed inside of me. I loved my mother so unconditionally, like I loved no one else. I am so much like her in looks, personality, and attitude that a part of me died along with her. She was my hero, my inspiration, and my best friend. I will never be the same again. My mother was loved by so many. She touched people's lives—just by being herself

and doing what she believed in. She taught by example and practiced what she preached every day. She was so strong, but the demons that have haunted her all her life finally took over, and she could fight no more.

I feel that I have been lost in a whirlwind since August, still not knowing when it will end or where I will end up. I constantly feel lost and empty inside, but the strength I derive from my mother keeps me going, even if that means ignoring my true feelings. I miss the love that I shared with her and feel the need to bond with someone else, but who? My daughter is the light of my life, and I love her unconditionally as well, but I need more than a six-year-old can provide at this time.

I need to love and desperately want to love with everything in me. I have spent the last ten years with two very different men. In both relationships, I have been "the best thing that ever happened to them" but never gave myself completely to either one. According to them, I am beautiful, intelligent, strong, confident, professional, and could have anyone I wanted. Both felt honored to have been "chosen" by me. I don't want to be anyone's "best thing" for these reasons. I may be these things, but if one doesn't feel loved, how can that be "the best"? A clean, comfortable home and good home-cooked meals do not make me a good wife. How can one be so desperately in love when they're getting nothing in return? I want to be the best thing that ever happened to someone by making them feel loved like never before. I want to love so completely and openly that nothing else matters. I'm tired of feeling empty and cold when that's not who I am, tired of going through the motions when there is no end.

I am in search of who I am. I believe that only love truly defines our person and, most importantly, our soul.

While I searched for myself, my husband waited in misery and uncertainty, blaming himself for my pain, because I let him. He was giving me time and, as always, never giving up.

Heidi,

I married you for better or worse. It looks like it has gotten pretty bad. You feel that I betrayed you as a husband and I am extremely hurt that I have made you feel this way. I don't know where I went wrong or how it has gotten this far. If you need me to leave and let you sort things out, then I respect that. Part of me wishes that it was me who died rather than your mom. The same part of me realizes the hard truth that you would be better off with your mother for the next 30–40 years than with me. I am so confused right now.

This past weekend I looked through old cards and letters that you had written to me. God, I loved getting those letters. You have a way with words that I have never encountered before. It reminded me of how we used to be, not saying it was all perfect, but it was true. I don't know what will happen to us, and it terrifies me. It terrifies me because I don't want to lose or be without you and because I know that we are good together and meant for each other. I have some serious doubts right now about where we are headed. I see the hurt in your eyes and hear the pain in your voice, and it tears at my heart to think that I am responsible for this.

We have discussed many issues in the past two weeks, and like you said, "Everything is on the table." Now all I can do is sit back, wait, and hope we get through this as a couple. I hope this is simply another test in our long line of tests, that we can make it through and be stronger people both individually and as a couple. No matter what, I will always be here for you. Whatever you need me to do, please just ask. I love you more than my life itself, and I would lay it all on the line for you. Just don't give up on us.

Love,
Jarrod

It breaks my heart to read those letters now, for the first time in twenty years. I was so broken and so angry, taking it all out on the person beside me. It was my turn to be angry at modern medicine that could not save my mother and angry at a husband who could not fix the hole in my heart. I desperately wanted him to make me whole, but that was not his job. I blamed him for my inability to love, and he took it. I blamed him for being lost when all I needed to do was reach out for his hand; it was always there. Our young marriage had struggled from its very first day. I will tell you now, getting married on that day was the best thing I have ever done, but it was not the best day of my life. It was hard. And the hard just continued to plague us. We fought, we lied, we hurt each other, we separated, we made mistakes, we sidestepped issues, we swept things under the rug, and we made amends that perhaps did not include forgiveness. But we decided to move forward and love at all costs.

We agreed to hang up the anger, and as spring arrived, we began to heal, individually and together. The business was growing, and we decided it was time for new surroundings. We bought a house and moved out of our apartment. It was a new beginning for us in many ways. We painted and hung wallpaper border without killing each other, decorated, and made it a home.

In July, the seven of us journeyed back to Michigan for a week. We returned to all her favorites, explored new ones, and watched fireworks on the Fourth. The sun warmed our souls and tanned our skin as the breeze whispered gently in our ears. The sand molded like clay around my feet as I spent hours procuring the most perfect keepsakes from various beaches. We sat on the porch in the familiar rockers and reminisced, telling stories sometimes late into the night. Every picture seemed to be missing someone. But together, as a family, we found healing. As if Mom had planned it herself, late in the week Jarrod and I discovered new life on the shores of Lake Michigan. This year would not be a goodbye but, rather, a hello to a child growing inside me. This place was, indeed, a sanctuary of mystique, renewal, and hope. Mom had introduced us to this place, and this place had introduced us to our son, who would undeniably change us forever.

CHAPTER FORTY

The Connection

We survived our year of firsts. Holidays, birthdays, and anniversaries came and went with varying amounts of anguish. Jarrod's grandmother died within that year; and being in a funeral home again was nearly debilitating. I found joy in being pregnant, preparing a nursery, and watching Jordan's constant anticipation for what she hoped would be a baby brother. After losing my job in October, I began to inch my way into the family business, the place I had planned to land following a maternity leave anyway. I also began an exercise and weightlifting routine. My initial motivation was to avoid excess weight gain during my pregnancy, but I quickly adopted a routine that became a way of life for me. For the majority of my life, my mother appeared to be weak and unhealthy. My assumption had always been that her poor health was mostly circumstantial, a product of her life experience, but I made a vow to myself to keep my body strong and prepared to fight. This was one thing I could control. I would do everything in my power to protect my children from what I had just gone through.

Caleb Matthew entered our lives on March 3; he took his time joining the world and arrived without a breath or a cry. The nurses swept him away and squeezed air into his lungs. His first cry, from across the room, matched mine as my body trembled with a combination of fear and joy. When they laid him on my chest, all was right with the world. My baby boy was fine, perfectly healthy, and would continue to make noise for the rest of his life!

Jordan was enamored, and our lives were quickly consumed by this beautiful child. He had made us whole and completed our family. Jordan has been his great protector since day one and remains that way yet today. They are as different as night and day, but their love for each other is fierce and unusual. They can respectfully argue politics, religion, and social status and remain completely smitten with each other in the end.

As devoted as he is to his sister, Caleb's favorite person in the world is his great-grandmother, affectionately known as his Mommycede. They are partners in crime and thick as thieves, genuinely defending each other to the mischievous end. On the day he was born, she fussed that she'd never spell his name right and she'd never live to see him grow up. I know she has never misspelled his name, and last May, at the healthy age of ninety-two, she attended his high school graduation. Come hell or high water, she will see both of my children get married.

For six years, we lived and breathed our growing family alongside our growing business. In 2009 tensions escalated; pent-up frustration, hurt, and anger all collided on the outside. In true Karen fashion, we decided we were smart, educated people, and we could counsel ourselves into a healthy marriage. We bought books, learned our love languages, and put the Band-Aid back on for a few more years. In fall 2012, buried within the chaos of new office construction, we hit a rough patch. I don't know that there was a specific catalyst or if we had simply resigned ourselves to the complexity of life. We were no longer serving each other as husband and wife but merely coexisting. We weren't arguing, but worse yet, we were barely speaking, going through our daily routines with little acknowledgment of one another.

As I wrote in the prologue, things that are buried don't stay buried forever. Things that get swept under the rug without resolution work their way out, speck by speck. I needed a breather, and following a few harsh words, I left for a weekend with Sara. I was determined to have fun, and that we did. We ate and drank and danced until they locked the doors. Both nights, I went back to the hotel and cried to my best friend about how miserable my life was. I came home, not refreshed but, rather, with a chip on my shoulder. Jarrod and I shut each other out for a few days, and then our voices broke through.

Life, parenting, owning a business, working together every day—it all seemed impossible, and I wasn't sure I wanted to do it anymore. I had what looked like a perfect life on the outside, but I didn't want it because I didn't feel I should have to work so hard to simply be happy. Didn't I deserve to be happy? I remember a tearful argument, the kitchen island representing the distance between us, when I told my husband I would rather live in a cardboard box and be happy than be unhappy in this beautiful home with him. It was heart-wrenching. We had come so far from where we began. But that night, we looked at each other with cold, empty stares; there was nothing left.

Later in the same conversation, he looked at me and said, "Maybe I should just let you go."

Without a word, tears streaming down my face, I got in my car and drove. It was dark, and the back roads were empty. I had no idea where I was going, I just needed to be alone. At some point, I called Sara. "I think he's going to leave me," I whispered.

"Is that what you want?" she asked.

My brain and my heart could not agree. "I don't know," I choked out and went home to figure it out.

Funny how I am the one with the degree in psychology with training in counseling, mediation, and reconciliation, and Jarrod was the one who insisted that we go to therapy. He had pleaded with me not to give up without even trying. And so, by referral from another therapist, we found Randy, our disheveled, quirky, unorganized, but strangely competent marriage counselor! Weekly, toward the end of the day, we left work together and went to counseling. It was painful. For the first time, we were speaking truth to each other, words that had been swallowed because they were too hurtful to say. We were forced to look each other in the eyes and be brutally honest. Some days I felt like we left in worse shape than we had arrived, but we vowed to continue the brutal honesty once we got home. Those two words became our motto for healing. Progress seemed slow, but we were in the trenches together. Some evenings, we cried; some we talked further; and some we simply, respectfully had no words.

On the nights without words, I hit the treadmill with my worship music in my ears. This routine saved my life during these days of darkness. The perfect artists were revealed to me, and lyrics rang out as if they were written only for my ears and my heart. Jeremy Camp wrote an entire album after losing his wife. Songs like "Empty Me" and "Revive Me" permeated my being and brought me to my knees. Sidewalk Prophets gave me songs like "Help Me Find It" and "Keep Making Me" which pleaded, "Make me broken so I can be healed, 'cause I'm so callused, now I can't feel." Casting

Crowns sang out my truth in "If We've Ever Needed You, Lord It's Now." And Tenth Avenue North brought me a song titled "Worn" that just made me ache. It included these words:

> And I know that you can give me rest
> So I cry out with all that I have left
> Let me see redemption win
> Let me know the struggle ends
> That you can mend a heart that's frail and torn

This was my anthem, and it still brings tears to my eyes today. The list became long; songs of hope were branded into my memory. In turn, I began to empty myself so I could be filled.

Homework brought a new challenge. We were to write letters to each other and then read them aloud in our session. It was a daunting task. Don't leave anything unsaid. Lay it all on the line. We had written letters to each other for years but never like this. These letters would either save or destroy our marriage. It was the most raw, awful, truthful, painful, healing experience. Hurts were shared that had been camouflaged for years, and hurts were revealed that we never knew existed. But hope was alive on both sides. We both yearned for something better together. We learned the meaning of true forgiveness, how to give it and put skeletons to rest, promising to never wake them again. We learned how to be sensitive to each other's needs, how to respect insecurities, and how to calm fears. Most importantly, we learned that we could not do this alone. We needed to put Jesus in the center of our marriage, and we needed to put each other first on the priority list.

Randy intuitively probed me on my relationship with my mother. And for the first time, I told the story in its unlovely entirety to a trained professional. In forty-three years, he was only the fifth person I had told. I remember him sitting back in his chair, looking up at the ceiling and saying, "Heidi, I don't think I've ever heard a story quite like yours."

I was overcome with a sense of relief. I had not won a prize for the best story, but he had validated me in saying that my story was unique and affirmed that, decades later, I was still feeling the ripples of *my* trauma. I had never seen myself as a victim of my mother's story. She had abandoned me in her death, but I had never dug deep enough to comprehend that I had been abandoned long before that. My husband had not failed me. I hated to admit it, but my mother had been the one to miss the mark. I had never come to terms with that reality and, therefore, had never allowed myself to grieve or heal. It had always been about her—her trauma, her pain, and her healing. I had never stopped to let it be about me, to acknowledge my own pain and realize my own need for restoration. I had spent countless years with a void in my life and had blamed the people who had loved me the most for not being able to fill it, to make me whole. I had been searching in all the wrong places for attention, for comfort, for a love I would never find. This revelation did not excuse bad choices, miserable behavior, or regrettable years of my life, but it did explain them; and somehow, that was enough.

Now it was my turn to work on forgiveness. Jarrod and I had worked honestly to melt the anger and soften our hearts again, but I had yet another task. I needed to begin by forgiving myself. For years, I had justified anger and dismissed guilt, but the further I strayed from the path, the less grace I felt I deserved. Perhaps this was just who I was, alone and unworthy. My love for the Casting Crowns connected me to a book written by Mark Hall titled *The Well: Why Are So Many Still Thirsty?* I was fascinated with the title because I was always thirsting, for something. In my life, I had created my own familiar wells that I went to routinely for sustenance. When these wells continually left me feeling empty, I blamed them for their failure and searched for others. As I read this book, I realized that I was filling my life from the wrong wells and attempting to fill the hole in my heart from a hole in the ground. People, things, jobs, attention, and accomplishments would never satisfy my thirst. Jesus had caught me in my brokenness; lifted my face; and told me that, if I drank from the one true well, I would never go thirsty. If I trusted the living water to fulfill me, He would not just bless me but also transform me. If I drank deeply, I would simply be enough.

There was no book to guide me through the process of forgiving my mother, who had been dead for thirteen years. She had been dragged down the dusty road to hell, and for ten years, she had steadily crawled her way out. For a long time, I used the phrase, "through no fault of her own." But at some point, I became uncomfortable with it. Even in death

I needed to let her accept responsibility. In my mind, it was wrong to find fault with her, even harder to blame her for merely trying to stay alive. But in my heart, I had to come to terms with the fact that she had still made choices. In her misery she had chosen to escape one life and live another. She'd made a choice that presented a different, more tolerable pressure. The bottom line I resigned myself to was that she did not choose me. In my childhood, I was unaware of her choice; she just wasn't there. As an adult, I have forgiven her for not choosing to be my mother.

Jarrod and I continued to move forward as a couple, while Randy and I spent some additional time together. One thing I needed to do for my husband was to let go of my safety nets of the past. Years ago, I had formed the misconception that the only people I could turn to were the people who knew my history. History held such an importance for me but had given me a false sense of security. I had been unwilling to allow anyone new into my heart because they didn't "know me." What I didn't understand was that my history was holding me back and preventing me from growing in other relationships. When I needed a friend, I was still relaying on only two people—Sara and Tyler. Sara had been and always would be my safe place. She remains my emotional refuge and my nonjudgment zone even if we only see each other once a year. But I realized that Sara could not do this alone. I had to invite other women into my intimate circle.

Tyler was a different story all together. Off and on for twenty years, through two marriages, even though I hadn't seen him, I continued to turn to him for emotional support. I had maintained the illusion that he was my knight in shining armor, and he had a power to save me that no one else did. It was unhealthy and unrealistic and because of this fallacy, I had never allowed my husband to be that person. I had always reserved a small place in my heart for Tyler—because he "knew me." The reality was he didn't know me at all. It was time to let go of the past. I willingly turned the corner and wholeheartedly have never looked back. The day I made that decision, something very powerful changed in me. A weight was lifted, and a new being crawled out from underneath.

CHAPTER FORTY-ONE

Reading and Writing

Randy encouraged me to start reading the journals again. I had still not read them from start to finish. He invited me to read them from a different perspective, to see myself and my life as I read about hers. In the past, I had always read for information, trying to absorb her story, but now I needed to read for personal context. I needed to parallel my life against hers and read from the perspective of the little girl, the teenager, the young mother, and the grieving daughter. And so, I read. It was a completely different experience from what I had encountered before. One journal at a time I read, transcribing pertinent entries into a typed document and adding notes from my own memory. It was a remarkable five-year journey full of hardship, lessons, epiphanies, and rewards.

As I read, I began to experience what I call "gentle nudgings" to tell her story. Her words were urging me to share this journey, and Sunday morning sermons were telling me that everyone has a story. I had the itch to write, I knew I had her blessing, and so I took to my fairly selective social media page with tidbits and pieces of what I had in my possession. I did not disclose details and never used the word "rape," but I brought her to life and gave her a voice. In the process, I developed a following of friends who validated my cause and encouraged me to continue.

> *December 9, 2017.* In honor of the Silence Breakers, I offer a "Me Too" for my mother, who passed away sixteen years ago. In 1987, she wrote these words in her journal: "If I should die, I want my story to be shared." So I have her permission. For fifteen years, she wrote. It was her dialogue with life and eventually with death. She taught me to write, not on purpose, but inadvertently she advised

me how to pour myself and my soul into words. I have her struggles and her victories, her pain and her joy, her hatred, and her grace all at my fingertips. It's her story, but it eventually becomes mine. I did not read or fully comprehend these words until recently, but I know they were meant for me. I argued enough with her in my earlier years, there is no argument now. It's all about honoring her. It is deeply personal and ugly in parts but courageous and resilient in others. I have been praying—scared but full of hope, cautious but overflowing with purpose. Someday, Mom, I will be your vessel, and together we are going to tell this story. With God's strength and grace, we are going to touch people and change lives.

This was the day, the moment I knew I had to tell her story. It would be my mission and my honor to write more than just a tribute but, rather, to tell it in its entirety.

February 11, 2018. She would be seventy-four today. It's been a quiet weekend, and I've been reading more of her journals. Sometimes, I feel I know her better now than I did twenty years ago when these words first took shape. She wrote with such intimacy, pages that have just invited me in, wanting me to know her spirit no matter how broken or joyful she was. At one point she wrote, "I come to the end of another journal book, and I wonder, have I written anything of value?" Oh, Mother, if you only knew the value of this gift you have blessed me with! Your words are carefully chosen and full of lessons, your descriptions vibrant and potent. I love you so much for the insight into your soul. This is who you are and who you remain within me. Today is your birthday, but I am the continuous recipient of this powerful gift.

I closed Mom's final journal in March 2018. The completeness of my venture was overwhelming. I had read and absorbed; visualized and remembered; cried; and, ultimately, healed. I filled in the blanks, answered questions, let go of bitterness and found redemption. As I have mentioned in earlier chapters, I heard words I desperately needed to hear and found reconciliation without having to read between the lines. In her own way, she had admitted to her absence and questioned its consequence in my life. Most importantly, I had earned her approval as a mother and regained her respect as a person. She was somehow telling me that, if she was not here to witness my life, she knew I would be OK. There will always be unanswered questions and conversations that simply never took place. But in the end, I have a sense of wholeness, and I am at peace.

> *May 13, 2018.* My journey through these fifteen years is complete. I have finished of all her journals, and because of this, my Mother's Day this year feels different. I have closure. There were things I had questioned, confirmations I needed, and words I desperately wanted to hear. In my last month of reading, I got all of this as if she knew exactly what I needed. In one entry she said that she wrote with such honesty so at least one other person could know the depth of her story. I am honored to be that one person, and because of her honesty, my unfinished business has found its end. Mom, you are my hero, the bravest person I know. I thank you for your words, in their truest and purest form; you have shared your soul with me.

She did choose me; I feel very confident of this. Ultimately, she had faith that, without instruction, her words would end up in the right hands. She trusted my father implicitly and left her journals in plain sight. She could have destroyed them prior to her death, but her story was never meant to go up in flames without being told. Fifteen years of contemplating life and death were not meant to satisfy her soul alone. A friend of hers told me once that my mother planned everything until the day she died—the journals, her memorial service and even my father getting remarried. She orchestrated the important things, the things that would preserve her memory and preach her legacy.

August 14, 2018. I was recently asked what motivates me to stay healthy. It's simple; I want to *live!* I know that eating right, exercise, and mental health awareness do not guarantee me anything. But I know that keeping my body strong gives it a greater capacity to fight. I lost my mother when she was fifty-seven, and I am now less than ten years away from that. Her weakness was not her fault, not a result of her failure to try. Her mind was plagued with depression, and her body, weakened by chronic fatigue and a compromised immune system. She had the will (sometimes) but not the ability to fight. Seventeen years ago today, I told God that she was tired and asked him not to let her suffer any longer. He listened. I am very much who I am today because of who she was, but sadly I have lived the best seventeen years of my life without her. She never saw me in the wedding dress I put on four days later; never met the bright, beautiful boy who came along in two years; and never got to watch the granddaughter she adored live out her love for music. It's a void that I live with, but I hope with everything in me that my children don't have to experience it. And so, I will fight, with every ounce of healthy food, every pound I lift, every hour of sleep, and every minute of peace I can find, because I want to live!

Every year I seemed to write on the same three days—her birthday, Mother's Day, and the anniversary of her death. What I couldn't figure out was how to take this desire to write to her, about her and turn it into her complete story. These entries were beautiful and heartfelt, but I wanted more. She deserved more.

February 11, 2019. This is why I love Michigan. It was "her place" in the world, and I can always feel her there. It was her annual baptism, the annual renewal of her soul. The waves brought her peace, and the sun surrounded her and made her feel safe. She would be seventy-five today.

It's impossible to think that she has been gone nearly eighteen years. I try to imagine what she would look like today—beautiful and petite, with silver hair and almost no wrinkles. She would have the softest hands and the best fingernails for back scratching. Her voice would be strong and confident but gentle like a storyteller. She would be retired but busy, baking bread and volunteering with children. She would be an active public speaker for the "Me Too" movement, gracefully sharing her story with the strength and bravery that her life embodied. She would be faithful to the God Who healed her broken spirit and the best grandma ever, because she loved nothing more! Happy birthday, Mama! May heaven be your eternal Michigan. May the beaches be plentiful and the waves refreshing. May there always be sand for your feet and stones in your hands. I love you.

May 12, 2019. Mother's Day, it's bittersweet. These children fulfill me like nothing else. My love for them is sometimes incomprehensible. They are my reward and my light every day, but especially on this day every year. As much as I love the promise that I have created and nurtured good, beautiful human beings, the pain of being motherless is real today. Thirty years may seem like a long time, but it's not when the reality is I've spent eighteen years without her. In her presence, but maybe more so in her absence, I have learned the lessons of motherhood. I have made decisions in my life not in spite of her but because they are choices she did not make in mothering me. Trauma is debilitating, and emotional pain robs you of normalcy in life. I have long since forgiven her for choosing self-preservation at times over motherhood. In that sense, she taught me about faith, strength, tenacity, determination, and acceptance. I see her when I look in the mirror and when I close my eyes. She speaks through me in my words, as well as my actions. My children are a reflection of her because I have taught them the qualities that she embodied most.

∾

September 15, 2019. I have stewed over this post for a few days, because that's just what I do. When I hear something that resonates with me, something that touches me deep within, I can roll it around in my mind for days, wondering if I should write publicly about it. Is it too personal to share? But after a few days, if it's still on my mind, then maybe it will touch someone else as well. Maybe it's important.

I heard an excerpt from Demi Moore's new book where she writes about her childhood and her mother's multiple suicide attempts. She describes digging pills out of her mother's mouth with her tiny little hands and knowing that was the moment when everything shifted in her life. Now in her fifties, as she writes this book, she can see how so many choices, actions, and reactions stem from that day—the day that everything changed. I instantly felt a connection with her.

I wonder how many of us can pinpoint a day, an event in our lives when everything shifted. A day that no one can ever take back, but you know that because of it, you were never the same. You know deep down that it changed you and affected choices you made later in life. I know my day. I was fifteen years old. And then another day, a few months later, twisted the knife that had been stuck in originally. I know that I am different because of this. For moments, I am weaker because of these events, a soul full of emotion and longing. But overall, I am stronger and healthier because I recognize the shift that occurred so many years ago. There is perspective in healing. I have chosen to make mine into something positive, but it took a long time to get here. Maybe in my fifties, I'll write a book like Demi did. But for now, just understanding who I am and why is enough.

This is when I began to burst at the seams. I literally felt like I was overflowing with her story. I became obsessed with her words, "If I should die, I want my story to be shared." But I didn't know how to honor their request. Internally, I was inundated with questions. Was it too much? Would people look at me differently? Was it really my story to tell? I wanted desperately to write, but I didn't feel like I could do it on my own. Who would help me and who could I possibly reach out to with such a private and personal testimony? My father has always supported me and my desire to respect her wish. He thought he could point me in the direction of someone. But that someone would still be a stranger. This ugly but beautiful story was not meant for a stranger, and so I tucked it back into my heart for a while.

CHAPTER FORTY-TWO

The Perfect Season

A Time for Everything

There is a time for everything, and a season for every activity under the heavens. A time to be born and a time to die, a time to plant and a time to uproot, a time to kill and a time to heal, a time to tear down and a time to build, a time to weep and a time to laugh, a time to mourn and a time to dance, a time to scatter stones and a time to gather them, a time to embrace and a time to refrain from embracing, a time to search and a time to give up, a time to keep and a time to throw away, a time to tear and a time to mend, a time to be silent and a time to speak, a time to love and a time to hate, a time for war and a time for peace.

—Ecclesiastes 3:1–8

On January 1, 2001, amid stage 3 colon cancer, this verse gave my mother a new sense of hope. At the beginning of a new year, she could not visualize her future, but the inability to see was not an inability to move forward. As much as I wanted to tell this story in 2019, I was not ready. I am a firm believer in the sentiment that everything happens for a reason, but consequently, we are not in charge of the timing. Perfect timing is introduced when we are ready—when the season is right.

Over the next two years I sat quietly and listened for God to speak and prepare my heart. Sunday after Sunday, He spoke to me through sermons about unlikely heroes, normal people being used for extraordinary things, and waiting on God. I learned that, when God most desires us to listen, he requires us to wait; in the waiting He does his most important work.

In late May 2021, a flier made its way to my desk asking our business to sponsor a speaking engagement for a local author. She had recently written a book about her very personal experience of being abducted, raped, and found in the trunk of her car. It was her story of survival, healing, grace, and gratitude. I was drawn in, offered financial support for the night, and decided to attend with a few friends from my book club.

Michelle was beautiful and graceful as she told her story, but most importantly she was honest about the pain of surviving the twenty-five years since her attack. My heart ached for her, and I cried openly as she spoke. Her presentation included a PowerPoint with pictures and speaking points. One slide in particular struck me squarely in the gut. As a part of her physical and mental healing process, she referred to the secondary victims/survivors in her life—the boyfriend / eventual husband who stayed by her side, her devastated mother, and her impending children who would know every detail. I had never known what to call myself, but I, too, had been a secondary victim and was now a secondary survivor.

As the evening drew to a close, I lingered. I waited at the end of the book signing line with my already signed book. As I approached her, I said, "I would love to spend some time talking with you, but I can't do it now because I will cry." I continued, "My mother was a trauma survivor, and I am grateful to learn the term 'secondary survivor.'" We chatted for a few minutes, exchanged emails, and I promised her I would be in touch. I went to dinner with my book club ladies and never said a word, but I went home and started reading Michelle's book. I finished it in three sittings.

It took me less than twenty-four hours to formulate my email. I thanked her again for the terminology and the sense of unity I shared with her. I gave her my story in a one-paragraph nutshell and told her I'd toyed with writing a book over the years. I then added these few sentences: "My youngest is leaving for college in August, which will leave a large void in my life. In a conversation with my dad on Father's Day, he asked what was next for me. At that point, I really didn't know. I just wanted to take time for myself to read a lot and maybe write a bit. God is sneaky, and I have a feeling that He introduced me to you yesterday for a very specific reason!"

We set a breakfast date for a few weeks down the road, and I set a dinner date for the night before with one of my dearest long-term friends. I drove two hours, checked into my hotel, and headed to dinner. It was a perfect night as Tricia and I sat outside, shared hugs and compliments, and caught up on each other's children. As our glasses of wine arrived, she almost instinctively looked at me and asked, "So why are you in town?"

It was not uncommon for us to have dinner a few times a year, but I had told her that I had a breakfast meeting in the morning. I explained how I'd met Michelle and then went into the story of why I felt my upcoming date was so important. For three hours, she listened and asked questions, and we cried until they kicked us out of the restaurant. Perspective again is illuminating. In the mid '80s, while I was suffering in my own little personal hell, Tricia's parents were in the middle of a divorce. From the outside, we saw each other's families as more appealing and begged to spend time in the other's home. That night last summer was the first time she had seen my family as anything other than normal. Before we parted, she took my hand and said, "Heidi, you have to write this book!"

Back in my hotel room, it was strange but comforting to be alone with my thoughts. They kept me awake most of the night! Exhausted but excited, I arrived for breakfast and had a three-hour meal similar to the one from the night before. Michelle was warm and inviting, as if we were old friends. I was completely vulnerable, and she put me at ease while I told my story. At one point, she asked me if I liked to write, and I pulled out my phone and read her my December 9, 2017, post where I offered a "Me Too" for my mother. As I read and occasionally choked up, her eyes filled with tears. Again, someone I trusted looked at me and said, "Heidi, you need to write this book!" The difference this time was that Michelle had just navigated this road herself, and she was willing to share all of the tools from her experience with me! I was no longer alone in this adventure.

On my drive home, I called my father and told him about my six hours of storytelling. He is by far the most significant secondary victim and survivor, but his story is much different from mine. From day one, he has been a supportive force behind my desire to put her words on "new" paper. That day, the conversation was different. I was ready. I had an idea for the structure. I had literary people and tools at my disposal. And I had been empowered by incredible women who promised to be first in line for my book signing. I was also about to have an empty nest. I could dedicate creative time and was indeed ready to embark on the adventure I had been planning in my heart for twenty years. After thirty-five years and only trusting seven people with the details of our truth, it was time to share it in the way my mother had intended. Hearing the story verbally is powerful, but it needs to be read. To fully absorb the gravity, the words have to be seen on paper. God had told me to wait. And now he was telling me to run. To everything there is a season, and this would be my season to write.

July 20, 2021. Entangled is what he called it.

My dad said that my mother and I are entangled by our stories. Her story becomes my story, and what happens in mine and who I become all lead back to her. She didn't get the chance to tell her story but made it clear that it was to be told. She was emphatic in her words that seem to be directed only at me. I have a duty. There are many things I could not or chose not to do for my mother while she was alive, but who am I to deny her this request? There are countless victims out there, and for every victim, there are multiple secondary victims—those of us who stood on the sidelines and helplessly watched the aftermath of trauma wreak havoc on the lives of our loved ones. We have stories as well. Our lives are never the same.

What does a fifty-year-old do when her baby goes to college? She decides to take the first steps in becoming a writer. My mother gave me life, a unique story, and the gift of writing. Maybe with the grace of God, I'll figure out how to put it all together!

ACKNOWLEDGMENTS

To my mother. What can I say that hasn't already been said? Thank you for speaking so clearly, so that I could better understand myself. Thank you for picking up your pen, divulging your soul, and leaving it for me to discover. It's not like you to give no instructions, but you trusted that your story would be placed in the right hands, that your words had been written for a distinct purpose. This has been my charge, my act of faith, as I, too, am an ordinary person with an awesome responsibility. I knew deep within that you would guide me as the ink began to flow. I now have faith that *our* story will reach far beyond the two of us and that our voices will speak to those who need to hear them.

To my husband, thank you for knowing there was a better person tucked away below the surface and for pushing me to find her. You offered patience, which is not your strong point, and grace when I felt I was less than deserving. You have continually encouraged me to learn my story and walked hand in hand with me through the journey. I am forever indebted to you for giving me the freedom, time, and space to write without ever making me feel like I was neglecting you. You are my anchor, always, and the wind that takes me to faraway places. I am eternally grateful to you for a life I could have never dreamed of and for loving me through every day of it.

To my father, thank you for loving when it was difficult, when you didn't want to. I am confident that it was your tenderness and gentle spirit that saved my mother time and time again. Thank you for making our far from normal childhood seem nothing but normal. I will forever be grateful to you for your intuition that the journals were intended for me. My life would be incredibly different today without them. I appreciate your continuous support and your willingness to allow me to tell this story in its raw, unfiltered version. You understand fully the scope of its truth.

My dearest Jordan, you came along at exactly the right time! You gave your grandma the opportunity to grandmother and taught her to love on an entirely new level. Her six years with you were likely the best years of her life. Thank you for always believing in me and being my biggest cheerleader. You are a rare gem, a beautiful spirit, a servant to the "widows and orphans." I know Grandma Karen is immensely proud. I'll love you forever. I'll like you for always.

My darling Caleb, the one Grandma Karen missed out on. She would have loved you, your curiosity, your gentle nature, and your nonstop talking. You are my bright spot, my proof of compassion and faith. Thank you for your confidence in this venture by asking what you will get when I make *The New York Times* Best Seller list! I love you with every ounce of my being.

My sweet Madeline, you are a gift. I love your passion for life and the energy that radiates from your soul. You have been excited for this book since the beginning. Your hunger to know your grandma and to understand her role in our family is so inspiring. I hope this book is everything you had hoped it would be.

To my big brother. We shared a mother but very different experiences. Thank you for having faith in me to tell her story, as well as my own. I appreciate you for listening and not being afraid to tell me what I didn't want to hear. I am grateful that you protected me without sheltering me. Thank you for teaching me that I did not simply deserve to be happy but also that true happiness is learned, discovered, and found within.

To Michelle. Our meeting was not by chance. God certainly put you in the right place at the right time. Without you, these pages would not exist today. Thank you for bravely telling your story so others like me could hear it and see ourselves within your words. You are a true, beautiful survivor, and you taught me that I, too, am a survivor. I will forever be grateful for our breakfast on that sunny July morning, for your open heart that told me my story needed to be shared.

To Emily. You made yourself available to me before I had the chance to overthink my dream. You eliminated the fears that had pushed me away in the past and gave me the necessary tools to put my soul onto paper. Thank you for empowering me in my different approach and convincing me that I *am* a writer. I appreciate that you gave me constructive feedback and then let me loose to just write. I am grateful for your assurance that this story would touch countless people and allow them to recognize their own footprint on the journey of the survivor.

To Sara, my rock, the one who has been on this journey with me since *day one*. Thank you for the days of sweet tea, rummy, and ice cream on the railroad trestle. You were my escape in so many ways. You have loved me through years of bad choices and countless mistakes and never left my side. You were always the one with a word of encouragement and a lack of judgment. Somehow, you knew a bulb had been planted, and with the right sustenance, it could sprout and eventually bloom. Thank you for your nourishment and allowing me to grow.

To Tricia and Cheree, my oldest and dearest friends. Sometimes life takes us in different directions, and then the winds of change blow us back to the people we truly need. Sadly, we share a bond of deep loss, but it was in our grief that we were reunited. We share a faith that is everlasting and a desire to serve others through our own experience. Thank you both for the intimate opportunities to share the story that you never knew existed during our childhood. I am grateful for the tears, the insight, and the questions that made me think even more deeply. The front-row seats will be reserved for you!

To Susan. You are the one I needed to let in so I could then let others go. Thank you for letting me share piece by piece and for allowing me to be vulnerable and trusting in my weakness. Thank you for teaching me that you don't need to be a part of my past to understand and appreciate my present. You are my inner circle, my family, my people.

To Randy. From the bottom of my heart, I am grateful. You helped us put in the work and save a marriage that I, at the time, didn't think was worth saving. You gave us the tools to support, respect, love and be honest with each other in all circumstances. Thank you for digging into my story with me, for recognizing its unique but common threads, and for connecting the pieces that had been misplaced over the years. Thank you for encouraging me to go back to the journals and to read my mother's story in hopes of learning my own.

To my pastor, Marc, thank you for hearing God's voice and answering the call to plant a church when we desperately needed one. I am grateful for an environment where I can be immersed in my faith and comfortable in my expression. With you, I am able to listen and relate, to seek, to digest, and to fully absorb God's Word. Through your invitation into relationship with Jesus, I have become confident in my story; the understanding of its purpose; and the truth that, in the waiting, it has become perfect.

To Kathy, thank you for offering to read and edit so many months ago. I'm not sure you knew what you were getting in to, but I'm grateful that you stayed the course through forty-two chapters. Thank you for loving the process and for getting to know the complete Heidi and still wanting to be my friend.

To Karen and Britta, my constant female and one of "my kids." What a joy it has been to take this journey with you. Thank you for your insight and clarity as we digested page by page. I am grateful for our necessary time together, for your affirmation of my emotions, your validation of my story, and your perspective as mother and daughter. I feel like our lives have come full circle and I love you both dearly.

To the countless survivors and secondary survivors of sexual assault. You have a voice. Your experience does not define you. Your past connects you to your present and gives you hope for a future. Perhaps you can risk seeing yourself somewhere within these pages, you can envision the freedom of wholeness, and you can find the words to start your own conversation.

REFERENCES

Ashe, Arthur, and Arnold Rampersad. *Days of Grace: A Memoir.* Ballantine Books, 1994.

Ban Breathnach, Sarah. *Simple Abundance: 365 Days to a Balanced and Joyful Life.* Grand Central Publishing, 1995.

Bass, Ellen, and Louise Thornton. *I Never Told Anyone.* Harper Colophon, 1983.

Bridges, William. *Transitions: Making Sense of Life's Changes.* Da Capo Lifelong Books, 2019 (1979).

Corraro, Michelle, and Emily Sutherland. *Found: Triumph over Fear with Grace and Gratitude: The Michelle Corraro Story.* Morgan James Publishing, 2021.

Duerk, Judith. *Circle of Stones: Woman's Journey to Herself.* Innis Free Press, Inc., 1999.

Field, Eugene. *Wynken, Blyken, and Nod.* North-South Books, 1995 (1945).

Hall, Mark, and Tim Luke. *The Well: Why Are So Many Still Thirsty?* Zondervan, 2011.

Hays, Edward M. *The Ascent of the Mountain of God.* Forest of Peace Books, 1995.

Jacques, Florence Page. *There Once Was a Puffin.* North-South Books, 2003 (1957).

Kubler-Ross, Elizabeth, and David Kessler. *On Grief and Grieving: Finding the Meaning of Grief through the Five Stages of Loss.* Scribner, 2007.

Martin Jr., Bill, and Eric Carle. *Brown Bear, Brown Bear, What Do You See?* Henry Hold and Co., 1996 (1971).

Nouwen, Henri J. M. *Out of Solitude: Three Meditations on the Christian Life.* Ava Maria Press, 1974.

Piper, Watty, and Mabel Bragg. *The Little Engine That Could.* The Platt & Munk Co., 1930.

Rupp, Joyce. *Praying Our Goodbyes, A Spiritual Companion through Life's Losses and Sorrows.* Ava Maria Press, 1988

Simon, Sidney B., and Suzanne Simon. *Forgiveness: How to Make Peace with Your Past and Get on With Your Life.* Grand Central Publishing, 1991.

Ten Boom, Corrie, Elizabeth Sherrill, and John Sherrill. *The Hiding Place.* Chosen Books, 2006 (1971).

Wise Brown, Margaret. *Goodnight Moon.* Harper & Brothers, 1947.

Songs

Camp, Jeremy. "Empty Me." *Carried Me: The Worship Project.* Capitol Christian Music Group, Inc., 2004, track 7.

Camp, Jeremy. "Revive Me." *Carried Me: The Worship Project.* Capitol Christian Music Group Inc., 2004, track 10.

Casting Crowns. "If We Ever Needed You." *Until the Whole World Hears.* Provident Label Group, LLC, a unit of Sony Music Entertainment, 2009, track 2.

Chisholm, Thomas, and William M. Runyan. "Great Is Thy Faithfulness." Hope Publishing, 1923.

Dauermann, Stuart, and Steffi Karen Rubin. "The Trees of the Field (will clap their hands)." Lillenas Publishing, 1975.

Gillard, Richard. "Will You Let Me Be Your Servant?" Universal Music, Brentwood Benson Publishing, 1977.

Joncas, Michael. "On Eagle's Wings." OCP, GIA Publications, 1978.

Lowry, Robert. "My Life Flows on in Endless Song." *The New York Observer*, 1868.

Schutte, Daniel L. "Here I Am, Lord." OCP Publications, 1981.

Sidewalk Prophets. "Help Me Find It." *Live Like That*. Word Entertainment, LLC, A Curb Company, 2012, track 7.

Sidewalk Prophets. "Keep Making Me." *Live Like That*. Word Entertainment, LLC, A Curb Company, 2012, track 5.

Sleeth, Natalie. "In the Bulb There Is a Flower." Hope Publishing, 1986.

Sleeth, Natalie. "Joy In the Morning." Hope Publishing, 1977.

Tenth Avenue North. "Worn." *The Struggle*. Provident Label Group, LLC, a unit of Sony Music Entertainment, 2012, track 3.